Japan's Asia policy

From the end of the Second World War to the end of the Cold War Japan had little room for manoeuvre in terms of conducting its foreign policy because of its close association with the United States. Beneath the surface, however, Japan sought to develop an independent policy towards Asia. In the 1990s it can no longer count on the Cold War structures to provide the frame of reference for its foreign policy.

Wolf Mendl explains the historical roots of Japan's foreign policy, especially the Asia-versus-the-West debate. The book provides a readable and up-to-date analysis of Japan's relations with the countries of North-East and South-East Asia. It also makes comparisons with the policies of powers of equal status in the post-war world. Various policy options are discussed as well as the determinants and characteristics which are likely to govern the conduct of Japan's external relations.

The book underlines the importance of the international environment in shaping the direction of Japan's foreign policy. It has become part of the Japanese tradition in the post-war era to steer the ship of state with the view to keeping open as many options as possible and adjusting to circumstances as they arise.

Wolf Mendl is Emeritus Reader in War Studies at the University of London. He is also an Associate Fellow of the Asia–Pacific Programme of the Royal Institute of International Affairs.

Japan's Asia policy

Regional security and global interests

Wolf Mendl

ROUTLEDGE

London and New York

First published 1995
by Routledge
11 New Fetter Lane, London EC4P 4EE

Simultaneously published in the USA and Canada
by Routledge
29 West 35th Street, New York, NY 10001

Typeset in Times by Pure Tech Corporation, Pondicherry, India

Printed and bound in Great Britain by
Mackays of Chatham PLC, Kent

British Library Cataloguing in Publication Data

A catalogue record for this book is available from the British Library

Library of Congress Cataloguing in Publication Data

A catalogue record for this book has been requested

ISBN 0-415-09648-0

Contents

Foreword by Michael Leifer vii
Preface and acknowledgements viii
Tables xi
Japanese names xii
Abbreviations xii
Map of East Asia xiv

1 **Introduction** 1
The enigma of Japanese policy 1
Regionalism versus globalism 5
Methodological problems 7
Summary 13

2 **The historical dimension of Japan's Asia policy** 14
The early period 14
The Tokugawa era (1603–1868) 18
The first stage of modernization (1868–1945) 21
The second stage of modernization (1945–89) 25
Summary 36

3 **The breakdown of the post-war international system and its impact on Japan's Asia policy** 39
The breakdown of the post-war economic order 39
The collapse of the Cold War structures 41
The consequences 43

4 **Regional interests and policy in North-East Asia** 50
Introduction 50
Relations with Russia 52

Relations with Korea 61
Relations with China/Taiwan 77
Summary 91

5 **Regional interests and policy in South-East Asia** 96
Introduction 96
Bilateral relations 97
Relations with ASEAN 104
Relations with Vietnam and Indochina 112
Summary 119

6 **Regional policy in the global context** 124
Introduction 124
The shifting foreign policy debate 126
The domestic dimensions 130
Japan's options 140
Making the choice 152

7 **Conclusion** 161

Appendices

I *Treaty of Mutual Cooperation and Security between the United States of America and Japan, Washington DC, 19 January 1960* 166

II *Treaty of Peace with Japan, 8 September 1951* 170

III *Japan–Korea Treaty on Basic Relations, Tokyo, 22 June 1965 Agreements between Japan and the Republic of Korea: Concerning Fisheries; Concerning the Settlement of Problems in regard to Property and Claims and Economic Co-operation; Concerning the Legal Status and Treatment of the People of the Republic of Korea residing in Japan* 187

IV *Treaty of Peace and Friendship between Japan and the People's Republic of China, 12 August 1978* 204

Notes 206
Select bibliography of books in English 217
Index 220

Foreword

In the wake of its defeat in the Pacific War, the succeeding Cold War provided the frame of reference for Japan's conduct of foreign policy and for its remarkable economic recovery and achievement. A half a century later in a very different strategic environment and in a revised relationship with its American victor and mentor, Japan has become one of the three major Asia–Pacific powers with an evident aspiration to assume a global role. That aspiration has been registered in a request to occupy a permanent seat on the United Nations Security Council. The legacy of the Pacific War persists, however, in Japan's reluctance to make the kind of conventional contribution to international peace and security required under Article 23 of the United Nations Charter. One reason for such reluctance is the knowledge that the kind of contribution required would not be welcomed within the Asian region which Japan once dominated.

This volume provides a timely and expert analysis of Japan's Asia policy as the country continues to address the future through trying to cope with the burden of a chequered past. Dr Mendl locates his exposition of Japan's policy towards both North-East and South-East Asia in a full historical and cultural context and importantly takes due account of the underlying and potent factor of national identity in shaping international outlook. He begins his study with a discussion of the enigma of Japanese policy expressed in debate over whether or not that policy expresses a calculated grand design. A corresponding enigma emerges in Dr Mendl's exposition of Japan's policy towards a part of the world with which it shares a geographical location and a measure of identity but one which, he maintains, cannot be separated from its engagement at the global level. In exploring the theme of how Japan is confronted by the problem of reconciling its relations with Asia with pursuing a global role in uncharted post-Cold War waters, Dr Mendl makes a lucid and scholarly contribution to the debate about Japan's place in a world which it has helped to shape through its economic performance and example.

Michael Leifer

Preface and acknowledgements

This book analyses Japanese policy in its Asian and global contexts and ends with a discussion of Japan's options in the current state of flux in world affairs. When I first set foot in the country in February 1955, my knowledge of it was sufficient to fill the back of the proverbial postage stamp. It had only just emerged from the isolation of post-war occupation and was largely unknown in Europe. Today, Japan has a truly global presence and cannot be ignored. A great deal of scholarly attention has been devoted to the phenomenal rise from the ashes of war and defeat, but that is not the purpose of this study. Instead, my main objective is to discuss the present state of Japan's relations with its Asian neighbours and how they are linked to its interests and policies as a global economic power.

To talk of a country's foreign policy is to beg a difficult question: how can any large conglomeration of people and sectional interest groups have *a* policy? What passes for the 'national interest' is often no more than the articulation of the perceptions of the dominant group or groups in society. Their policies, in turn, are modified and adjusted to respond to the pressures of other groups, of public opinion and of the international environment. At least, that is largely true of those states in which there exists some degree of democratic accountability through a system of periodic elections.

The importance of domestic politics in shaping Japan's external relations cannot be exaggerated and they form the background of this study. Although Japan can be counted among the pluralist states and exhibits many of the traits of a modern, technologically advanced democracy, its people also have an unusually strong sense of national identity, which is based on a widespread belief in their social and cultural homogeneity. Whether well founded or not, this perception undoubtedly has a bearing on the way the Japanese view their relations with the world outside. In spite of the so-called 'internationalization' of the Japanese economy and the changes in the lifestyle and outlook of the Japanese over the past fifty years, we ignore that phenomenon at our peril. The sub-theme which runs throughout the book is that Japanese ethnocentrism is a force to be reckoned with in any discussion of external relations and that it could be a hindrance to the development of a policy of positive and constructive engagement with the world outside, but that it need not necessarily be so.

Japanese exclusiveness has its roots in the country's geographical position off the coast of the East Asian mainland, from which it is separated by some one hundred miles of water at the nearest point. It has been strengthened by periods of deliberately imposed seclusion in its history and it also reflects a tendency towards the identification of the individual with the group, whether it is the family, village educational institution, company, bureaucracy or political faction, which becomes the main point of reference for his or her relations with the world outside. The factor of group-centred orientation has been extended to the state in modern times and has had an important bearing on Japan's conduct in international relations. Such characteristics may seem to justify the references to Japan in the singular, as if it were a monolithic or coherent unit. Although I follow this practice for the sake of literary convenience and to avoid constant and clumsy qualifications, I hope that the text shows that the making of foreign policy is a complex and untidy process.

Finally, the reader may be surprised that I offer no firm conclusion about the future course of Japanese policy in the Asian region or elsewhere. Possible options are outlined, each of which has its appeal as well as its problems. There are some indications of the direction Japan will take in the immediate future: a strong inclination to hang on to its close relationship with the United States, an emphasis on the Asia–Pacific region rather than on an exclusively Asian orientation, and a determination to work for recognition and acceptance as a major player in world politics, without having a very settled idea of a new world order or its role in it. However, none of the choices can be taken for granted. If anything, this study underlines the importance of the external environment in shaping the course of policy, for it has become part of the Japanese tradition in the post-war era to keep open as many options as possible, to be flexible and to adapt to circumstances as they arise.

If I were to name all the people to whom I am indebted in one way or another, the list would be endless, for it will be apparent that I owe a great deal to many scholars and others who have laboured long and fruitfully in this field. Rather than indulge in invidious naming, I prefer to record my general but none the less sincere thanks to them as a group. This applies especially to those in Britain, Japan and the United States, many of whom have become personal friends over the decades and some of whose works are listed in the bibliography.

But I must mention a few. Michael Leifer first suggested that I might try my hand at writing this book for the series of which he is editor. He bore my ditherings and hesitation with good-humoured patience and made most helpful suggestions and comments on the penultimate draft. Gordon Smith, Rebecca Garland, James Whiting and their colleagues at Routledge have been unfailingly considerate and thoughtful in seeing the book through the lengthy process from gestation to production. Susan Boyde and her colleagues in the library of the Royal Institute of International Affairs have provided invaluable and invariably cheerful assistance in my search for material and information. Tomoyuki Ishizu provided some very useful additional information. My wife helped with Japanese language material and, as always, cheered me on and sustained my efforts whenever they were flagging.

To all I express my deep gratitude. None bears any responsibility for the final version of the book.

W.M.
September 1994

Tables

5.1 Comparative ODA flows in ASEAN and China ($ million, net disbursement) 108
6.1 Source of primary energy (percentage share of total) 130

Japanese names

The order of Japanese names is in Western style, i.e. given name followed by surname.

Abbreviations

APEC	Asia–Pacific Economic Cooperation
ARF	ASEAN Regional Forum
ASEAN	Association of South-East Asian Nations
CCP	Chinese Communist Party
CSCA	Conference on Security and Cooperation in Asia
CSCE	Conference on Security and Cooperation in Europe
DPRK	Democratic People's Republic of Korea
EAEC	East Asian Economic Caucus
FAO	Food and Agriculture Organization
FDI	Foreign Direct Investment
FS-X	Fighter Support Experimental
G-7	Group of Seven Industrialized States
GATT	General Agreement on Tariffs and Trade
IAEA	International Atomic Energy Agency
IBRD	International Bank for Reconstruction and Development
ICBM	Inter-Continental Ballistic Missile
IHT	*International Herald Tribune*
ILO	International Labour Office
IMF	International Monetary Fund
INF	Intermediate-range Nuclear Forces
JDA	Japan Defence Agency

JET	Japan English Teaching Programme
JICA	Japan International Cooperation Agency
JOCV	Japan Overseas Cooperation Volunteers
JT	*The Japan Times*
JTW	*The Japan Times Weekly*
JVTA	Japan–Vietnam Trade Association
LDP	Liberal-Democratic Party
MEDSEA	Ministerial Conference on the Development of South-East Asia
MITI	Ministry of International Trade and Industry
MSDF	Maritime Self-Defence Force
NIC	Newly Industrialized Country
NIE	Newly Industrialized Economy
NPT	Nuclear Non-Proliferation Treaty
ODA	Official Development Assistance
OECD	Organization for Economic Cooperation and Development
OECF	Overseas Economic Cooperation Fund
PMC	Post-Ministerial Conference
RIMPAC	Training exercises by armed forces of countries of the Pacific Rim
ROK	Republic of Korea
SCAP	Supreme Commander of the Allied Powers
SDF	Self-Defence Forces
SDI	Strategic Defence Initiative
SDPJ	Social-Democratic Party of Japan
UDI	Unilateral Declaration of Independence
UNTAC	United Nations Transitional Authority in Cambodia
WHO	World Health Organization
WEU	Western European Union
ZOPFAN	Zone of Peace, Freedom and Neutrality

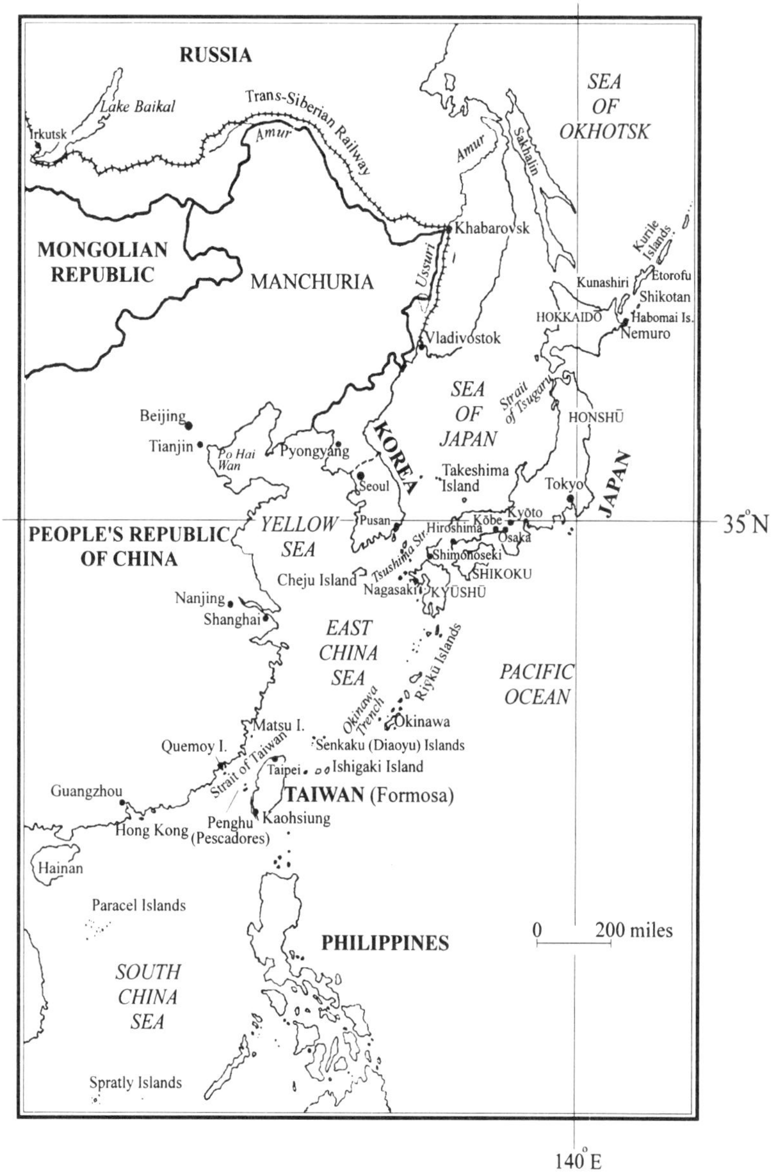

Source: *Issues in Japan's China Policy* (London: Macmillan for The Royal Institute of International Affairs, 1978)

Reproduced with minor alterations by permission of The Royal Institute of International Affairs and Macmillan Press Limited

1 Introduction

THE ENIGMA OF JAPANESE POLICY

Japan drifted along the currents of international politics in the post-war era without any particular purpose or sense of direction; or so it seemed in contrast to other states of similar importance. France was bent upon the restoration of a leading role in Europe through the containment of German power within the structures of the European Community. Britain's priority was to consolidate the 'special relationship' with the United States as the precondition of its continued influence in world affairs and of the balance of power in Europe. After it had joined the European Community in 1972, British policy sought to strengthen the ties between the United States and Western Europe and thus to contain the influence of France and Germany. Reunification with the Soviet-occupied eastern part of the country was the principal objective of West Germany.

While each of the three European states had basic policies which were evident at the time and which they pursued with varying degrees of success, Japan appeared to have no clearly defined objectives in its external relations. In part this was due to the nature of the post-war occupation. Unlike Germany, it did not become the football in the political game of four occupying powers. And again unlike Germany, the state and government retained their legitimacy and remained intact. Japan's isolation under American occupation from the rest of the world, and particularly from its Asian neighbours, meant that it emerged largely unknown and closely tied to the United States when it regained its formal sovereignty in 1952.

The structures of the state and society had been reformed. The emperor had lost his divinity and could no longer be exploited for political purposes. Some of the key players in the political system, notably the military and the descendants of the clans which had led the Meiji revolution, had been removed. The power of the landowning class was broken and the great industrial conglomerates, the *zaibatsu*, were broken up. In their place, the Diet and the political parties occupied centre-stage in the political scene. Yet, in spite of the wide-ranging changes, there was a remarkable continuity in the basic processes of the political system. The bureaucracy retained its influence over policy; the uniformed bureaucrats of the prewar era having given way to the sober-suited officials of the Foreign Ministry (*Gaimushō*), the Ministry of International Trade and Industry (MITI), and the Ministry of Finance (*Okurashō*). In place of military factions there were political and bureaucratic factions. Just as pre-war Japan was governed by the shifting alliances of cliques, so post-war Japan was governed by shifting alliances of political factions. The elder statesmen, *genrō*, who served as power brokers in the Meiji, Taishō, and early Shōwa eras, were replaced by the elder statesmen of the Liberal-Democratic Party (LDP). The pre-war *zaibatsu*, groups of financial, commercial and industrial enterprises controlled by a holding company which was owned by one family, revived in the shape of enterprise groups (*keiretsu*) without the domination of family, but clustered around a bank. The old landlord class may have disappeared, but farmers still wielded great influence over policy through an electoral system that favoured the smaller rural constituencies.

Nor has the Japanese way of doing things changed. Modern communication and information technology and a much greater familiarity with the Western (especially American) way of thinking and doing things among bureaucrats and businessmen – much less so among the politicians – as well as the popularity of Western (again chiefly American) life-styles among the young, certainly give the impression that Japanese society is not so different from the societies of North America and Western Europe. Nevertheless, the convolution and hesitancy of Japanese decision making and the many checks and balances within the system, whether in economic or political affairs, are both baffling and frustrating to those who have to deal with the Japanese.

With the partial exception of Shigeru Yoshida, Japan cannot boast of an Adenauer, a de Gaulle or a Thatcher, each of whom exercised strong personal leadership and influence over national policy. Yasuhiro Nakasone was the only other post-war prime minister who was well known in the world at large and he seemed to fit the bill as a forceful national leader, but he remained a prisoner of the system. He was long on rhetoric abroad, but short on action at home. His achievements were modest and he could only manage to stay in office for five years.

Yoshida was exceptional. Most of his time as prime minister was spent under the American occupation and he saw his principal tasks as preserving the continuity of the state, extricating Japan from the disaster of the war and restoring its status as a sovereign power. Looking back on his term in office and the following decades, it is possible to see the emergence of a distinctive line of policy which set the main direction of Japan's external relations for more than thirty years after his resignation.[1] Nakasone tried to close the post-war chapter, but the real challenge to the 'Yoshida Doctrine' did not come until the end of the 1980s with the collapse of the Cold War system.

There were three elements in Yoshida's policy. The first was concentration on economic and social reconstruction within the parameters of the new constitution of 1946. In the early years of the occupation he sought to moderate the impact of the radical reform plans that emerged from the Headquarters of the Supreme Commander of the Allied Powers (SCAP) in Tokyo. His primary objective was to achieve economic recovery (Japan did not reach pre-war levels of production until the mid-1950s) and social stability as necessary foundations for building a prosperous and independent Japan.

The second element was the creation of a strong economy which could hold its own among and might eventually surpass most if not all of the advanced economies of the West. This became the policy of his successors in the 1950s and 1960s. Yoshida was convinced that economic strength and technological achievement were the keys to future power and influence in the world. That view arose from a mixture of lessons learnt and a certain far-sightedness about the requirements of security for a country as exposed and vulnerable as Japan. It led to the third element in his policy: a decision to rely on the United States for Japan's basic security. There was no alternative in the circumstances of defeat and occupation, and the argument for such a dependence was strengthened by the beginning of the Cold War, when Japan was still under American tutelage. But it was also a shrewd calculation of where Japan's interests lay. Yoshida had been among the 'Anglo-American faction' in the Foreign Ministry before the war and had favoured accommodation rather than confrontation with the great maritime powers of the Pacific.

The identification of a 'Yoshida Doctrine' as the strand that runs through Japan's post-war policy is a fairly recent development in scholarly analysis and discussion of Japan's external relations.[2] Before then, foreign commentators tended to argue that Japan had no particular objectives other than to keep out of trouble and wax rich under the protective mantle of the United States. Most attention was given to analysing those factors in the political system which make it so difficult to discern any clear direction in its external policy.

The thesis of a post-war Japan drifting along in the wake of the West and taking what opportunistic advantage it could to benefit economically from such a passive stance was countered by another thesis that emerged in the 1970s, when people began to feel the global impact of Japan's growing economy. It was argued that, under cover of political inaction, Japan was deliberately laying the foundations for a new bid to 'conquer' the world. Having failed to do so in the past by military means it had learnt the lesson and this time would use money, management, and technology as the chief instruments with which to establish its hegemony. This 'neo-mercantilism' is now seen as a major threat. The trickle of books forecasting such a development has become a veritable torrent since the end of the Cold War, each study or polemic adding new variations to the theme.[3]

Both the 'Japan has no policy' argument,[4] encapsulated in the epigram: 'economic giant – political dwarf', and the 'Japan out to dominate the world economy' theses make sense within the framework of ideas that place the political ambitions of states at the centre of international politics. Within this context, the Japanese political culture as well as the inhibitions imposed by the post-war constitution and its relationship with the United States have prevented Japan's leaders from making any but the vaguest, blandest and most ambivalent statements of policy. And yet, behind the low political profile, there has been a relentless pursuit of economic interest which has led to Japan becoming the second largest economy in the world. Surely, this could only end in a bid for global domination.

'Japan has no policy' and 'Japan aims at global domination' are, of course, very simplified descriptions of the two main explanations of Japan's post-war external relations. A number of subtle variations of those theses exist in between the two extremes. However, the so-called 'Yoshida Doctrine' is closer to the second thesis: i.e. having achieved its post-war objectives – wealthy country and stable society – Japan is now ready to launch itself in new directions in its search for a major role in the conduct of world affairs.

REGIONALISM VERSUS GLOBALISM

The view which is advanced in the following chapters can be located somewhere in the middle of the line which links the two poles of analysis. If we look upon the post-war era (1945–89) as an interlude in which Japan was first in isolation (1945–52) and then came slowly out of isolation in subordination to the United States (1952–73) and finally became a major economic player in the world (1973–89), then the beginning of the 1990s sees a return to the basic issue which has dominated Japanese foreign policy since the country emerged from two and a half centuries of seclusion under the Tokugawa regime. The issue concerns the connection between Japan's policy towards neighbouring Asia and its aspiration to be a player in the Great Power league of the world.

There can be no doubt that geographically, culturally and historically Japan belongs to Asia, but once it began to modernize in the mid-nineteenth century, it acquired a distinct position as the only independent state in the region which strove successfully to become an equal of the great imperial powers. In so doing, it entered the 'Great Game' of global politics. Henceforth there emerged a tension between its regional and global interests; an issue that was temporarily in abeyance in the first two decades of the post-war era. It re-emerged gradually towards the end of the 1960s, but was overlaid by the Cold War structures which greatly inhibited Japan's freedom of manoeuvre. Following the collapse of the Soviet Union, the issue has again become the major problem in Japan's external policy.

Several factors have to be borne in mind when considering the issue. The first is the evolution of a Japanese national self-awareness whose roots go back to the pre-Tokugawa era. It was an awareness that Japan had a unique identity, although it belonged to the sphere of Chinese civilization. The Japanese adapted and assimilated the fruits of that civilization: the confucian ethic, law, architecture, urban planning, art, calligraphy, but without the concept of universalism which was based on a vision in which relations between states were like those between members of a family. That would have implied acceptance of a position subordinate to the ruling dynasty in China.

The second factor arose from the challenge of the West in the nineteenth century. Just as Japanese rulers had tried to keep a distance from China in the past, they were now faced with the same problem in relation to the imperial powers of Europe and North America. Americans would have been horrified to be placed in the same category as the European imperialists, but their part in the forcible opening of Japan, their demands for special privileges in commerce, and their rivalry with the other powers for influence in East Asia, culminating in the annexation of the Philippines in 1898, were, in the eyes of the Japanese, clear evidence of imperialism on a par with British, Russian, French, Dutch, and German activities in the region. Once more they tried to adapt and assimilate the technology and methods of the Western industrialized states without succumbing to their economic, political and ideological domination. The struggle between the 'Westernizers' and 'Japanists', who emphasized the unique identity of their country and people within the context of East Asian civilization, was played out in domestic and foreign politics. The debate was conducted against the background of Japan's struggle to maintain its independence and then to extend its influence and domination over the region.

Defeat, surrender and occupation after the Pacific War had a double effect on Japan's position. For decades it was effectively removed as a major actor in the international politics of East Asia and at the same time the dramatic change in its circumstances gave it the opportunity to catch up and become an equal of the industrialized powers, with the result that it was able to penetrate the global economy to the extent that its leading financial institutions, trading houses, and manufacturers have become household names throughout the world.

Finally, as a third factor, the end of the Cold War between the United States and the Soviet Union and their respective allies has launched Japan into new and uncharted waters and has had the effect of reviving the Japan-in-Asia versus Japan-as-a-Western-power debate in a new context. The main difference between the renewed debate and the earlier one is that Japan now has greater freedom to choose than it had in the era which ended in 1945. Not only has it acquired the means to become a truly global power, but the international environment is such that Japan could move equally well in either direction: to consolidate its position in the East Asian region or put its principal effort in assuming a global role. However, these are not rigidly exclusive options. The time for such simple and stark alternatives is over. Instead of being conflicting aims they could be regarded as complementary, and it can be and is argued here that Japan's position in East Asia cannot be separated from its constructive engagement in global politics. Nevertheless, the relative importance attached to regional and global policies will have a significant bearing on the course of Japan's external relations.

METHODOLOGICAL PROBLEMS

Before embarking on a detailed examination of Japan's Asia policy in the global context, it is necessary to address some methodological problems, not because they can be resolved completely, but in order to establish the parameters of this study and to avoid misunderstandings.

Japan's relations with such a vast region as East Asia require a conceptual framework of its geography. An obvious solution would be to divide it into two sub-regions: North-East Asia and South-East Asia. The former would comprise the Far Eastern and Maritime provinces of Russia, Korea, north-eastern China down to the Yangtze, Japan, and Taiwan. The latter would include south-eastern China, Hong Kong, the six members of the Association of South-East Asian Nations (ASEAN), the three states of Indochina, and Burma/Myanmar.

Japan has maritime borders with a number of countries in North-East Asia and therefore has to define its relations with each, whether it wants to or not. For instance, much as it might prefer to avoid becoming entangled in the problems of a divided Korea, it cannot escape them. South-East Asia, on the other hand, is sufficiently far away to offer Japan a choice of where and how to be involved or whether to stay out of regional politics altogether.

These sub-divisions are geographical expressions and are not necessarily relevant to all the issues of foreign policy. The East Asian region can be divided differently depending on what aspect of external relations one is talking about. If one thinks of Japan's territorial security, it is sufficient to consider only relations with Russia, Korea and China/Taiwan. But if one thinks in terms of economic security, i.e. access to important markets and free passage along the sealanes, it is necessary to include the routes that pass through South-East Asia, particularly the Straits of Malacca and Singapore between Malaysia, Indonesia and Singapore, and those that cross the Pacific eastwards to North America and southwards to Australia and New Zealand, which raises the question whether the term 'East Asia' should not be extended to embrace the Western Pacific as well. Most studies of contemporary Japanese foreign policy place the main emphasis on the economic dimension and therefore include the Pacific as part of the regional analysis.[5]

Moreover, if we were to confine our attention to East Asia and its two sub-regions as defined above, we would still have to recognize that it is wholly artificial to think of them in isolation from each other. China, for example, straddles both North-East and South-East Asia and Japanese relations with China in one sub-region have a direct bearing on policy towards China in the other. It follows, therefore, that the geographical context will change according to the issues of Japan's external relations.

If the primary focus is on Japanese economic interests, we also have to take into account the emerging economic zones in the East Asian region. They include the south China–Hong Kong–Taiwan triangle, often referred to as 'Greater China', the Japan Sea area, and the potential of an ASEAN/Indochina free market zone, all of which cut across established political boundaries.

If the chief concern is with Japan's political and economic security, the focus will be on Japan's immediate neighbours and on the waterways around Japan, especially the Soya/La Pérouse, Tsugaru, and Tsushima straits as well as the passages through the screen formed by the Kurile island chain between the Sea of Okhotsk and the Pacific, and the main supply routes to North America, the Middle East and Europe. Alternatively, if one concentrates on Japan's political influence and its place in the balance of power in the north Pacific, the main attention will be on its interaction with the three major powers in that area: the United States, Russia and China.

The discussion of geographical definitions leads us to a second methodological problem: the linkage between the economic, political, and security dimensions of foreign policy and where to place the emphasis. The short answer is to say that to concentrate on one at the expense of the others would be misleading and unrealistic. The three are intricately linked and to insist on the separation of economics from politics in relations with particular countries, as governments are wont to do when it suits their purpose, is a nonsense. Indeed, to say that one can make such a separation is in itself a political statement, for one is setting limits to the extent to which one is prepared to go in applying political pressure. But it is equally misleading to deny the differences between the three dimensions or to suggest that only one or the other matters in a study of foreign policy.

For example, the post-war concentration on building up Japan's economic strength was not a carefully worked out plan to achieve world domination via that route. It was the only possible policy forced on Japan by the circumstances at the end of the Second World War. It acquired its competitive thrust as a result of the 'catching up' mode which it had adopted since the Meiji Restoration. However, the policy of economic reconstruction after 1945 had political, diplomatic and security implications which soon began to exercise an influence on the course of Japan's external relations.

Ever since the discovery of the 'Yoshida Doctrine', the theory has been that the primary factor that determines Japan's power and influence in the post-war world is the strength of its economy. Of course, this is not a new idea and it can be traced back to the mercantilism of the seventeenth century, which received a further impetus from the rise of the industrial state in the nineteenth century.[6] Traditionally it was thought that economic strength would inevitably be followed by the build-up of military/naval strength, which was regarded as the principal indicator of national power. Nevertheless, over-reaching one's economic strength by an excessive diversion of resources to military ends usually leads to exhaustion and collapse, with the Soviet Union providing the latest example of such a fate.

The evolution of post-war Japan has so far followed a different course. As a result of its defeat and of subsequent constitutional constraints, the military component of Japan's power has all but disappeared and is likely to remain in the background for some time to come, if not for always. This means that the present debate in Japan turns around the question of how to convert economic muscle into an instrument of power and influence; how to turn its financial, industrial and technological assets into means which support its political and diplomatic objectives. Those objectives include ensuring national security, maintaining the country's prosperity, enhancing its status as a major power, and spreading its cultural influence.

Bearing in mind the complex linkage of national objectives, the main focus of this book is on the political and security factors in Japanese foreign policy. Economic factors are dealt with only in so far as they affect these dimensions of Japan's external relations. All this, however, raises a prior, and perhaps the most difficult, methodological problem: the analysis of a country's foreign policy. There are rare moments in history when we can discern a clear and unambiguous line of policy which is followed with single-minded determination. Bismarck's pursuit of the unification of Germany under Prussian leadership is one example in modern times. The decade of de Gaulle's attempt to restore France to a leading role among nations is another. The drive to establish Japan as the dominant East Asian power in the first half of the twentieth century could also be cited as an example, though, characteristically, this was not the work of a pre-eminent leader, but rather an enterprise of collective leadership.

In the technologically advanced democracies of the present age, lines of policy are usually confused and hesitantly applied. They tend to veer between alternatives and follow a zig-zag course. British attitudes towards membership of the European Community are a good example. First there was the hesitancy surrounding the question of whether and under what conditions to join. Then, after entry, there has been the continuous tug-of-war between the American and European tendencies in foreign policy. Japanese policy since the war illustrates such hesitancy and apparent lack of direction to perfection. Where a direction was discernible, as in the build-up of the security forces, it operated on the principle of two steps forward and one step back. It can be asked whether Japan had a policy at all or simply reacted to events.

An attempt to describe and analyse foreign policy is fraught with difficulties, especially when dealing with contemporary affairs without full access to the official and confidential records of government. What passes as the national interest is often little more than the articulation of the lowest common denominator on which the dominant groups in society can agree. They will usually define it in terms of their particular aspirations and objectives. But in societies which have democratic accountability built into their structures through a system of regular elections, policy has to be adjusted to take some account of pressures from the political opposition, although elections are usually fought on domestic issues. Such issues form the background against which those responsible for managing foreign relations have to operate. It is, however, possible to isolate a number of factors which to a greater or lesser extent influence policy orientation. One of them is the self-image engendered within the nation, especially among the élites. It is the product of historical and cultural experience. When using the word culture, I adopt the definition of Akira Iriye, who describes it as a consciousness of common traditions within defined geographical boundaries; a sharing of religious, artistic, and literary roots;

generally accepted customs and ways of life; and the existence of myths and symbols with specific meanings, held in common by those who belong to the national society.[7] Thus, the historical evolution of Japanese society and the distinctive culture that emerged over many centuries have combined to form both a Japanese self-image and a Japanese view of the world which have exercised a powerful influence on Japan's response to changes in the international environment.[8]

Among the distinctive features of Japanese culture are the myths surrounding the emperor. They made the Japanese peculiarly susceptible to the personification of the state and gave the impression of a cohesive polity pursuing a single-minded and ruthless policy. The aftermath of the war exposed the complexities and contradictions of a society where power is much more diffuse and no longer the possession of one group, such as the military in pre-war Japan. None the less, the personalized view of the state continues to linger. Japan shares this characteristic to some extent with other long established states, whose leaders also operate within the traditional concepts of the nation's personality and sovereignty; ideas which are increasingly shown to be illusory under the pressure of technological, economic, and social change.

A second factor is the clash of interests and the divergent pulls among élite groups within a society. Their impact depends, of course, on the relative strength of the various components of the policy-making élites. In post-war Japan they included the bureaucracy, business circles, and politicians of the ruling LDP, though the influence of the opposition parties has also been significant on certain occasions. The media constitute a fifth component, though one that is more of a restraining than a positive force. It is essential to bear in mind that the balance and relative importance of these groups is not static but is constantly shifting.[9] Furthermore, none of them is monolithic. Each is composed of sub-groups, such as the factions within the LDP or different ministerial bureaucracies, which compete among themselves. For example, business interests were divided over relations with China before 1972; some in favour of expanding trade with the mainland, others deeply entrenched in the economy of Taiwan. Again, after 1978, Japanese economic relations with China were often driven by the competition among Japanese enterprises. Similarly, policy towards the rearmament of Japan and relations with the United States was influenced by the conflict of interests between the Gaimushō, MITI, the Japan Defence Agency (JDA), and the powerful Okurashō.

Newspapers and commentators on current affairs play a significant part in a nation of avid readers of what we would call the quality papers, whose circulation puts that of the most popular British tabloids to shame, and of the numerous periodical journals. In one respect they act as pace-setters in the formation of the national consensus as, for instance, in the acceptance of the Self-Defence Forces (SDF), when they acted both as a brake on government policy and as a conduit for the gradual acceptance of their existence by a distrustful public. Their restraining influence was noticeable in 1960, at the time of the mass protests against the revision of the Security Treaty with the United States. Although the popular demonstrations failed in their immediate objective and the treaty was duly ratified, the public outburst, strongly supported by the press and intellectuals, not only forced Prime Minister Kishi out of office, but ensured that the low-profile external policy with its concentration on economic expansion was again on course. It was not until the mid-1980s, under Nakasone's premiership, that the government tried to place security, the alliance with the United States and the build-up of the SDF in the forefront of its policy. The fact that Nakasone could pursue policies that would have provoked national uproar two decades earlier, is in part due to the widespread, if resigned, public acceptance of the SDF and the Mutual Security Treaty with the US. In this respect, the turn-around of prominent intellectuals and critics, who had been leaders in the clamour of 1960 and had now become defenders of government policy and, indeed, in some cases advocates of substantial rearmament, was significant. They helped to set the ideological climate surrounding these issues.

Finally, the pressure of the international environment is an important influence on the course of any country's foreign policy. It is a complex phenomenon and concerns events beyond Japan's direct involvement and control. The impact on Japanese policies, mainly in the form of reaction to such events, promotes a feedback from outside which again influences Japanese perceptions and reactions. This essentially circular process occurred during the Arab-Israeli (Yom Kippur) War of 1973 with the accompanying Arab oil boycott and the subsequent Japanese switch of policy over Palestine. It could also be seen in the Nixon–Kissinger policy of *détente* and the dramatic reversal of American policy towards China. The Japanese were offended by the lack of consultation and the extremely short notice given of this move and they reacted accordingly.

Similarly, Japanese economic policy and, more precisely, the ever mounting trade surpluses have created friction with other industrialized countries and aroused anti-Japanese sentiment and pressures which, in turn, have provoked a more nationalistic reaction in Japan. The collapse of the Soviet Union and of the Cold War structures are the latest examples of events which have a profound effect on Japan and require some response.

SUMMARY

For the purposes of this study, the East Asian region is divided into the North-East Asian and South-East Asian sub-regions, bearing in mind that such divisions are bound to be somewhat arbitrary and that they are linked through China which straddles both. Moreover, in terms of economic development, one can discern the formation of at least three major zones in the region which cut across the chosen geo-political lines of demarcation. However, since the main emphasis of the book is on the political and security aspects of Japan's policy in Asia, the more usual sub-division of the region is the most convenient.

Although the discussion will concentrate on the diplomatic and security elements in Japanese policy, it will be impossible to ignore the influence of the economic factor, especially as it has been the principal driving force behind Japan's involvement in Asia in the post-war era. Yet, as Japan faces the need to adjust to the changing environment of the 1990s, the political and security dimensions loom much larger and have begun to assume an autonomy of their own.

The importance of the domestic determinants of Japan's foreign policy can hardly be exaggerated, but they will only be considered in so far as they are likely to affect the nature of Japan's relations with its Asian neighbours. Both the economic and domestic factors have been the subjects of many substantial studies on which I will rely for this analysis.

Finally, while the main focus of this book is on Japan's Asia policy, an attempt will be made to place it in the wider context of international politics and to unravel the connections and tensions between regionalism and globalism in Japan's foreign policy.

2 The historical dimension of Japan's Asia policy

The history of Japanese relations with the neighbouring continent can be divided into four phases:

1 The early period up to the end of the sixteenth century;
2 The Tokugawa era (1603–1868);
3 The first stage of modernization (1868–1945); and
4 The second stage of modernization – the post-war era (1945–89).

Japan is now on the threshold of a fifth phase, the post-Cold War era, which is the main focus of the subsequent chapters of this book. Some understanding of the past relationship between Japan and its neighbours is however necessary because historical experience and tradition, in the shape of myths and images, continue to play a part in influencing the contemporary approach to Asia.

THE EARLY PERIOD

To discuss Japan's relations with Asia in the centuries before the Tokugawa era really means talking about Japan's relations with China via or over Korea. The concept of international relations as the relationship between sovereign states, equal according to international law but unequal in size and power, whose territorial extent is defined by clearly demarcated boundaries and whose intercourse is regulated by formal treaties and the management of a balance of power, was absent in the Chinese conception of world order in which the 'natural' and 'social' order of things were indistinguishable. They saw it as an essentially harmonious world under Heaven. Nor did the Chinese conceive Heaven to be a transcendental or supra-natural force, responsible for all creation and taking an active part in the management of events on earth. They believed instead that 'the Way of Heaven' lay at the root of the five fundamental and permanent human relationships between male and female, father and son, elder brother and younger brother, friend and friend, sovereign and subject. Peace and harmony depended on the right ordering and conduct of these relationships. The transfer of such ideas to the relations between China, which was thought of as the centre of civilization, and other countries meant that they were seen in hierarchical terms on the principle of superordination and subordination.[1]

Accordingly, all the countries and peoples surrounding China, whose first appearance as a centralized state, roughly within the boundaries of present-day China, dates from the Ch'in dynasty in the second century BC, were regarded as being in varying degrees of subordination to the Middle Kingdom. When a Japanese envoy presented an official letter to the Chinese Emperor in 607 AD, which was couched in the following terms:

> The Son of Heaven in the land where the sun rises addresses a letter to the Son of Heaven in the land where the sun sets. We hope you are in good health.

it was noted in the dynastic records that:

> When the Emperor saw this letter, he was displeased and told the official in charge of foreign affairs that this letter from the barbarians was discourteous, and that such a letter should not again be brought to his attention.[2]

On another occasion the dynastic history records that the Chinese Emperor was annoyed on hearing reports from his envoy in Japan that:

> The King of Wa (Japan) deems heaven to be his elder brother and the sun, his younger. Before break of dawn he attends the court, and, sitting cross-legged, listens to appeals. Just as soon as the sun rises, he ceases these duties, saying that he hands them over to his brother.

The chronicle continues:

> Our just Emperor said that such things were extremely senseless, and he admonished [the King of Wa] to alter [his ways].[3]

The stories symbolize a number of features in the relations between China and Japan, faint traces of which may still be observed today. The Chinese emperor insisted on his superior status under the Mandate of Heaven and was angered by the egalitarian tone of the letter addressed to him. He was also irritated that the Japanese ruler should presume to adopt working practices outdoing those of a Chinese emperor, who displayed his virtue by conscientiously attending to his duties *at dawn* and not before. Perhaps most annoying of all was the presumption on the part of the Japanese emperor of a special relationship to Heaven and the sun. In keeping with his claim to superior status and the belief that he should exercise his governance by precept and example, he admonishes the King of Wa and urges him to mend his ways. The Japanese, on the other hand, while observing the formalities (the bearer of the offending letter had also brought tribute), claimed an equal status and maintained a sturdy independence.

Such patterns of behaviour have their echoes in the post-war relations between the two countries, albeit in a very different context and based on very different ideologies. For example, the issue of a Japanese apology for the suffering inflicted during the war against China in the 1930s and 1940s, reflects a Chinese attempt to seize the moral high ground and a Japanese reluctance to conform. The prickliness between neighbours with ancient and proud traditions may not be surprising, but it has not prevented the development of a close and involved relationship; a relationship that remains the dominant factor in the politics of East Asia.

From earliest times, Japan's intercourse with China had three aspects: the cultural nexus; the political relationship; and the economic interest. Because of the delicate and occasionally stormy nature of the political relationship there were periodic attempts to separate it from economics, though in practice this proved difficult to do.

No Japanese would deny the enormous influence of Chinese civilization on the cultural history of Japan. Religion, philosophical traditions, the written language, art and artifacts, institutions of government, architecture, and other elements of culture were introduced to Japan from China, often through Korean intermediaries, though the Japanese, under the influence of the hierarchical confucian view of the world order, have in the past been less willing to recognize their cultural debt to Korea.[4] These importations were not simply copied, but were adapted and assimilated to the distinctive Japanese culture which had evolved over the centuries. This characteristic persisted with the introduction of Western artifacts, institutions, technology and ideas in the nineteenth and twentieth centuries, when Japan was erroneously seen as nothing more than a skilled imitator.

Political relations, in contrast, have fluctuated and alternated between an acceptance of their inferior status *vis-à-vis* the Chinese court and a certain show of independence with the hint of equality, as shown in the letter quoted above. From 894 AD until around the middle of the twelfth century there were no strictly official relations between the two courts, although a brisk trade had developed between the fiefdoms in western Japan and the eastern seaboard of China. Indeed, during this earlier period of a largely self-imposed Japanese isolation, the Chinese had taken the initiative both in seeking trade and in trying to establish formal relations. For example, an official mission in 945 AD had been very coolly received by the Japanese and was not encouraged to proceed.

Commerce was another matter and under the guise of tribute became quite substantial, although the terms of trade were favourable to Japan. In 1369 the Ming emperor wanted to bring Japan into the Chinese sphere by making it a tributary state, chiefly in order to control the Japanese pirates who were causing such depredations on the coast. The shogun Ashikaga Yoshimitsu cooperated and was invested as tributary sovereign early in the following century, which served the purpose of increasing his status at the expense of the emperor of Japan, but he was also motivated by the desire to acquire copper coins through increased trade.[5] Yoshimitsu's successor, Yoshimochi, severed relations with the Ming, but the fief of southern Kyushu continued to trade privately with the Chinese. By 1432 official relations were re-established, but the Chinese complained of the increasing volume of Japanese goods sent for sale. In the sixteenth century the trade all but ceased, though piracy and smuggling, in which Chinese merchants connived, continued to flourish.[6]

In addition to official relations and commerce, the Korean peninsula was a third factor in the relations between Japan and China. The Han emperors' conquest of north Korea at the end of the second century BC drew the attention of some tribal rulers in west Japan to the power and civilization of China, and they sent missions to the nearby established colonial government. Henceforth, Chinese cultural influences reached Japan via Korea. With the collapse of Chinese power in the third century AD, Japanese armies began successful incursions aimed at controlling south Korea. In the middle of the seventh century AD the rising empire of the T'ang dynasty had re-entered Korea and defeated the Japanese armies there.

A more striking example of Korea's place in the relationship with China was provided by the expedition of Hideyoshi Toyotomi at the end of the sixteenth century. Korea was merely the pathway to the conquest of the Ming empire. Hideyoshi intended to establish himself in Peking and had laid detailed plans for the government of the new dominions under a 'Civil Dictator'. The enterprise came to an end with his death in 1598. Hideyoshi's scheme should be seen not so much as an expression of Japan's national aspirations but as an expression of his acceptance of Chinese concepts of universalism, although he had envisaged a China organized on the lines of the feudal regime with which he was familiar in Japan.[7]

On the eve of the installation of the Tokugawa shogunate and the policy of *sakoku* (closing the country), several distinct features had emerged from the long history of Japanese contact with the neighbouring continent. They include: the central importance of China and its civilization in Japanese eyes, but a resistance against being drawn into a subordinate relationship; the distinction between official and commercial relations, even though they were linked in the eyes of the Chinese court through the tribute system; the fashioning of an indigenous culture, however much it owed to Korean/Chinese influences; and the strategic importance of Korea as the route to the mainland and, conversely, to Japan.

THE TOKUGAWA ERA (1603–1868)

The two centuries of seclusion between 1639 and 1854 did not interrupt Japan's intercourse with the neighbouring mainland. The Tokugawa shogunate retained relations with several north-east Asian countries. Korea had diplomatic relations with Japan on an equal footing. Twelve Korean embassies were sent to Japan in this period. The Kingdom of Ryūkyū also retained official relations, though its status was peculiar as it was simultaneously regarded as a vassal state by China and Japan. China itself had commercial relations with Japan without diplomatic ties. The only other foreigners allowed to have contact with Japan were Dutch merchants confined to the tiny island of Deshima.[8] Indeed, through the port of Nagasaki, Chinese and Korean traders developed the links that integrated Japan into the trading system of the region. However, a subtle qualitative change in Japanese attitudes towards neighbours across the seas took place during this period.

In the settled and relatively undisturbed environment provided by the official policy of keeping the outside world at arm's length, there developed a strong sense of national self-awareness, which seems strange at first sight. It is usual for such sentiments to emerge among a people under pressure or attack from outside. In the case of Japan, national self-consciousness arose with reference to Chinese philosophical influence and not as a result of a threat from Europe or America. It is true that the seclusion policy was the direct consequence of the fear of Christian subversion, but that fear was concentrated primarily on the threat to the authority of the shogun and not on a threat of attack by a foreign power.

The Tokugawa era witnessed a revival of interest in Confucian ideas, coupled with a new emphasis on the native Shintō religion and the classics of Japanese history, the *Kojiki* and *Nihongi* – themselves inspired by the chronicles of the Chinese dynasties. The singular characteristic of this intellectual movement was the adaptation of the Confucian ideal to the ideal of a 'pure' Japanese society which, it was assumed, existed before the impact of Chinese influences. Those influences were seen as having had largely evil consequences. Although the philosophy of Confucianism had its origins in China, the Japanese nationalists argued that the Chinese themselves were bad at heart and that their ideas had led to a rejection of the true sources of the Japanese tradition. From this mixture of nativism and return to an untainted Confucianism there emerged the belief in Japanese cultural superiority. Unfavourable comparisons were drawn, for example, between the succession of dynasties in China, each eventually overthrown as a result of its corruption and the withdrawal of the 'Mandate of Heaven', and the unbroken reign of Japan's ancient dynasty.

The real source of the intellectual revolt was a growing dissatisfaction and discontent with the Tokugawa regime, which had begun to weaken and decay in the late eighteenth century. It was, therefore, not directed against China itself, with which relations remained calm, but, in true oriental style of indirect criticism, against the alleged impact of corrupt Chinese teaching. Thus, this early manifestation of Japanese nationalism, which focused on the myths surrounding the emperor system and the role of the emperor in society, developed in an East Asian cultural environment and was not a response to Western ideals and principles.[9]

One interesting consequence of the long years of settled conditions under the Tokugawa was the emergence of a civil society which laid stress on rule by virtue rather than force. It was a society which had been established by force of arms and whose dominant class were warriors. Under the strict control of the shogunate, the daimyō (feudal lords) and samurai were turned into administrators. The samurai were allowed to retain their swords, but that was because the sword was a status symbol and occupied a special place in Japanese aesthetics.

In the context of the new nationalism, Norinaga Motoori (1730–1817) and Nobuhiro Satō (1769–1850) were the leading exponents of ideas about the unique qualities of the Japanese and their pre-ordained mission to dominate the world. This view rested on a belief in divine favour bestowed through the direct succession of the imperial line from the Sun Goddess, and on the strength of the spirit of the Japanese whose moral fibre would enable them to overcome all obstacles. This may be an extreme way of putting it, but such a philosophy laid the foundations for a concept of Japan's place in the world, which must, however, be distinguished from the kind of supra-national *Weltanschauung* which is part of the Western philosophical tradition. In other words, in the Japanese view of the world, Japan was at the centre and there was no suggestion of an over-arching system of values which did not distinguish between one nation and another.[10]

Through intercourse with the Dutch traders, Tokugawa Japan was also open to European ideas, science and scholarship. Knowledge of the world outside became widespread among the literati and men of culture, though it was personally hazardous to have contact with foreigners. The Japanese were, therefore, not wholly unprepared when the European and American powers made their appearance on the doorstep.[11]

Before the mid-nineteenth century, Japanese officials and thinkers had begun to discuss geo-political issues in terms which would have been familiar to any advocate of *Realpolitik*. At first the focus was on Russian power advancing from the north. There were those who advocated counter-measures, which included state intervention in industry and commerce, the construction of a strong navy, colonization of Hokkaidō and expansion into the Kuriles, Sakhalin, Kamchatka, the Aleutians and even North America. One political thinker advocated moving the capital from Edo (Tokyo) to Kamchatka for better control over an enlarged empire.[12]

By the time of the Treaty of Shimoda (7 February 1855), which partly delimited the boundary between Russia and Japan, Japanese leaders were considering which of three options it would be best to pursue: to seek an alliance with Russia; to open Japan to all comers; or to continue with the policy of exclusion. Russia at that time seemed to pose less danger than the United States, whose

'Black Ships' had already made their appearance in 1853. Other themes in the national debate included the expansion of Japan into Asia, the idea that the defence of China and Japan should be seen as a single strategic problem, and the more general question of whether Japan should seek accommodation with Russia or the maritime powers in the Pacific.[13]

At the beginning of the Meiji era, the Japanese had acquired a concept of unique national identity within the compass of sinic civilization and had also adopted a view of world politics based on power rivalries in response to European and American pressures. These perceptions, combined with the emergence of a centralized state and a proto-capitalist economy under the Tokugawa, had laid the foundations for the rapid modernization of Japan in the latter half of the century and for the debate over its identity in relation to Asia and the West.

THE FIRST STAGE OF MODERNIZATION (1868–1945)

The immediate concern of the leaders of the Meiji revolution was to build a modern state which could withstand the onslaught from the West, avoiding the fate of China, and would eventually bring Japan into the circle of the Great Powers which dominated the world. This ambitious programme required primary concentration on the reconstruction of society before Japan would be ready to claim equality with the other empires.

To achieve these ends, the reformers naturally looked to Europe and the United States for their models. The catching up syndrome became the driving force behind official policy and has continued to guide it ever since. It was encapsulated in such slogans as *Datsu-A nyū-Ō* (Out of Asia, into Europe) and *Fukoku Kyōhei* (Rich Country, Strong Army). An example of this determination was the short interval between Japan's first acquaintance with steam navigation through the arrival of Commodore Perry's squadron in Tokyo Bay in 1853, and the passage of its first independently built and navigated steamship across the Pacific seven years later.

Emulation of the Western countries stimulated the controversy between the 'Asian' (or oriental) and 'Western' schools among the Meiji élites. The clash was not between those who resisted all Western influences, a die-hard and rapidly dwindling minority, and those who wanted to introduce Western technology and methods, the overwhelming majority of the new leadership. The conflict was subtler than that. As in China, where there was an attempt to counter the challenge from the West by adopting 'Western Function' (*Yung*) and retaining 'Chinese Essence' (*T'i*),[14] the Asianists in Japan wanted to make use of Western technology and practices in order to strengthen what they regarded as the naturally and morally superior indigenous culture of Japan. On the other hand, some of the new leaders went further and urged the incorporation of Western ideas and philosophy, insisting that Japan could not become a truly modern state without identification with the West. The leading advocate of this course was Yukichi Fukuzawa (1834–1901), whose portrait adorns the highest denomination (¥10,000) of the current series of banknotes. His admiration for the West had no bounds and the principles of Christianity won his whole-hearted approval. In his view Japan would only become 'civilized' if the influence of Chinese-style education could be driven out.

> The true reason of my opposing the Chinese culture with such a vigour is my belief that as long as the old retrogressive doctrine of the Chinese school remains at all in our young men's minds, our country can never enter the rank of civilized nations of the world.[15]

There were, of course, many variations of the theme and it would be misleading to insist on a simple dichotomy between 'Asianists' and 'Westernizers'. However, the underlying confrontation was reflected in Japan's external relations. The Asianists not only sought modernization as a means with which to confront the West more effectively, beating it on its own ground, but saw in Japan's success a vindication of its superiority in Asia and a justification for assuming the role of leadership of the Asians in their struggle against Western imperialism. Those who wanted to go further and introduce the 'essence' of Western civilization had a more ambivalent attitude towards Japan's place in Asia. While it was culturally and historically inseparable from its neighbours, Japan's geographical location enabled it to remain somewhat detached from the mainland. Thus it could manipulate Asian politics to suit Japanese interests without claiming to be the leader of Asia or being the defender of the Orient against the rapacious Occident.

In practice such attitudes were reflected in the differences between those who favoured establishing a dominant position on the Asian mainland and those who preferred a policy of containment, principally of Russian/Soviet power, in association with the Anglo-American maritime powers. The Asianists in this debate tended to use arguments about the moral and cultural superiority of Japan and its divine mission to lead Asians, to cover more earthy motives of economic exploitation and gain. High-flown principles came strangely from the mouths of militarists, adventurers, freebooters, and shady operators. None the less, the vacillations of policy in the first stage of Japan's modernization mirrored the problems of national identity and interest.

The first clash came soon after the Restoration. It arose over the question whether Japan should advance into Asia and seize Korea as a first step. Takamori Saigō (1827–77) was disturbed by the rapid pace of Westernization, particularly as it affected the samurai class, and was convinced that Japan could not withstand the West without having Korea and China on its side. He made an ingenious proposal for provoking war with Korea, partly to divert attention from domestic strife and to unify the nation. His old friend, Toshimichi Ōkubo (1830–78), opposed this policy on the grounds that priority should be given to the modernization process. In terms of foreign relations, he argued that such an adventure would expose Japan to threats from Russia and England, the one poised to seize advantage in the north, the other finding a pretext to interfere because of Japan's dependence on loans from Britain.[16]

Although one can trace a conflict of interest between advocates of a forward position in Asia, on the one hand, and those who preferred domestic reconstruction, on the other, it is important to note that both placed greatest emphasis on building up the strength of Japan in order better to be able to remove Western domination. The difference was over the means with which to achieve this objective.

The perceptions of the Western and Asianist schools were fundamentally the same: of a Japan faced with a challenge from the Western powers in a world of fiercely competing nations and empires. The divergence over policy was between those who thought Japan could best meet the challenge by establishing its primacy in East Asia – by force if necessary – and those who favoured a policy of accommodation and cooperation with the Western powers, among which Russia and even the Soviet Union were occasionally included.

The extreme example of the Asia first policy was the attempt to establish a Greater East Asia Co-prosperity Sphere during the Pacific War, a concept spelled out in detail in a secret planning paper of January 1942.[17] An example of the opposed internationalist position, which rejected any attempt to seize colonies or impose an East Asian 'Monroe Doctrine', is to be found in a speech by a Mitsubishi executive in December 1929, espousing the cause of peaceful commerce and international cooperation:

> It is essential to make all foreigners feel that the Japanese have been converted from their old religion [of liking war and being militarists] and have become advocates of peace.

The heyday of Japan's 'conversion' was in the 1920s when it embraced the League of Nations and the naval disarmament treaties of Washington. Wilson's principles of 'new diplomacy' became guidelines for Japan's international behaviour.[18]

The epitome of both points of view and the common ground from which they sprang is to be found in the contents of a letter written by Aritomo Yamagata (1838–1922) to Prime Minister Ōkuma at the outbreak of the First World War, in which he painted a grim picture of the future while urging a moderate policy. Yamagata foresaw an inevitable racial clash between the white and coloured peoples, a view influenced by recent events, including the wave of anti-Japanese feeling in California. It was therefore essential for Japan to court Chinese cooperation and trust, not by military aggression but by winning its support for establishing a common defence. At the same time there should be no needless aggravation of the United States, which was rich and strong. Instead, he concludes:

> I consider it more prudent, as far as China is concerned, not to raise the issue of a league of coloured peoples. Our empire is now in alliance with England; it has agreements with Russia and France; and we are mutually striving to promote both the peace of the Orient and the independence of China. But we must also realize the need to negotiate with America. Our politicians must be sternly warned against raising the issue of racialism which would hurt the feelings of other countries and impair their friendship for us. The crux of the matter is that China must be won over by hints and suggestions, and only gradually before we can realize our plans in the future.[19]

Here we have it in a nutshell: a sombre appreciation of the nature of world politics, which Yamagata thought would lead to a war of the races. It called for a long-term policy of Asian solidarity and, by implication, leadership in a Sino-Japanese association. However, the strength of the Western powers and the spread of Japan's interests, in which its dependence on foreign trade was no doubt a major consideration, required a policy of tact and negotiation in dealing with the West.

The issue of harmonizing policies of involvement in Asia, which meant essentially Korea and China, and cooperation with the West, especially Britain and the United States, is the main theme of Japan's external relations in the seventy years of this period. Relations with Russia/Soviet Union were a sub-theme, alternating as they did between extreme hostility, attempts at reaching accommodation over North China and Korea, and manoeuvring between the giant northern neighbour and the Anglo-Saxon maritime powers, as in the era of the Anglo-Japanese Alliance and during the Second World War.[20]

In spite of its ambivalence, Japan's external policy was remarkably successful until the 1930s. By then it had acquired a dominant position in North-East Asia and had achieved Great Power status. First it had fought a successful war against China, its only possible Asian rival. In 1902 it forged an alliance with Britain, the world's greatest empire. Next it defeated Russia in the war of 1904–5 and followed that with the annexation of Korea in 1910. After the First World War it was one of the 'Principal Allied and Associated Powers' in the negotiations over the Treaty of Versailles and gained a prominent place in the League of Nations as one of the five permanent members of the Council, alongside Britain, France, Italy and the United States. The last-mentioned, of course, never took its seat. The Council of the League did not have the kind of powers vested in the Security Council of the United Nations, and Japan left both the Council and the League in February 1933 over the report of the Lytton Commission on the 'Manchurian Incident'.

Yet all this time it was in effect little more than a regional power. The vacillation between Asia and the West, which had imposed a check on its ambitions, was temporarily removed in the 1930s and 1940s, when Japan made a disastrous bid to establish its hegemony over East Asia and the Western Pacific. This was followed by a crushing defeat which brought it back to the near helpless position of the mid-nineteenth century. And so ended the first phase of the attempt to come to terms with the conflicting pulls of Asia and the West.

THE SECOND STAGE OF MODERNIZATION (1945–89)

The early years of Japan's post-war history were dominated by the impact of defeat, surrender and occupation. The atomic bombing of Hiroshima and Nagasaki, which hastened the collapse and surrender of Japan, was a traumatic experience that has left its traces to this day. The psychological effect was, however, complex. It provoked a deep-seated revulsion against war and particularly nuclear weapons; a revulsion that has weakened considerably in the past decade with the change of generations. It strengthened the tendency towards racialism among the people in the feeling that the Americans would not have launched such weapons if the Japanese had belonged to the white race. It confirmed the sentiment that the Japanese are a unique people, for only they have been the victims of an atomic attack and thus have acquired a special status. Finally, it was seen as the culmination of a disastrous episode in Japan's modern history for which the military were primarily to blame. Hence a determination that the men in uniform should never again acquire a position of influence in the formation of national policy – an anti-militarism which bridged the divide between left and right in politics.

The occupation (1945–52), nominally by the allies in the war against Japan but in reality by the United States, has had an even more profound effect. This, too, was a first in Japanese experience. Real power resided in SCAP, in the person of General MacArthur. The basic structures and institutions of the state were retained, though substantially modified in the new, largely American-imposed constitution of 1946.[21] Among its most important and fundamental effects were the reduction of the emperor's status to that of 'symbol of the State and of the unity of the people, deriving his position from the will of the people with whom resides sovereign power' (Article 1). His very limited functions became those of a constitutional monarch. Political power shifted decisively to a Diet elected by universal suffrage and to the cabinet, which was responsible to it. The text of Article 9:

> Aspiring sincerely to an international peace based on justice and order, the Japanese people forever renounce war as a sovereign right of the nation and the threat or use of force as means of settling international disputes.
>
> In order to accomplish the aim of the preceding paragraph, land, sea, and air forces, as well as other war potential, will never* be

* The meaning of 'never' is not indicated in the Japanese text, which can be taken as implying the weaker sense conveyed by the word 'not'.

maintained. The right of belligerency of the state will not be recognized.

has led to it being popularly referred to as the 'Peace Constitution', and the so-called 'no-war' clause has remained a major influence on Japan's foreign and security policy.

Many other reforms ordered by the occupation authorities affected land ownership, labour relations, education, economic and social structures. All added to the revolutionary changes in post-war Japan. And yet, in spite of all the innovations, the subsequent history of Japan has again proved in many respects that *plus ça change, plus c'est la même chose.*

The emperor may have become a constitutional monarch in a democratic society, but the Imperial Household Agency has been busy trying to restore some of the mystery of the imperial institution and to keep him from too close a contact with the people. Shintō may have been divorced from the state, but it still plays a part in official ceremonies. The huge family-owned financial/industrial conglomerates may have been broken up, but they have regrouped around a bank. The educational system may have been reformed on American lines, but it has retained its hierarchical characteristics with the former imperial universities at the apex of the pyramid and the methods of instruction little changed. The Imperial Army and Imperial Navy may have disappeared, but Japan has acquired respectable military forces whose permitted area of operations has been gradually extended beyond the confines of the national territory and the surrounding waters. They have become almost self-sufficient in the production of armaments, and in terms of expenditure Japan had the third largest defence budget in the world by the end of the Cold War.

The revival of some of the traditional Japanese institutions and practices, albeit in a new garb, owes much to the cohesion of state and society under the occupation. In contrast to Germany, where the state disappeared completely and which was divided among the victors who quickly became enemies, Japan kept its central government with all the echelons down to local level. Unlike Germany, it was not divided into zones of occupation in which each occupying power pursued distinctive policies which were only loosely coordinated in the very early years after the war by a Central Control Commission, soon to be reduced to impotence by discord between the Soviet Union and the West. Moreover, even in the early years of vigorous punishment and reform, the United States pursued a limited objective: to readjust the balance in Japanese society in favour of the 'peaceful and democratic forces', while many of the basic elements were left largely untouched.[22] With the beginning of the Cold War, these objectives were pushed into the background to make way for a policy of converting Japan into a secure and reliable bastion of the anti-communist front. It was to occupy a key position in the American containment strategy in East Asia.

The biggest change from the first stage of its modernization was in Japan's foreign and security policy. The defeat at the hands of the American armed forces (though one can argue about the contribution to its collapse of the war of attrition in China or the largely British operations in South-East Asia) and the subsequent American-dominated allied post-war policy towards Japan led to a fundamental shift in the course of its external relations.

Although it is generally held that Japan has always regarded czarist Russia and later the Soviet Union as its principal enemy, relations with the northern neighbour included periods of friendliness and cooperation and there were times when the Japanese saw the Russians in a more favourable light than some of the Western powers. They were aware of their key position in the rivalry between Russia and the United States in the northern Pacific; a rivalry which was already apparent to them in the 1850s.[23] Hostility and conflict have indeed loomed larger in Russo-Japanese relations than in American-Japanese relations, but there had also been periods of hostility and tension between the United States and Japan. The arrival of the Black Ships in the mid-nineteenth century had hardly been welcomed with open arms. American immigration laws in the early years of this century had caused resentment and American policies in China had been a source of friction. American pressure had also helped to undermine the popular Anglo-Japanese Alliance of 1902.[24]

As a result of the defeat and occupation of Japan, the United States dominated Japanese foreign policy to the extent that American policy became the principal point of reference in the conduct of Japan's external relations, a habit that lasted well into the 1980s. From 1945 until 1951, Japan was virtually isolated from the rest of the world. All its relations with outsiders were filtered through the sieve of the American occupation authorities. The only foreigners of whom the Japanese were aware were Americans, leaving aside the relatively small impact of the British and Commonwealth occupation forces concentrated around Kure. Japanese who wanted to have contact with the world outside and who wanted to escape the drab life in their war-devastated and impoverished country, looked to the United States. The pro-American element among the élites was in the ascendant. More generally, the Japanese leadership had learnt the lesson of the past decade: do not rely on the superiority of the Japanese spirit to defeat the most powerful industrial nation on earth. The 'Yoshida Doctrine' was founded on such sentiments.

American influence was not, of course, confined to policy alone. It permeated all aspects of social and economic life and created a network of close personal relationships which influenced the thinking and attitudes of the dominant social groups. The majority of entrants to the diplomatic service in the early years after the war received part of their training in American establishments. By the 1990s, about a quarter of some eighty Gaimushō trainees are sent for two to three years to the United States. Many of the best and brightest post-war graduates of Japanese universities also spent several years of postgraduate study in American universities and institutes. It was a two-way traffic, and among foreigners Americans became by far the most knowledgeable in the language, culture and institutions of Japan.

The pre-eminent place acquired by the United States in the management of Japan's external relations continued for more than three decades after the return of full sovereignty in 1952. It was reinforced by the shift of economic relations from East Asia to North America. In contrast to the important place occupied by China and other East Asian countries in Japan's foreign trade before the war, those markets were all but closed to Japan under the occupation and in the 1950s and 1960s. This change of direction was due partly to economic factors: the war-damaged economies of East Asia, the fact that the United States was the only economy strong enough to assist the recovery of Japan and, most important, the impact of American requirements after the outbreak of the Korean War in 1950. Japan became the rear base and recuperation centre for the United Nations forces in Korea and the repair centre and workshop for their *matériel*.

Political factors also played their part in the reconstruction of Japan. The onset of the Cold War blocked off normal trading relations with the Soviet Union, China, and other areas under communist control. Obstacles to economic relations with the countries of South-East Asia, stemming from Japanese aggression and behaviour during the war, were not removed until a series of reparation agreements had been negotiated in the 1950s, and not until 1965 in the case of South Korea. Once the United States had switched from a policy of punitive reform to a policy of reconstruction in order to anchor Japan firmly in its containment system, everything was done to hasten its economic rehabilitation, a process facilitated by American requirements in the Korean War and, a decade later, by the needs arising from its involvement in Vietnam.

Among the domestic factors which furthered Japan's recovery, its disarmament and slow rearmament after 1952 played an important part. In spite of strong American pressures, successive governments made haste slowly in building up Japan's defence capability. In this they responded not only to strong domestic resistance, but used these inhibitions, including the existence of the American-inspired Article 9 of the constitution, as an excuse for concentrating on economic development. Never more than 1.8 per cent of the GNP was devoted to defence even at the height of the preliminary stages of rearmament in the 1950s.[25] The government knew that whatever the American complaints about Japan not doing enough, the United States could not abandon Japan without undermining its whole strategy in East Asia.

The same conditions that had enabled Japan to make a successful economic recovery in the 1950s, enabled it to embark on an economic expansion which elevated it to the rank of the third largest economy in the world, after the United States and the Soviet Union. Towards the end of the 1960s serious friction had developed with the United States, and for the next twenty years the dialogue between the two countries was dominated by the need to keep a balance between Japan's economic interest and the American strategic interest. As long as the Cold War was the prime focus of United States policy, Japan was able to mitigate its economic advance with increased contributions to American defence costs and general support for its global policy.

Japan took its place in the global system in two steps: first as a member of international organizations and then as a more clearly identified member of the Western group of powers clustered around the United States.

Just before and immediately after the end of the occupation, it joined a number of international agencies of the United Nations family. It became a member of the International Labour Office (ILO), the Food and Agriculture Organization (FAO), UNESCO, the World Health Organization (WHO) in 1951, and of the International Monetary Fund (IMF) and the International Bank for Reconstruction and Development (IBRD) – commonly known as the World Bank – in 1952. In 1955 it joined the General Agreement on Tariffs and Trade (GATT) and in the following year Japan was admitted to the United Nations and then joined the International Atomic Energy Agency (IAEA) in 1957. In 1964 it became a full member of the Organization for Economic Cooperation and Development (OECD).

Its emergence as a recognized member of the West was slower. In the 1960s the practice of regular consultations with the United States over security, political, economic, and cultural affairs, from cabinet level downwards, was extended to regular exchanges with the foreign ministers of other Western powers. In 1975 Japan became a founder member of the Group of Seven (G-7) industrialized powers. Earlier, in 1973, the unofficial but influential Trilateral Commission was established, linking the United States, the European Community and Japan. The trilateral dialogue intensified throughout the 1970s and 1980s and led to meetings between Japanese and NATO officials. It became commonplace to refer to a trilateral partnership and to dwell on the need to strengthen the European-Japanese side of the triangle, so as to make it more equilateral, and to talk of Japan as a member of the 'Western Alliance', although strictly speaking that was untrue.[26]

Throughout the post-war era Japan acted as if it were an external power in Asia. The process of normalizing relations with the non-communist countries, which had been enemies in the Second World War, was not completed until Japan had reached a settlement with its former colony in South Korea. Diplomatic relations with Mongolia and China (in that order) were established in 1972, and with North Vietnam in 1973, although it did not open its embassy in Hanoi until October 1975, after the North had conquered the South. Negotiations for the establishment of relations with North Korea were still in progress at the time of writing.

The legacy of the war, fear and suspicion of Japan's intentions, and the impact of the Cold War combined to keep Japan at a distance from the politics of East Asia. Economic relations were another matter, but at the official level the Japanese government maintained the fiction of separating economics from politics when dealing with communist countries, except the Soviet Union where its position was the reverse, i.e. there could be no separation of economics and politics. Japan's official position was aligned with that of the United States and regularly supported it over issues in the United Nations. Indeed, Japan's voting record in plenary sessions of the General Assembly in the years between 1956 and

1963 revealed it to be a typical member of the Western and Latin American bloc of countries, especially in the later years.[27]

While Japan stayed outside the main events in Asia during the post-war era, most Asian countries saw it as little more than an American vassal in the region. Below the surface, however, there were stirrings of an independent stance among important elements in the leadership and among the population at large. This inclination had already appeared over the preparations for the peace conference in San Francisco in the closing years of the occupation. In the end, American pressure and fear of the communist threat, heightened by the outbreak of war in Korea, prevailed and Japan followed the American lead over China, though not without significant reservations which left the door open for private and semi-official contact with the mainland in the following two decades. For many Japanese the barrier between their country and China seemed not only unnatural, but went against fundamental Japanese interests. Sentimentality, anti-American feelings, and economic interest were mixed in this view, but it also signified a widespread opinion that it was wrong for Japan to be cut off from a people and cultural sphere with which it had more in common than with the people and culture whose origins were basically European.[28]

In the twenty years up to 1972, Japan kept in step with American policy towards China. When the United States suddenly quickened the pace in 1971, it caught Japan by surprise and neglected to consult its partner before the momentous announcement of President Nixon's forthcoming visit to China. The Japanese learnt the lesson: the United States could not be relied upon always to take into account the views and feelings of its allies before making major changes in its policy. Although the partnership continued as before, and even deepened in the military/strategic field during the period of heightened Cold War tension between the Soviet invasion of Afghanistan in 1979 and the advent of Gorbachev in 1985, there were unmistakeable signs of a greater assertiveness on the part of Japan.

The first open indication of greater independence came in policy towards the Middle East, when economic considerations – in this case Japan's dependence on Middle East oil – led it to break ranks over the recognition of the Palestine Liberation Organization (PLO) in 1973. Eight years later, in October 1981, Prime Minister Suzuki became the first political leader of a major Western state to receive the Head of the PLO, when Yasser Arafat was on an 'unofficial' visit in Tokyo. A further intimation of Japanese self-assertiveness was the interest during the 1970s in fostering the Euro-Japanese dialogue within the triangular relationship between the United States, Western Europe and Japan. This tendency became particularly marked during the twin Iran hostage and Afghan crises at the turn of 1979–80.[29] Another sign was Japanese persistence in maintaining some trade relations with the communist North throughout the war in Vietnam and disagreement with American policy towards that country when the war ended in 1975. Japan's refusal in the 1980s to be drawn into periodic revivals of tension between China and the United States over Taiwan was a further example.

In general, there was a tendency to steer clear of involvement in American quarrels with other countries. The one exception was in relations with the Soviet Union, where the territorial dispute led Japan to adopt a hard-line position, especially after 1973, in the wake of Prime Minister Tanaka's fruitless visit to Moscow. Even then, at times of heightened tensions, as in 1979–80, Japan sought to coordinate its position with that of the European Community in the hope of exercising a moderating influence on American policy.

At home, the centre of gravity in the debate over the purpose and extent of Japanese rearmament shifted from pacifist versus political realist – the latter advocated a modest, defensive rearmament in the context of the security treaty with the United States – to a debate between political realist and military realist, who saw beyond the American alliance and advocated a substantially rearmed Japan which would be ready to assume an independent role in international affairs. A smaller group, an offshoot of the military realists and sometimes rather misleadingly referred to as 'Gaullists', went further and advocated Japanese nuclear armament as an indispensable element of global power status. It is instructive to compare the movements in the security debate with the movement of policy. The latter reveals a gradual progression from measures aimed at minimal self-defence to an expansion of the concept of security and of the role of the SDF within the framework of the American alliance (see the chart on pp. 34–5). Behind these debates and gestures, which focused mainly on the nature and future of the relationship with the United States, one can detect a resurrection of the Asianist versus Westernizer debate in modern guise. Should Japan become ever more deeply embedded in what was loosely termed the Western Alliance or should it concentrate on developing its role as leading power and champion of East Asia?

A CHRONOLOGY OF THE POST-WAR SECURITY DEBATE IN JAPAN

	Policy	*Trends in the Debate*
1946	Promulgation of Constitution (3 Nov.)	*Dominance of 'Pacifist'* (unarmed neutrality) and *left-wing ideological* (people's defence) *positions*: defend the Constitution; abolish SDF; and scrap the Security Treaty
1950	Establishment of National Police Reserve	
1951	Signature of Security Treaty with US (8 Sept.)	
1954	Law establishing Self-Defence Forces (SDF)	
1957	Basic policy for national defence formulated	
1960	Treaty of Mutual Cooperation and Security with US (19 Jan.)	Emergence of '*Political Realists*': Defend the Constitution; maintain SDF, but as secondary element in a comprehensive security policy; and support the Security Treaty
1967	Qualified arms export embargo by ordinance	
1968	Enunciation of three non-nuclear principles (30 Jan.)	
1970–1	Nakasone, Director-General of Defence Agency, issues first Defence White Paper (Oct. 1970); wants to develop 'autonomous' defence	
1975	Sakata/Schlesinger Agreement (29 Aug.)	*Dominance of 'Political Realists'*
1976	Comprehensive arms export embargo guidelines (Feb.); establishment of Japan–US Sub-Committee on Defence Cooperation (8 July); National Defence Programme Outline (NDPO) (29 Oct.); defence expenditure not to exceed 1% of GNP (Nov.)	
1980	MSDF participates in RIMPAC exercise (Feb.–Mar.); Inoki Report on Comprehensive National Security (July)	*Rise of 'Military Realists'*: revise Constitution when practicable; develop SDF as principal element in security policy; support Security Treaty on terms of full equality (some against nuclear armament and for integration into US strategy; others for 'defensive' nuclear armament and support for US, but decide on own priorities)

1981	Suzuki/Reagan Summit (7–8 May) (use of word 'alliance', acceptance of sealane defence)	
1983	Decision to transfer military technology to US (14 Jan.) – Agreement signed (8 Nov.)	
1985	Mid-term defence build-up programme (1986–90) – breach of 1% of GNP ceiling	*Challenge from 'Modern Militarists/Gaullists'*: revise Constitution; develop SDF as dominant element in security policy; support Security Treaty for time being, but aim at autonomous defence
1986	Cabinet Security Council established	
1987	Agreement on participation in SDI research signed (22 July)	

The various aspects of the debate reflected competing interests among the Japanese élites. Such conflicts were myriad, criss-crossing the political spectrum. They divided big business from medium and small enterprises in the China versus Taiwan debate. They pitted giant enterprises against each other over competition in the China market. They led firms to flout government policy, as over the export of machine tools to the USSR by Tōshiba in 1987. They led to differing policies between the Foreign Ministry, with its prime concern over the state of relations with the United States, and MITI, with its more nationalistic concern over the health of Japanese enterprises. Within ministries, too, there were differences. The Foreign Ministry had its American faction and its China faction. The politicians of the ruling Liberal-Democratic Party were also divided, not according to the factions, which were primarily concerned with the acquisition of funds and office, but according to interest groups which had links to politicians in other countries, such as Taiwan, China, and Korea. Nor were the opposition parties free from internal divisions over policy. On the whole, their influence was marginal, with the exception of some individuals who had close relations with leading politicians of the LDP and with key figures in other countries.

The diffusion of power in post-war Japan, where the prime minister was one chieftain among several, some of whom were more powerful than he, where there was a frequent change of ministers in all departments of state, and where consensus-building was an essential part of the policy-making process, meant that foreign policy was not easy to define in terms of a clear line or sense of direction. Moreover, the prosperity of the country and the general satisfaction of the people inhibited any diversion from the principles of the 'Yoshida Doctrine'. It seemed best to leave things as they were and to avoid adventures. The startling changes in the external environment at the end of the 1980s interrupted the placid course of policy and have challenged its validity.

SUMMARY

The geography, history and culture of Japan tie it to Asia. Over the centuries its indigenous culture absorbed and was refined by the influences of Buddhism and Confucianism coming from the mainland. However, these religious, intellectual and cultural imports were assimilated to a strongly rooted native tradition which favoured a pragmatic eclecticism. Thus, while the confucian ethic was the umbilical cord that tied Japan to the civilization of East Asia, it was adapted to serve the needs and interests of the ruling class. Until 1945, one might say that it was an 'imperial Confucianism' in the service of the military caste. Since the war it has become a 'merchant Confucianism' which reflected the interests of the political and industrial élites.[30]

The introduction of Western rationalist thought and technology followed the same course. The Japanese did not copy, but were learners and adapters. Consciousness of being Asian and that Japan's destiny lay with Asia struggled with the attraction of the West and the adaptation of Western ways which made Japan the first 'modern' state in Asia and gave the Japanese a sense of superiority over their fellow Asians that compensated for their inferiority complex in the face of Europe and America.

The disastrous outcome of Japan's expansion into Asia and its return to near isolation under American domination temporarily overlaid the Asia versus the West debate. However, the Japanese never lost a belief in their uniqueness. The tradition of eclecticism and pragmatic adaptation, combined with a refusal to be philosophically or ideologically hidebound, enabled them to adjust to altered circumstances.

The characteristic of sitting lightly on ideological systems is illustrated by the ease with which intellectuals have moved from one position to another. For example, Katsuichirō Kamei (1907–

66) turned from extreme left-wing radicalism to the advocacy of a pacifistic Asianism in his later years. Ikutarō Shimizu (1907–88), on the other hand, moved from support of the Imperial Rule Assistance Association during the war to become a left-wing pacifist after the war, only to return to a strident nationalism in the 1970s and 1980s, which led him to call for a nuclear-armed Japan.

The general tendency among thinkers was to return to the Asian roots of Japanese culture, often after having been strongly attracted to the West in their earlier years. This trend is also noticeable among novelists such as Junichirō Tanizaki (1886–1965), Jirō Osaragi (1897–1973) and Yukio Mishima (1925–70). Their nostalgia took the form of a Japanese version of East Asian culture, as in the case of Tanizaki and Osaragi, or of a cruder nationalism as with Mishima. The phenomenon was neatly encapsulated by Kamei:

> We are all familiar with how Asian culture, transformed or more highly refined, became part of the flesh and blood of Japanese culture. However, like most young men of the past sixty or seventy years, I used not to consider Asia as being necessarily primary to us. My ignorance of and indifference to China and India did not trouble me in the least, and I was constantly fascinated by Europe. I thought that to learn from European knowledge was our first task, and I neglected the matter of learning from the wisdom of the East.[31]

The early manifestation of national identity as well as economic and social developments in the Tokugawa era facilitated the rapid modernization of Japan under the impact of the West in the nineteenth century. Of course, other factors also influenced the process, such as the introduction of universal education, the development of modern communications, the creation of a mass conscript army, and the government-led industrialization. Thus began the 'catching-up' syndrome, which dominated the ruling élites, with its concomitant attempt to distance Japan from a backward Asia. These attitudes continued during the period of economic revival after the Pacific War. Throughout, Japan has sought to play a role in the region which was commensurate with that of a first-class power.

The rise of Japan as a modern nation state passed through three stages. In the first it tried to ward off attempts at outright domination by the West. At the same time it asserted its equality with the other imperial powers in Korea (1876) and China (1895). The next stage began after Japan had finally removed the threat of domination through the abolition of extraterritoriality in 1899. It spanned the first forty-five years of the twentieth century during which Japan sought to establish its hegemony over North-East Asia through the expulsion of Russian influence (1904–5), the annexation of Korea (1910), the Twenty One Demands (1916), the domination of Manchuria (1931), and the attempted conquest of China (1937). In a parallel process, Japan tried to win recognition as a world-class nation through the alliance with Britain (1902), participation in the First World War on the allied side, membership of the 'Big Five' in the peace settlement of Versailles, participation in the founding of the League of Nations, and later through association with the Axis powers in the 1930s and 1940s.

After an interval of about two decades, the third stage began when Japan joined international organizations such as OECD and GATT. Japanese participation in the annual meetings of the Group of Seven industrialized powers and an ever closer association with the Western alliance marked its acceptance into the circle of the world's leading states. As Japan gained in economic strength and influence during the 1970s and 1980s, the old Asia versus West debate revived at a practical level. It had rumbled on in the early period of post-war obscurity, but was largely confined to intellectuals and academics. Since the end of the Cold War the debate has continued and become more acute. It reflects the interplay of many competing needs and interests as well as the absence of a single, identifiable, and undisputed centre of power in post-war Japan, which could give its external policy a clear sense of direction.

3 The breakdown of the post-war international system and its impact on Japan's Asia policy

THE BREAKDOWN OF THE POST-WAR ECONOMIC ORDER

The post-war economic order emerged with the Bretton Woods Conference of July 1944, which created the International Monetary Fund (IMF) and the International Bank for Reconstruction and Development (IBRD). The idea behind the establishment of these institutions was to avoid a repetition of the currency chaos and 'beggar-my-neighbour' policies of the 1930s, which were thought to have been a major factor contributing to the outbreak of the Second World War. The IMF was intended to finance short-term imbalances in international payments, while the World Bank was to make available long-term capital loans to states in urgent need.

Under the system the value of a national currency was expressed in terms of gold, which meant in essence the dollar value of gold and the convertibility of the dollar. Fixed exchange rates, pegged to the United States dollar, gave an economic advantage to Japan during the first twenty-five years of reconstruction and expansion after the war. With its increasingly undervalued currency it was able to penetrate and eventually dominate foreign markets. On the other hand, the rules emanating from the Bretton Woods agreement enabled the government to avoid current account deficits in the balance of trade so as to prevent a devaluation of the yen in the early post-war years.

The measures taken to preserve the post-war international monetary order had the effect of creating a financial system in Japan which included strict controls over imports and capital flows and ensured that there was little borrowing from overseas. As a result, an economy emerged that was 'owned, operated, and supplied by Japanese firms' – an arrangement which echoed policy in the late nineteenth century, when Japan was preoccupied in escaping foreign economic domination.[1]

Bretton Woods ensured stability during the early post-war decades, but inflationary trends began to appear as a result of the outflow of dollars, beginning with massive aid for reconstruction in Europe under the Marshall Plan, followed by increasing military expenditures with the development of the Cold War. All this assisted the resurgence of the European and Japanese economies, but the mark and the yen remained undervalued while dollar scarcity turned into dollar surplus. The basic flaw was the overvaluation of the dollar at a parity with gold, which had been fixed in 1934. This worked well enough as long as the dollar's pre-eminence was backed by the gold reserves in Fort Knox. By the end of the 1950s these had begun to dwindle, so that inflationary pressures and American balance of payments deficits eventually led to the devaluation of the dollar in the 1970s, precipitating the break-up of the post-war international financial regime.

By the time the Bretton Woods system had come to an end with the floating of currencies in 1973, the relative positions of Japan and the United States were reversed. From being the world's creditor nation after the war, the United States economy was weakening and the value of the dollar declined, while an impoverished post-war Japan had become rich, with a currency whose value rose rapidly. Soon Japan became the world's leading creditor nation.

There were, of course, other factors which accounted for Japan's rise to economic pre-eminence. The liberalization of international trade through the GATT system, which was protected by American hegemony, and the availability of cheap raw materials, especially oil, enabled Japan to make rapid strides in rebuilding its industries and begin its progress as a major exporter, first to the North American market and then to Western Europe, once American resistance had placed restraints on the uninhibited import of Japanese manufactures. Another factor in Japan's economic success had been the demand for supplies and services by the American military establishment in East Asia.

After the steep rise in the price of oil, on which Japan depended for more than seventy per cent of its energy requirements in the 1970s, a pattern was established in which Japan balanced a large deficit in its trade with resource-rich countries, particularly the

Middle Eastern oil producers and Indonesia, by accumulating substantial surpluses in its trade with the industrialized world of North America and Western Europe.

Friction emerged first with the United States and then spread to Europe. The strong economic nationalism of Japan clashed with the weakening economic power of the United States and there began an endless series of disputes over Japanese market penetration and threatened dominance, in textiles, automobiles, ball-bearings, VCRs and microchips. In return, the United States and the European Community pressed for the opening of the Tokyo financial market and the removal of structural impediments to foreign penetration of the Japanese economy, especially the so-called non-tariff trade barriers against imports in the Japanese market.

The demise of the post-war economic order, therefore, preceded the end of the Cold War by nearly two decades. While the structures of the international security system, which rested on the complex relationship between the superpowers, were still in place, the bilateral and trilateral relations among the three principal partners of the West, the United States, the European Community and Japan, were dominated by economic disputes.

THE COLLAPSE OF THE COLD WAR STRUCTURES

Fixing precise dates for the end or beginning of certain periods in human affairs is bound to be arbitrary and artificial. We may date the end of the post-war economic order, which began in 1944, with the collapse of the fixed exchange rate mechanism in 1973, but the signs of change had already begun to appear in the 1960s with the rising economic power of Japan and West Germany. Similarly, it is possible to date the end of the Cold War era, which had begun in 1947 with the Truman Doctrine, with the breach of the Berlin Wall in 1989 or, alternatively, with the demise of the Soviet Union in 1991. Yet, with the benefit of hindsight, we can trace the events which precipitated the collapse of the post-war political and security structures to the appointment of Mikhail Gorbachev as Secretary-General of the Communist Party of the Soviet Union (CPSU) in 1985.

The Cold War system rested on the competitive/cooperative relationship between the United States and the Soviet Union. Again with hindsight, it is easy to see that the two giants were far from being equal in strength and that at the beginning the principal weapon of the Soviet Union was the attraction of its ideological position, first in the war-devastated and impoverished regions of Europe and northern Asia, and later in the successor states of European colonial empires. The economic primacy of the United States was never challenged throughout the Cold War era and its military superiority was only gradually eroded until a rough strategic parity was established in the 1970s. The next twenty years were marked by the seemingly interminable arms control negotiations between the superpowers, whose main objective was to establish a system of mutual nuclear deterrence within the context of a continuing arms race.

Towards the end of the 1960s it became fashionable to talk of an emerging multipolar world in which the states of Western Europe, China and Japan were regarded as new centres in the power constellation of the world. Nevertheless, the security structures were still dominated by the two superpowers whose nuclear armouries set them apart from all other states. The incalculable dangers of a conflict between them and their associated alliances encouraged caution in their mutual antagonism. They accepted the delimitation of informally understood spheres of influence between them and they shared a determination to prevent any of their allies or of the non-aligned states from upsetting the stability of the balance between them.

Within this over-arching global structure, the Japanese-American security system was embedded in the terms of the revised Treaty of Mutual Cooperation and Security of 1960 (see Appendix I). It was a distinctive feature of this treaty that mutual assistance applied only in the event of aggression against either party 'in the territories under the administration of Japan' (Article V). An attack on the United States and its armed forces elsewhere in the world would not oblige Japan to come to its assistance. However, the wording of Article IV and the undertaking in Article VI, which grants the use by American 'land, air and naval forces of facilities and areas in Japan' for the purpose of maintaining 'international peace and security in the Far East', placed Japan under some moral obligation to take note of threats to peace and security within the East Asian region and to support the United States in its attempt to deal with them. A subsequent exchange of letters between the then Prime Minister, Nobusuke Kishi and Secretary of State Christian Herter, gave Japan a kind of veto through the requirement of 'prior consultation' over the use of American bases in Japan for combat operations in pursuit of this objective.[2]

After the Treaty had been in force for ten years, either party could give one year's notice to the other of its intention to abrogate it (Article X). Technically, therefore, the Treaty could have been terminated within a relatively short space of time. In the light of developments since the end of the Cold War and the increased role of the United Nations in international security, it is of interest that the wording of Article X also provides for mutual agreement to scrap the pact if 'there shall have come into force such United Nations arrangements as will satisfactorily provide for the maintenance of international peace and security in the Japan area'.

The circumstances of 1960 and the situation in North-East Asia at that time could lead to only one conclusion about the objectives of the Treaty: to provide the United States with a forward position in the containment of the communist powers and to tie Japan into this policy. The Sino-Soviet split of the 1960s and 1970s complicated matters to some extent, but there was never any doubt, at least on the Japanese side, that the principal threat came from the Soviet Union.

The shared strategic objective of the two governments ensured that the growing economic competition and friction between Japan and the United States would be kept under control in the interest of their common diplomatic and security policies. The collapse of the Soviet Union has raised the question of the purpose of the Mutual Security Treaty and has threatened to disturb the balance between shared politico-security interests and economic friction in the Japanese-American relationship. Moreover, a divergence in their foreign policies had already become apparent under the comparatively stable conditions of the Cold War. We have noted such differences over China, Vietnam and the Middle East as well as a Japanese reluctance to shoulder a greater burden within the Western alliance, due to constitutional and legal constraints and the force of public opinion (see pp. 32–6).

THE CONSEQUENCES

The disappearance of the communist regimes in central and eastern Europe in a series of relatively bloodless revolutions and the final disintegration of the Soviet Union into sixteen republics, each claiming full sovereignty and independence, destroyed the structures of regional security in Europe which had evolved in the Cold War years. Under the old order, Europe, like Caesar's Gaul, had been divided into three: the members of the Atlantic Alliance, the Warsaw Pact, and a group of neutral or non-aligned states. The stability of the system depended on the leadership of the two blocs by the two superpowers and their relationship of mutual deterrence. The system was managed through endless negotiations conducted between them and their alliances in the main cities of the neutral/non-aligned countries: Geneva, Helsinki, Vienna, Stockholm and Belgrade. The whole process was institutionalized by the Conference on Security and Cooperation in Europe (CSCE) at Helsinki in 1975.

In the 1990s the Europeans were suddenly faced with the task of reformulating the functions and structures of the CSCE, the Atlantic Alliance, the European Community, and the Western European Union (WEU) in the face of mounting disorder and violence in the countries that had been within the orbit of the Soviet Union or had been dominated by independent communist regimes like those of Yugoslavia and Albania. The recrudescence of extreme nationalism and ethnic hatreds presented the leaders of the most important European states with problems very different from those of the Cold War.

East Asia was not unaffected by these upheavals, but the transition to the post-Cold War era was less abrupt and violent. One explanation of the more gradual process of change lies in the fact that the disappearance of the Soviet Union has meant that it has simply been replaced by Russia. No independent republics have emerged in the Soviet Far East close to Japan. Mongolia, the only country in the region comparable to the Soviet satellites of eastern Europe, made a relatively smooth and trouble-free transition to full independence, although the future remains uncertain. It could easily become the battleground of a renewed struggle for influence and domination between Russia and China.[3] Furthermore, with the exception of Russia and Mongolia, the old communist dictatorships were still firmly in place in China, North Korea and Vietnam. The political landscape, therefore, did not change so dramatically as in Europe. With China in the forefront, each of these regimes is trying to combine elements of a liberal market economy with the maintenance of ideological rectitude. However, the European experience has shown that liberal economics and the application of Marxist dogma are incompatible in the West and that sooner or later one of them must give way.

None the less, exactly the same conclusion may not apply to East Asia. Its post-war history has shown that authoritarian government, as in South Korea, Taiwan or Singapore, can be combined with fast and effective modernization and growth. Even Japan bears witness to the success of government intervention in the management of the economy, which is anathema to the theorists of free markets. The extraordinarily rapid development of the south China region near Hong Kong suggests that governments claiming to be the guardians of Marxist orthodoxy are perfectly capable of pursuing pragmatic policies which encourage economic freedom and enterprise. Such policies have their risks and the pro-democracy movement in China or the periodic student and worker disturbances in South Korea illustrate the problem of reconciling liberal economics with an authoritarian style of government. Those who benefit most from the reforms are most likely to demand a greater share of political power and those who benefit least are equally disaffected by the frustration of their rising expectations. Both the military-dominated government in South Korea and the communist oligarchy in China responded to the pressures for political change with a mixture of repression and concessions – more of the former in China and of the latter in Korea. It remains an open question whether the three communist regimes can in the end be transformed without the rupture of revolution and without an absolute disavowal of the ideology which they have professed since the war. The European experience would suggest that the answer is likely to be in the negative.

When they first established themselves, the communist leaders in Asia shared the same Marxist ideology as their colleagues in Europe and elsewhere, but the new regimes soon displayed distinctive characteristics. This was due to a combination of factors. The revolution in their countries had been based on the peasantry and not on an urban proletariat; it had merged with a nationalist anti-imperialist movement; and it carried with it elements of the east Asian cultural tradition which was dominated by the confucian ethic.

Once Mao had become leader of the Chinese Communist Party (CCP), he embarked on a sinification of Marxism, which emphasised its compatibility with 'Chinese peculiarities'.[4] During the Cultural Revolution, stress was laid upon the continuity of the revolutionary tradition in Chinese history and its links with the people's right to withdraw the 'Mandate of Heaven' from unjust and corrupt rulers. When Chinese communists rejected confucianism they had in mind the élitist and corrupt manifestation of confucian governance that sustained an oppressive feudal system. The confucian 'thesis' was discarded, but they did not accept the Western 'antithesis', which had overthrown the old order in China at the beginning of the twentieth century. Instead, they fashioned a 'synthesis' and called it communism with Chinese characteristics.[5]

Their view of the world also differed from traditional concepts. In the early years they accepted that the source of their new civilization lay outside China and that China occupied a status inferior to that of the Soviet Union, the homeland of communism. Later, especially after the break with the Soviet Union in 1960, there was a semblance of a return to traditional concepts with the insistence that China was the true home of revolutionary enlightenment. Some traditional characteristics of government also made their appearance. Zhong-nanhai, the seat of the party leadership in Beijing, became more like the old 'Forbidden City' of the emperors, and nepotism and corruption were rife in the ranks of the CCP. Nevertheless, in its foreign relations the new China accepted the world of nation states, the machinery of international diplomacy, and the principles of international law and organization.[6]

The combination of ideological and philosophical flexibility with economic pragmatism could mean that, unlike its European counterparts, the Chinese regime may transform without the dislocation of a revolution. Moreover, communism in China was never divorced from nationalism since it was born out of the nationalist movement at the beginning of the century. It retained its legitimacy when it openly rejected its subordination to Soviet leadership in the 1960s.

A similar case can be made for the course of Vietnam's modernization. The technocratic and reformist leadership, with its eyes on the Japanese model, can also lay claim to the nationalist aspirations which had been so powerfully exploited in the struggle for independence, first against the French and then against the Americans. North Korea presents a rather different picture. Not only will its future be determined by the fact that it is only one half, and in many respects the weaker half, of a divided country, facing an ideologically opposed and economically successful regime in the south, but its late leader, Kim Il-sung, had gone a long way to establishing a Confucian-style regime with a dynastic succession.

During the Cold War, Japan viewed its communist neighbours in a different light from that in which West Europeans and Americans regarded the communist world. The ideological fears of the Japanese have been less pronounced, partly because of their own lack of ideological dogmatism and partly because they recognized a cultural kinship with other Asian peoples. The continued existence of at least nominally communist states in East Asia does not mean that they believe that the Cold War must continue in that region until the last vestiges of communism have disappeared from the scene.

The problems for Japan lie elsewhere. The disappearance of the confrontation between the superpowers transformed the situation in the two principal areas of tension: Korea and Cambodia. The Cold War stability in Korea, in spite of periods of heightened hostility between North and South, which were marked by incidents in the Demilitarized Zone (DMZ) and on the seas around the peninsula, was guaranteed by the two superpowers who shared an interest in avoiding the outbreak of a new war. This was also the interest of the two other states in the neighbourhood, China and Japan. The complex and conflicting relationships among the four powers, which included Sino-Soviet rivalry for influence over the North, the Chinese attempt in the 1970s and early 1980s to forge a common front with the United States and Japan against the Soviet Union, and the Japanese concern to retain a substantial American military presence in the South in the face of American attempts to reduce it, did not undermine their common determination to prevent the North–South confrontation from getting out of hand. Hence there was a strong likelihood that any tendency towards adventurism in either of the Korean states would be restrained. The Cold War, therefore, had the same stabilizing effect in Korea that it had in Europe.

The beginnings of a Sino-Soviet *rapprochement* in 1989 and the establishment of diplomatic relations between the Soviet Union and South Korea (30 September 1990), to be followed by China (24 August 1992), increased the isolation of North Korea. Although the basic interest of the four powers in Korean stability has not changed, the paradoxical effect of the changed international environment, coupled with the beginnings of an American withdrawal from the South,[7] has been to increase the autonomy of the two Korean states in managing their mutual relationship. A loss of control by the external powers over their clients in the peninsula raises the prospect of increased instability and the possibility of a violent confrontation.

The situation surrounding Cambodia is different. Since the American withdrawal from Vietnam in 1973, both superpowers have operated through proxies in South-East Asia. Their competition in the region was complicated by Sino-Vietnamese and Sino-Soviet hostility. Notwithstanding Great Power rivalries, the real protagonists in Cambodia were China, backed by ASEAN, and Vietnam. But this was not a simple equation. Some of the member states of ASEAN regarded China as potentially a greater threat to the region than a Vietnam backed by the Soviet Union. The end of the Cold War was marked by a substantial withdrawal of the Soviet Union under Gorbachev. The Soviet/Russian interest in South-East Asia had always been subordinate to the more important issue of relations with China. Once a Sino–Soviet *rapprochement* was in progress, the strategic objectives of the Soviet-Vietnamese alliance lost much of their relevance.[8]

Eventually, the four warring factions in Cambodia accepted the UN peace plan in September 1990 and signed a Peace Agreement in Paris in October 1991. Subsequent events have shown how fragile such arrangements can be. The removal of the Cold War context has opened the way for autonomous manoeuvre by the local actors, as it did in Korea, and it does not follow automatically that this will lead to greater peace or stability.

From the Japanese perspective, the security provided by the relatively stable Cold War structures, even when they shifted from a bilateral to a trilateral context, has been replaced by a much more fluid and unpredictable state of affairs. But Japan has also been released from the constraints imposed by the Cold War.

The chief rationale for the security treaty with the United States has been undermined. It does not follow that it will be abandoned lightly. The wording of Articles IV and VI justifies its continuation after the Soviet threat had disappeared. However, the pressures for a physical withdrawal from the region will become greater in the United States as the administration addresses the urgent needs of the domestic economy. Though Japan might be willing to continue with the security relationship, it cannot count on a similar commitment from the United States. It will in any case have the opportunity to pursue a more independent policy in Asia than hitherto without having the need constantly to look over its shoulder to assess American reactions. On the other hand, an independent policy is fraught with many uncertainties and hazards, which will be discussed in Chapters 4 and 5.

The opportunity provided by the current transitional stage in world politics is for Japan to develop and pursue a more distinctive policy in global affairs. There was much talk in the 1980s that it should play a political role commensurate to its economic and financial strength. In this it was encouraged by the United States and other friendly countries who saw that role in terms of a greater Japanese contribution to the Western alliance. But the domestic debate also stemmed from a feeling of national assertiveness which grew out of a new self-confidence.

How to convert this sentiment into practical policies has been and continues to be the great conundrum. One can detect indications of a more distinctive Japanese policy in world affairs, but the outlines remain hazy. This is due to a variety of factors, including domestic politics and the impact of external events in an environment which is changing with bewildering rapidity. Much will also depend on whether the old arguments of Japan as an insider versus Japan as an outsider in Asia remain valid and how it will try to reconcile its regional and global interests. These questions are the subject of Chapter 6.

4 Regional interests and policy in North-East Asia

INTRODUCTION

Russia, Korea, China and Taiwan are the neighbours of Japan in North-East Asia. Although it is surrounded by the sea, Russia and the Korean peninsula are close enough to raise questions about the territorial security of Japan. Policy-makers, and especially those responsible for national defence, face two sets of problems: how to protect the territorial integrity of Japan, including the waters close to the archipelago and the airspace in the immediate vicinity, and how to ensure stability in the region which would guarantee Japan unhindered access to its global markets.

A serious threat to the national territory does not exist at the time of writing and is not likely to emerge for the remainder of the century and the early years of the next. The situation in the seas around Japan is rather more uncertain. Japan has unresolved territorial disputes with all its neighbours. Most prominent is the issue of sovereignty over the Russian occupied 'Northern Territories', comprising the two southernmost islands of the Kurile chain, Etorofu and Kunashiri, and the smaller island of Shikotan and the Habomai group of islets which are a geological outcrop of the Nemuro peninsula of Hokkaidō. Japan is the claimant in this case. There is also a dispute with China and Taiwan over the even smaller, partially submerged islands near the Ryūkyūs, called the Senkaku by the Japanese (Diaoyu by the Chinese). Here the Chinese and the government of Taiwan, in rare agreement, are the claimants. Finally, there is Korean occupied Takeshima Island in the Sea of Japan, where Japan is the claimant. In addition and related to the disputes over the islands, but extending over a much wider area, there are conflicting claims over fishing rights and the exploitation of undersea mineral resources of the continental shelf, particularly oil and natural gas.

These clashes of interest affecting sovereignty over various islands and exclusive rights over the surrounding waters are potentially dangerous sources of friction. The claims to the Northern Territories and Takeshima are symbols of Japan's national assertiveness; the issue of the Senkaku Islands is an instrument of Chinese pressure. While not completely quiescent during the Cold War, these disputes were contained because none of the governments wanted them to escalate to the point where there was a danger of the outbreak of hostilities. Furthermore, the prospect of American involvement in the disputes acted as an important restraint on all the parties. That involvement has become less certain since the end of the Cold War.

The guarantee of stability in North-East Asia rested on two conditions. First, that a balance of power be maintained, so that none of the major states would be tempted to make a dash for hegemony in the region. Such a balance could, in theory, have existed among the three resident powers in the region: the Soviet Union, China and Japan. But the delicate position of Japan in the aftermath of its record of aggression and in the circumstances of the Cold War made it inevitable that the only outsider, the United States, would in fact ensure the maintenance of the balance. The second condition required the containment of local conflicts or revolutions in order to avoid their internationalization. Such disturbances might have jeopardized Japan's important lines of communication to South-East Asia, the Indian Ocean, the Middle East and Europe.

The principal threats to regional stability come from the division of Korea and the conflict between the authorities in Taipei and Beijing. Here, too, the role of the United States has been decisive. American policy during the Korean War ensured that it remained limited, in spite of Chinese intervention and political pressures to bring the Nationalists on Taiwan into the fray. The continued American presence in South Korea since 1953 and of the Seventh Fleet in the Straits of Formosa has prevented periodic crises from upsetting the basic stability of the region. The removal of the limits set by the Cold War structures has created the potential for an uncontrolled escalation of violence in local conflicts in the absence of external constraints, thus bringing about their gradual internationalization, as has happened in former Yugoslavia.

The relations between Japan and its neighbours in the post-Cold War era of transition will therefore be greatly influenced by the twin requirements of territorial security and regional stability. Its policy towards each is also determined by the special characteristics of the relationship, which have their roots in the past and are influenced by the international politics of the region as a whole.

RELATIONS WITH RUSSIA[1]

As the Japanese see it, Russia is a troublesome and threatening neighbour in North-East Asia. It is the most powerful state in closest proximity to Japan and culturally and ethnically the only non-Asian power in the region.

The Russian advance to the east and south in the eighteenth and nineteenth centuries brought it into contact with Japan and turned Japanese attention to the sparsely populated and poorly secured island of Ezo (Hokkaidō). After a century of skirmishes in the southern islands of the Kurile chain and around Hokkaidō, the boundary between the two empires was delimited for the first time by the Treaty of Shimoda in 1855. The line of demarcation was drawn between the islands of Etorofu and Urup. For the next hundred years the territorial disputes between the two empires centred on Sakhalin and the Asian mainland, where they vied for influence and control over Korea, which was annexed by Japan in 1910, and Manchuria, which became a Japanese puppet state in 1931.

The history of Russo-Japanese relations has been dominated by rivalry and armed conflict. First there were difficulties between the two communities on Sakhalin, which were settled by the Treaty of St Petersburg in 1875. Under its terms Russia received Sakhalin in exchange for the remainder of the Kurile Islands right up to the tip of Kamchatka. The next point of friction was the mainland, when Russia unwisely joined with France and Germany to force Japan to disgorge its annexation of the Liaotung peninsula after its victorious war against China (1894–5). The war of revenge against Russia (1904–5) ended with Japan's annexation of South Sakhalin and its unchallenged dominance over Korea.

After the Bolshevik Revolution, Japan joined with the United States, Britain, France and Canada in the occupation of the Russian Maritime Province and eastern Siberia, where it stayed after the allies had withdrawn in 1920 and extended its occupation to northern Sakhalin. It established its political control over a huge area, but withdrew in 1922, although North Sakhalin was not returned to the Soviet Union until 1925. Tensions were renewed after the Japanese advance into Manchuria (1931) and culminated in the border war on the Manchurian/Mongolian frontier, in which the Red Army emerged as the victor over the formidable Kwantung Army at the battle of Nomonhan in the summer of 1939.

In spite of its association with the Axis powers during the Second World War, Japan avoided conflict with the Soviet Union for strategic reasons. Under the Soviet-Japanese Neutrality Pact of April 1941, the two parties undertook to remain neutral if either was involved in conflict with a third party. Japan observed the pact when Germany attacked the Soviet Union two months later, and the Soviet Union did likewise when Japan launched the Pacific War at the end of the year. If either side wanted to give notice of its intention not to renew the treaty, it had to do so one year before the date of its expiry in April 1946. However, Stalin had agreed at Yalta to enter the war against Japan after the defeat of Germany. In April 1945, on the eve of the collapse of the Nazi regime and Germany's unconditional surrender, the Soviet government informed Japan that it would not renew the pact. A week before Japan's unconditional surrender on 15 August the Soviets declared war and the Red Army swept through Manchuria, Korea, South Sakhalin, the Kurile Islands, Shikotan and the Habomais.

In the territorial dispute over the Northern Territories, the Japanese case rests on a number of charges. On the first count they accused the Soviet Union of having violated the Neutrality Pact and maintain that, according to the terms, the Soviet Union was under an obligation to allow the pact to run its full course after having given a year's notice of the intention not to renew it.

The second charge is of 'treachery'. The Soviet government had entered the war in full knowledge that the Japanese were looking for a way out of it and had indeed approached the Soviet authorities to act as intermediaries between them and the allied powers. The whole episode is regarded as a stab in the back, made worse by the continuation of hostilities after Japan's official surrender. To this is added a third charge over the deportation of six hundred thousand Japanese soldiers to the appalling conditions and brutal treatment in Siberian prisoner-of-war camps, where some sixty thousand met their death.

Finally, and most important, the Japanese claim that the Soviet occupation of the four Northern Territories is illegal. This is a complicated matter and has at least three aspects. Stalin and Roosevelt had struck a secret deal at Yalta: in return for its entry into the war, the Soviet Union was to receive South Sakhalin and the Kurile Islands. The Japanese were, of course, ignorant of this arrangement when they surrendered. They had done this on their understanding of the Cairo Declaration of 27 November 1943, issued by Roosevelt, Churchill and Chiang Kai-shek, and adhered to by Stalin at Tehran a few days later. The Cairo Declaration was subsequently reaffirmed in Article 8 of the Potsdam Proclamation to Japan of July 1945.

The Declaration had stated that it was the purpose of the allies:

> that Japan shall be stripped of all islands in the Pacific which she has seized and occupied since the beginning of the first World War in 1914, . . . Japan will also be expelled from all other territories which she has taken by violence and greed.

Japan had manifestly not acquired the Kurile Islands, Shikotan and the Habomai group by 'violence and greed'. Furthermore, the territorial settlement of the Treaty of Shimoda had never been challenged in the course of the subsequent relations between Japan and Russia/Soviet Union. Not only did Japan have every right to consider the Northern Territories as an integral part of its empire, but the secret agreement at Yalta was illegal because Japan had surrendered in ignorance of this modification of the stipulations in the Cairo and Potsdam documents.

That argument is, however, rather weak. Article 8 of the Proclamation to Japan issued at Potsdam reads as follows:

> The terms of the Cairo declaration shall be carried out and Japanese sovereignty shall be limited to the islands of Honshu, Hokkaidō, Kyūshū, Shikoku, *and such minor islands as we determine* [emphasis added].

Whatever the meaning attributed to the original wording of the Cairo declaration, there was nothing to prevent the allies from modifying it later, a modification which Japan was bound to accept. After all, it had surrendered unconditionally and by doing so it had given up any right to question such decisions. This, of course, is the argument which was advanced rather brutally by Stalin and adopted by his successors until 1985: Japan had lost the war and it must accept the consequences.[2]

The other two aspects of the legal case are more convincing. In the negotiations preceding the peace treaty with Japan, the Americans found themselves in a cleft stick. They were quite content for the Soviet Union not to be a party to the treaty and were anxious to make Japan an ally in the struggle against the communist powers. On the other hand, they could not escape their commitments at Yalta. The final text of the Treaty of San Francisco (see Appendix II) reflected this American ambivalence, tempered by the harsher line of some of the allies against Japan as well as by Japan's aim to keep the territorial question open. Japan renounced 'all right, title and claim to the Kurile Islands',[3] but did not specifically transfer sovereignty over them to the Soviet Union. Furthermore, the Soviet Union never became party to the treaty – chiefly because of this issue[4] – and the territorial question was left open to be resolved either through bilateral negotiations for a peace treaty between Japan and the USSR or by some other means, such as recourse to arbitration by a third party or a ruling of the International Court of Justice.

Apart from the issue of sovereignty, there is also the question of the definition of 'Kurile Islands'. In this respect the Japanese claim to the two larger islands is weaker. Shortly after the Treaty of San Francisco was signed, a Japanese official had conceded in the Diet that the term included both the southern and northern Kurile Islands.[5] It can hardly be doubted that Etorofu and Kunashiri are part of the Kurile chain, although it can be argued that geologically Shikotan and the Habomai group are not part of the Kuriles at all. The government quickly retracted the official's 'slip of the tongue' and excluded all the Northern Territories from the terms of the Treaty, basing its position on the Treaty of Shimoda, since when there had been no doubt whatsoever that they were an integral part of the Japanese Empire. In fact, Shikotan and the Habomais were not mentioned in that treaty. They had never been part of the territorial dispute which had led to the delimitation of 1855 and had always been regarded as part of Hokkaidō. The Russians tried unconvincingly to get around this fact by referring to these smaller islands as the 'Little Kuriles'. Yet they appeared to have admitted, at least tacitly, the justification of a part of the Japanese case in Article 9 of the Soviet-Japanese Joint Declaration after the abortive attempt to negotiate a bilateral peace treaty in 1955–6. The text of the article is as follows:

> The Union of Soviet Socialist Republics and Japan agree to continue, after the restoration of normal diplomatic relations between the Union of Soviet Socialist Republics and Japan, negotiations for the conclusion of a Peace Treaty.
>
> In this connexion, the Union of Soviet Socialist Republics, desiring to meet the wishes of Japan and taking into

> consideration the interests of the Japanese State, agrees to transfer to Japan the Habomai Islands and the island of Shikoton [*sic*], the actual transfer of these islands to Japan to take place after the conclusion of a Peace Treaty between the Union of Soviet Socialist Republics and Japan.[6]

Since 1989 and especially in the later years of *glasnost*, prominent figures on the Soviet side admitted that Japan has a case over the Northern Territories, while not necessarily conceding it. Such a remarkable public acceptance, which would have been unthinkable under Gorbachev's predecessors, was more pronounced the further removed such personalities were from the centre of power. Those most influential in government, from Gorbachev down, were far more reserved and nuanced; a posture which emerged from close analysis of the text and context of their declarations, and did not justify the periodic outbursts of optimism among Japanese commentators and the media.

Following the dissolution of the Soviet Union and Japan's official recognition of the Russian Federation as its legal successor on 27 December 1991, the prospects of a solution to the dispute have hardly improved, although the atmosphere in which the two parties conduct their dialogue is better – a development that was already noticeable in the later years of the Gorbachev era.

It is puzzling that the territorial issue continues to occupy a central place in Russo-Japanese relations when it concerns a group of small and economically unimportant islands, which have lost some of their strategic significance after the end of the Cold War. Its salience is a reminder of the extraordinarily tenacious nature of such issues, especially when they involve settler populations and touch on strong nationalist sentiment. We need only look at the Falkland/Malvinas problem between Britain and Argentina, which suddenly flared into armed confrontation after some one hundred and fifty years. The dispute over the Northern Territories is only fifty years old, but the question of their population has become crucial.

The last of the Japanese residents had been expelled by 1949 and the three bigger islands have had two generations of Russian settlers since then. Russian nationalist feelings have been heightened since the collapse of the Soviet Union and were without doubt the main reason for the abrupt cancellation of President Yeltsin's planned visit to Japan in 1992 and its further postponement in May 1993. When he did finally arrive in Tokyo in the following October, it was noticeable that, despite the friendly personal atmosphere and the specific mention of all four territories in the text of the Tokyo Declaration on Japan–Russia relations of 13 October 1993, as well as reference to the 'constructive dialogue' over the peace treaty, there was no substantial progress. Its likelihood became more remote still since the rise of Mr Zhirinovsky's brand of extreme nationalism following the elections at the end of the year. On the Japanese side, popular demand for the return of *all* four territories has been officially fostered and is given a focal point by the annual celebration of Northern Territories day on 7 February, the date of the Treaty of Shimoda.

It was widely assumed in the late 1980s that a solution could be found once the Soviet Union had made a deal with Japan which would involve the exchange of at least some of the islands in return for substantial economic and financial assistance. The Russians are anxious to secure Japanese help in developing the infrastructure and primary resources of their Far Eastern territories and Siberia. Such aid would include massive loans at low interest rates, participation in joint ventures for the exploitation of sources of energy and other raw materials, the transfer of technology and managerial skills, and the development of the production of consumer goods whose export would generate a much needed income of hard currency.

Russia's main economic attraction lies in its almost limitless natural resources and thus in the prospects for a good return on long-term investment. Its geographical position is also advantageous when compared with the long distances that separate Japan from other sources of energy and raw materials. None the less, Japanese economic interest in the Soviet Union/Russia has been fitful and usually short-lived during the post-war era. Bilateral trade never amounted to much more than two per cent of Japan's total foreign trade and although there have been a number of joint ventures, few have been on a very large scale and many have not progressed beyond the stage of preliminary agreements with only small amounts of capital actually committed, chiefly in feasibility studies.[7]

Any likelihood of a substantial increase of the Japanese stake in the Russian economy would depend on determined government support, otherwise the uncertainties for the private investor are too great. The risks seem only to have increased since 1991 with growing political and economic instability in Russia and the other successor republics of the former Soviet Union. One sign of progress in the bilateral relationship has been some relaxation of the Japanese government's rigid position over the inseparability of politics and economics. It has switched to talk of 'parallel progress' over economic aid and the settlement of the territorial dispute. Another sign has been a tendency to hint that, while the demand for the return of all four territories still stands, Japan might be prepared to have the process take place in stages, with an immediate reversion of the two smaller territories and further negotiations over Kunashiri and Etorofu.

Another factor in Russo-Japanese relations is the ethnic/cultural dimension. The Soviet Union and Russia have generally had a poor press in Japan. This has been due partly to the many conflicts in their shared history. It has also been influenced by European and American propaganda. Ever since the nineteenth century, Europeans have never ceased to warn the Japanese against the northern barbarians. This kind of Western-inspired view of the Russians, which reflected European ambivalence whether to regard the Russians as belonging to their cultural sphere or as being Asiatic outsiders, was sometimes belied in practice by the better standards of Russian behaviour towards Japan when compared with the behaviour of other European powers.[8] It also tends to overlook those periods in the past when Russo-Japanese relations were quite cooperative and friendly, notably between the Treaty of St Petersburg and the tripartite intervention of 1895, and again during the First World War and in the years following Japan's recognition of the Soviet Union.[9]

From the end of the Second World War until the collapse of the Soviet Union, the atmosphere veered between cool and stormy. In contrast to the more positive attitude of Russians towards Japan in recent years, especially among the younger generation, popular Japanese perceptions remain predominantly sceptical or disparaging.[10] These attitudes are rooted in history. The Japanese propensity to see the world in terms of hierarchical structures has meant that while at first they equated Russia with the other European empires, they soon discovered that it was an empire whose outer shell was hard but whose core was rotten – an impression greatly strengthened by the experience of the war of 1904–5. Intellectuals might admire the world of Tolstoy, Dostoyevsky, Pushkin and Chekhov, just as many of them later admired the work and thoughts of Marx and his acolytes, but the ordinary Japanese tended to look upon Russians as boorish peasants. The backwardness of the country lowered its status in Japanese eyes to second rank among the 'civilized' countries. Such attitudes have largely persisted to the present and have been reinforced by the poor shape of the Russian economy.

Suspicion and fear of the neighbour is not one-sided. Although Russians today have a much more positive image of Japan than the Japanese have of Russia, Russian apprehensions of Japanese intentions have not quite disappeared and, if anything, are revived by their persistence in pursuing the territorial claim. Such suspicions can be traced to the long years of Japanese aggression on the mainland since 1894 and especially the attempt between 1918 and 1922 to entrench themselves in Siberia and to set up a buffer state through their support of the Whites in the Civil War.

In all this, the Russians have been acutely aware of the American factor in their relationship with Japan. However, their appreciation of the American role in the region changed in the course of the past one hundred and fifty years. Czarist Russia tended to regard the United States as a rival in North-East Asia. The Soviets, and notably Lenin, counted on US-Japanese imperialist rivalry as an important element in reducing the threat from Japan.[11] In the 1930s and during the Pacific War, American policy was seen as favouring the Soviet Union. During the Cold War, Japan was feared as a client of American power.

The prospects for a settlement of the territorial issue and improved Russo-Japanese relations will not depend primarily on the Northern Territories–economic aid equation. The idea that a solution rests on the price Japan is willing to pay for the return of the islands is not well founded. Russian nationalism and the attitudes of the population on the islands make it unlikely that a simple 'sell-out' would be politically acceptable. A further consideration would be the impact such a deal might have on other territorial and population problems on Russia's frontiers. Vociferous nationalist politicians in the early 1990s accused the Yeltsin government of betraying the Russian and slav people by the policy of cooperation with the West. The demand that the Russian minorities in the neighbouring republics should not only be protected but reincorporated in the motherland, suggests that any surrender of the four territories to Japan, no matter on what terms, would be unpopular and politically dangerous for the Russian government. The pressures that led to the sudden cancellation of Yeltsin's visit to Japan in September 1992 was a warning. Nor is it clear whether the Russian military, whose political influence was much strengthened by its support of President Yeltsin against parliament during the crisis in October 1993, would tolerate any abandonment of the islands which are a useful screen and springboard in the north-west Pacific.

On the Japanese side, too, the suggestion that territory might be bought back when it is regarded as having been wrongfully seized from Japan, would be politically sensitive. The uproar which greeted the proposal by one of the senior figures in the LDP, Shin Kanemaru, that Japan might buy back some if not all of the islands, and the immediate repudiation of such an idea by his colleagues and the Gaimushō, is an indication of how difficult such an arrangement might prove to be.[12]

There can be little doubt that Russia badly wants massive Japanese economic help. Nor is there much doubt that Japanese willingness to provide such aid would spring more from long-term economic and political calculations than from the immediate attractions of the Russian Far East. The immense technical difficulties and costs of Siberian development, the availability of alternative sources of energy and primary materials, including the potential of China's off-shore reservoirs of oil and natural gas, and the uncertainty about developments in Russia – civil war and further distintegration or the emergence of a new authoritarian-style and chauvinist government? – are grounds for caution before the Japanese become deeply involved in Siberian development.

The Russians have tried to counter the strong reservations on the Japanese side by holding out prospects of regional development in the Japan Sea area, which would embrace their Far Eastern province, North-East China, Korea and Japan. They have also tried to exercise pressure by suggesting that they could develop their east Asian region without Japanese help, relying instead on South Korea, Taiwan, Western Europe and other advanced countries as their partners.

The vista of the development of the Japan Sea area into another East Asian zone of rapid growth has yet to be translated into reality. Coastal and cross-border trade in the region has increased, but whether this can generate sufficient momentum to transform its economy remains doubtful.[13] It is also questionable whether South Korea, Taiwan or the other newly industrialized economies (NIEs) in East Asia could provide the same high technology and financial resources as Japan. As for Germany and its partners in the European Union, their primary focus is on European Russia and western Siberia. Russia must, therefore, look to countries on the Pacific rim for aid to its regions in Asia, and Japan is the key player in this area. The Russians may calculate that by drawing in Korean and other Asian interests they will lure Japanese enterprises into their market for fear that they might be left behind. This policy could have the desired effect if the behaviour of Japanese firms in China is any precedent.

There is also a political dimension to the interplay of Russian and Japanese interests in North-East Asia. The passing of the Cold War has not removed the problem of security. Russia's ties with South Korea and the improvement of relations between Moscow and Beijing are pointers to a policy which seeks a return of Russian influence in the peninsula and raises the danger of Japan's isolation in the region. Such a manoeuvre seemed to be indicated by Yeltsin's visits to South Korea in November 1992, shortly after he had cancelled the trip to Japan, and to Beijing at the end of the year. The possibility of growing Russian influence in Korea and of a new Sino-Russian *entente* must alarm Japanese policy makers, especially as they note the shift of tone by Beijing. China no longer explicitly supports the Japanese claim in the territorial dispute but openly speculates about a new threat from Japan.[14] Finally, it is no longer safe to assume that the United States will continue to support Japan unconditionally or even play the role of stabilizer in the region.

Considerations of the balance of power in North-East Asia and of potential threats to national security have not disappeared from Japan's relations with Russia, nor indeed from its general approach to the region, but they have to take into account a new context.

RELATIONS WITH KOREA

Korea is Japan's closest neighbour and their relations are no exception to the general rule of international politics that neighbours find it difficult to live in harmony. In the historical experience of Japan, Korea has been a dagger pointed at its heart as well as a bridge to the Asian mainland. The earliest contact between Japan and the world beyond the seas was via Korea, and the deep-rooted cultural and historical dimensions of the relationship affect their mutual attitudes today. But the period of Japanese colonial domination between 1910 and 1945 has been the single most important influence on their mutual perceptions in the twentieth century.

Until the beginning of the century they faced the usual problems that arise between neighbours, especially when one of them is surrounded by more powerful states. Korea is the Poland of East Asia. The Japanese have been involved in Korean affairs since ancient times, either as allies of some of the warring kingdoms on the peninsula or as invaders. The last such attempt had been the expedition of Toyotomi Hideyoshi (1592–8), which was conceived as the first step in the conquest of China (see p. 18).[15] On that occasion Korea was the bridge to Asia. Previously it had been the dagger pointed at Japan. It was the base from which the Mongols launched their abortive attempts to invade Japan in the late thirteenth century.[16] However, it was Japanese colonial policy in this century which has poisoned and injected a dangerous emotional content into Korean-Japanese relations.

Many of the great cultural influences that contributed to the formation of the Japanese state and society had come via Korea. In pre-historic times, Korean immigrants had played a major part in the settlement of Japan. Later they introduced many facets of Chinese civilization to the Japanese. There were no serious problems in the mutual appreciation of the two peoples. Indeed, amicable relations were retained with Korea during the centuries of seclusion. Korean embassies were received with great courtesy in Edo and trade was conducted through the daimyō of Tsushima.[17]

However, the combination of 'national learning', based on Shintō and the Japanese classics, and the Confucian concept of a world order in which the relationships between rulers and countries were defined in familial and hierarchical terms, led to the classification of Korea as an inferior state. When the decline of the Yi dynasty became obvious in the nineteenth century, the Japanese developed a mixture of condescension and contempt for the country and its people. It seemed natural to some nationalist thinkers in the later years of the Tokugawa era that Japan should conquer Korea as a counter to the looming threat from the Western powers.[18] Thus the stage was set for the struggle to control and eventually absorb Korea in the first phase of expansion after the Meiji Restoration.

This policy was justified not only as a necessary measure to protect Japan against the designs of the aggressive barbarians from the north and the west, but also as a historic mission. The interpretation of their earliest historical encounters became a source of fierce dispute between Japanese and Koreans. During the period of colonial domination, the Japanese military inculcated the idea that the gods of Yamato had ruled over Korea from the beginning and that the Empress Jingu had conquered the southern part of the peninsula and had established the principality of Mimana, thereby providing a precedent and justification for the annexation of 1910. Legends and myths were used to substantiate the later policies which tried to eradicate the native culture and force the population to become 'Japanese'.[19]

Those interpretations have been challenged by some Japanese scholars of the post-war generation. Instead of arguing for a mythical Japanese superiority, they pointed out that, according to acknowledged evidence, Japan had been conquered and settled by horsemen who came from Manchuria and Korea and whose cultural influence had a profound impact on Japanese civilization.[20] The dispute between the two schools continues. It may be academic, but it has served to embitter the mutual relationship, especially through the treatment (or mistreatment) of Korean history and the relations between Japan and Korea in the textbooks authorized by the Ministry of Education in Tokyo.[21]

The impact of attempts to provide historical and cultural proof of Japanese superiority and Korean inferiority has sustained feelings of contempt and dislike for Korea among the Japanese public right up to the present day. Conversely, the brutality of Japanese rule between 1910 and 1945 and its systematic effort to eradicate all traces of the indigenous culture with the compulsion to speak Japanese, to worship at Shintō shrines, to make their subjects adopt Japanese family names, to conscript them into the Japanese Imperial Army and to bring large numbers of Koreans to Japan to work as slave labour in the later stages of the Pacific War, has left an indelible hatred and fear of Japan in the minds of many Koreans of the older generation.[22]

Such sentiments might be expected to decline with the passing of the wartime generation. However, surveys of public opinion point to the contrary and although relations between Japan and South Korea have improved, especially since their normalization in 1965, resentments continue to fester and have been kept alive by subsequent events, in spite of attempts by political leaders in both countries, notably the late President Park Chung Hee and former Prime Minister Nakasone, to bury the past. The older generation of Korea's post-war élites were fluent in Japanese, and diplomatic intercourse between the two countries was conducted in that language. With the rise of a new generation in the 1970s and 1980s the language of communication became English. This is a symbolic break with the legacy of the colonial period, which might prepare the way for a relationship of greater mutual respect between the two countries, yet the past continues to haunt popular images of the other side.[23]

Japanese relations with Korea in the post-war years were essentially with the Republic of Korea (ROK) in the south. Some trade was conducted with the northern Democratic People's Republic of Korea (DPRK), but the orientation of Japanese policy was directed by the Cold War and the close association with the United States. The difficult process of normalizing relations with ROK was eventually concluded in 1965 after considerable American pressure.[24] Negotiations were officially opened in February 1952 and were suspended or interrupted six times before the Treaty on Basic Relations between Japan and the Republic of Korea and three separate agreements on fisheries, reparations and economic cooperation, and the juridical status of Koreans resident in Japan, were signed in June 1965 (see Appendix III). They met with fierce opposition in both countries before ratification. Criticism in Korea focused primarily on the insufficient recognition of and compensation for Japanese aggression and injustice. The opponents in Japan attacked the treaty and agreements on ideological grounds, principally because they would impede the unification process and represented a further step in Japan's integration into an American-dominated alliance in East Asia.[25]

The controversy over the terms of the normalization set the agenda for the issues in Japan's relations with South Korea during the subsequent decades. The most delicate problem stems from the impact of the Cold War and American policy in the region. As in its relations with other neighbours, the international context severely restricted the room for Japanese diplomatic manoeuvre. This does not mean that there were no differences with the United States, but they had perforce to remain nuanced. A good example was the Japanese attitude to the so-called 'Korea clause', originally inserted in the Nixon–Satō joint communiqué of November 1969, which stated that the security of the Republic of Korea was 'essential to Japan's own security'. To an extent it echoed the declaration of the joint Japanese-Korean ministerial meeting held in August 1968. At various times in the following years Japanese leaders tried to modify or remove the clause from joint statements with both the Korean and American governments.[26]

As in the case of China, Japan sought to keep the door open to relations with the communist regime in a divided country. Two methods were used. One was the policy of separating trade from politics. The other was through the wording of treaties with non-communist governments, in which Japan sought to avoid any outright recognition of their claim to be the sole legitimate authority in the whole country.[27] In the early 1970s, during the period of East-West *détente*, Japan briefly tried to move towards a policy of equi-distance in its relations with the two Korean entities, a policy that ceased with the renewal of Cold War tensions towards the end of the decade.[28] In relations with China this issue largely ceased to exist in the 1970s. But in Korea, where the division had been cemented by a civil war within the framework of the Cold War, it remains a significant element in the relationship between Japan and its nearest neighbour.

Other issues in the bilateral relations with the South include the economic nexus, disputes over territorial demarcation, which also affect fishing rights and the exploitation of the resources of the continental shelf, and the status of the Korean minority in Japan.

The 1980s saw the phenomenal growth and expansion of the Korean economy.[29] The process had begun in the 1960s and 1970s, but the fruits of success became apparent in the following decade. Between 1982 and 1988 the average annual growth rate of GNP in real terms was more than ten per cent. Between 1986 and 1988 it had climbed to more than twelve per cent and was achieved at a relatively low rate of inflation. The chronic deficit in the balance of foreign trade had turned into a large surplus by 1986, though it sank into deficit again in 1990. In the early 1990s the growth rate, rates of inflation, and the foreign trade balances marked a slowdown in the economy, reflecting general trends in the global economy. Nevertheless, Korea had emerged as the second largest economy in the region and as an important economic power in the world.

Japan and the United States between them account for more than fifty per cent of South Korea's foreign trade. Since 1965 Japan has become the main source of imports for the Republic of Korea and the US has become its chief export market, with the consequence that the balance of trade between Japan and ROK has consistently been in Japan's favour, while the Koreans have equally consistently run up a surplus in their trade with the United States. Japanese-Korean-American trade thus developed into a triangular structure. Although the content of trade has changed over the years, the pattern has remained the same; ROK imports machinery and components from Japan and exports finished goods to the United States.[30]

The Republic of Korea has also become a formidable economic competitor in the region and in the world at large. To cite one example: in 1987 South Korea replaced Japan as the world's largest shipbuilder, a position occupied by Japan since 1956. If the imbalance of trade with Japan persists and Korea continues its inroads in third markets, friction between the two countries will increase and assume the same characteristics as the friction between Japan and the United States. On the other hand, there has been a remarkable rise in Japan's imports from South Korea, which has moved from ninth place as supplier in 1985 to second place behind the US in 1988–9, though it was driven to fourth place in the following year.

A more immediate issue for Japan is the competition from South Korean investment in other markets, particularly in China and Asian Russia. The *rapprochement* between China and the Republic of Korea, which culminated in the establishment of diplomatic relations in August 1992, was largely the result of the rapid growth in economic intercourse between the two countries. South Korean investment in China trebled between 1991 and 1992 from US $170 million to over US $500.

In contrast to the buoyant outlook in China, the promise of a great expansion in Russo-Korean economic ties has faded ever since the establishment of diplomatic relations in 1990. The Koreans are experiencing the same difficulties as the Japanese in dealing with Russia. Both sides expressed disappointment over the lack of progress when President Yeltsin visited Seoul in November 1992. Russian complaints about a lack of Korean investment were matched by Korean complaints about insufficient guarantees for investors and the failure of Russia and other successor states of the Soviet Union to continue paying interest on a $3 billion loan. An agreement over these issues was reached during the Yeltsin visit, but the Koreans remain cautious for the same economic reasons that the Japanese have given to explain their reservations over large-scale aid and investment.

In Russia the giant conglomerates (chaebol) need to work closely with Japanese and other Western enterprises in the face of the enormous technical difficulties, the financial risks, and a background of considerable uncertainty about political developments in that vast country. In the China market, on the other hand, competition is the dominant feature in the relations between Japanese and Korean companies.[31]

Although economic developments in Korea pose a number of challenges to Japan, it remains and is likely to stay the economic powerhouse of the East Asian region. Korea may be number two and become a serious competitor in industries with a high value-added content in which Japan has been pre-eminent. The chaebol, such as Hyundai, Samsung, Daewoo, and Lucky Goldstar, which bear some resemblance to the pre-war zaibatsu, are becoming household names the world over. But in sheer size, the Korean economy lags far behind that of Japan. The Japanese economy has become mature and is less dynamic, with an average growth rate of four per cent in the decade between 1980 and 1990; low when compared with Korean growth in those years. Yet it remains the dominant economy of East Asia. The combined GNP of the NIEs of the region (South Korea, Taiwan, Hongkong, Singapore) and of the other five ASEAN countries is less than one third that of Japan. If China is added to the equation, Japan's GNP would still be more than twice their total.[32]

A more serious challenge to Japan could arise from an eventually reunited Korea. It is of course impossible to foretell when and under what circumstances this might happen, but it is thought that a unified Korea with a population of some seventy million could attain a level of economic output of about US $400 billion within five years and would become the third largest economy of Asia after Japan and China. According to some estimates, it could achieve the status of the tenth most powerful nation in the world in economic and military terms. Considerations of this kind must remain speculative, but they probably lurk in the minds of long-term planners among Japanese bureaucrats.

The competition between Japanese and Korean conglomerates in the region is likely to continue and intensify, but it is balanced by the convergence of economic interests, which is just as likely to lead to cooperation between the two countries. Apart from the importance of their bilateral relations, both have a strong motive in supporting a global free trade system, in promoting an Asia–Pacific economic zone, and in ensuring the safety of the maritime routes on which their economic prosperity depends. Above all, the ambitious project for the development of the Tumen river delta, not yet beyond the blueprint stage and feasibility studies, would draw Japan and Korea into a web of economic interdependence which could make the Japan Sea area one of the most dynamic economic zones in East Asia and the world. While Korea, along with China and Russia, would be more directly involved in developing the potential of the delta, the project would depend on Japanese capital and technology for its accomplishment and offers opportunities to tap the vast resources of the region to the benefit of the Japan Sea coast littoral with its centre in Niigata.

South Korea and eventually a united Korea pose an economic challenge to Japan, but would not necessarily be a threat. On the contrary, the Korean economy could be a stimulus to the Japanese economy and play an important part in furthering the integration of the North-East Asian region. Friction, tension, and conflict are more likely to arise between Japan and Korea over political issues and problems of security.

As already noted, the legacy of the past and mutual perceptions or, more accurately, misperceptions, continue to cast a shadow over Japan's relations with both Korean states. However bitter the animosity between North and South might be, they are united in their suspicion of Japan and in their demand for moral and material redress of past injustice. At meetings between the prime ministers of South and North in February and September 1992, Premier Yon Hyong Muk of the DPRK called for joint action against Japan and the establishment of a committee to look into ways and means to achieve it.[33] Such obvious political manoeuvres, designed to drive a wedge between ROK and Japan, were rejected by the South, but they indicate the common ground between them, which would be an important element in the relations between a unified Korea and Japan.

The political and psychological dimensions of Japan's relations with South Korea include the ongoing problems arising from the past. Korea demands apologies and compensation for the misdeeds of the Japanese militarists and the cessation of Japanese attempts to gloss over or ignore the dark side of the colonial era in school textbooks. A recent example of this kind of dispute concerns the treatment of Korean women and girls who were forced to provide sexual favours to soldiers of the Imperial Army. The women demand both an apology and compensation. The reluctance of the Japanese authorities to admit responsibility and therefore the justice of the claim for compensation fuelled doubts about their sincerity when expressing 'regrets' for the past. The tone of the short-lived coalition government of Mr Hosokawa (August 1993–April 1994) pointed to a more positive and conciliatory approach to these vexed issues. The cabinet headed by Mr Tomiichi Murayama went a step further in August 1994 when it allocated ¥100 billion to a ten-year programme of projects on the history of the peoples and countries of Asia, including extensive exchanges of scholars, young people and peoples at the grass-roots of society, as a general token of apologies to all the victims of Japanese aggression. Again, no specific recompense was offered to the 'comfort women' from Korea and other Asian countries, on the grounds that questions of individual claims had already been settled under various bilateral reparations agreements. There was however a hint that the government would back a ¥10 billion private fund for such women.

The psychological obstacles to a more cordial relationship may eventually disappear with the passage of time and the change of generations. Other substantive issues are likely to remain until they are formally resolved. They include a dispute over the ownership of the Takeshima Islands, two uninhabited islets of 0.23 km^2. South Korea claims the islands on the grounds that the occupation authorities excluded them from Japanese administration by order of SCAP on 29 January 1946, and had placed them outside the 'MacArthur Line', which delimited the operational zone of Japanese fishermen. The Koreans 'occupied' the islands in 1954, building a lighthouse and later a radio tower and artillery emplacements on them.

The Japanese base their claim on historical evidence which goes back to the Tokugawa period. On 28 January 1905, the Japanese government formally incorporated Takeshima into the national territory as part of Shimane prefecture. Japan refutes the Korean claims based on occupation rulings. The SCAP order stated specifically that 'nothing in this directive shall be construed as the policy of the Allied Powers concerning the final decision on the ownership'.[34] Moreover, the Treaty of San Francisco, which superseded all the orders issued under the occupation, made no mention of Takeshima.

As in most territorial disputes, the issue is extremely complex, involving differing interpretations of the historical background and of international law. In the case of Takeshima it is complicated further by the problem of fishing rights. In a proclamation of 18 January 1952, President Syngman Rhee declared Korean sovereignty over the continental shelf surrounding the Korean peninsula, extending up to two hundred nautical miles in places. The rights to exploit the resources of this zone, which include rich fishing grounds in the Japan and Yellow Seas, were reserved exclusively for Korea. According to the 'Rhee Line', Takeshima fell under Korean control. The Japanese naturally objected, citing the measure as a violation of the principle of the freedom of the seas.

In September 1954, Japan proposed to bring the territorial dispute before the International Court of Justice, a move rejected by South Korea. The 1965 agreements normalizing relations between Japan and ROK resolved the issue of fishing rights with the abandonment of the 'Rhee Line' and a series of measures which included provisions for cooperation and arbitration should disputes arise in the future (see Appendix III). The ownership of Takeshima, however, was not settled. The Korean side suggested and the Japanese accepted that it be left to negotiations in the future. In an exchange of notes it was agreed that remaining differences should be resolved through diplomacy and, failing that, through third party mediation. Although Takeshima was not mentioned specifically in this exchange, it was obviously on the minds of the two parties.[35]

The contention over Takeshima, fishing rights, and the right to exploit the underwater resources has flared up periodically. Incidents occurred around Takeshima in February 1977, May 1978, and August 1981; times when bilateral relations were strained for other reasons. More recently there was an incident in the spring of 1990 around Tsushima Island between vessels of the Japanese Maritime Safety Agency and Korean fishing and Fishery Agency boats.[36] The characteristics of these encounters are worthy of note. They occurred during periods of tension between Japan and the Republic of Korea and in the case of Takeshima were used by Japan as a means to exert pressure on the Korean side. Domestic political considerations were also among the motives that prompted the Japanese to revive the claim to Takeshima. In 1977 it was partly to distract attention from the embarrassment of leading politicians of the LDP over allegations that they had received bribes from the Korean Central Intelligence Agency (KCIA) and from Japanese firms operating in Korea. In the incident of 1978 it was partly in response to pressure from the fishing lobby in Japan.

There can be little doubt that the North would have supported the South over these issues as, in a broad sense, it also shares the South Korean position over the treatment of the Korean minority in Japan. The status of the six-to-seven hundred thousand residents of Korean descent in Japan (the largest 'foreign' minority in the country) is a delicate and emotional issue. The problem has two facets. One concerns the difficulties and discrimination which face second or third generation Koreans, many of whom have never been to their ancestral land and for whom Japan is the only home they know, but who are still not fully accepted into the community. The other concerns the problem of nationality. The great majority of Koreans in Japan, no matter whether they are first, second or third generation, remain Korean nationals and the question arises whether they are nationals of the Republic of Korea or of the Democratic People's Republic of Korea.

The first facet is closely linked to the legacy of the past and arouses all the emotions that stem from the colonial period. The second arose out of the Cold War division of the peninsula and will disappear once the country is reunited. The whole problem featured prominently in the negotiations over the normalization of relations between Japan and the Republic of Korea. It was largely settled by a series of complex measures in the Agreement of 1965, which laid down guidelines for the treatment of Korean residents in Japan (see Appendix III), but revealed an important difference in the approach of the two parties to the question of nationality.

The Republic of Korea regarded itself as the only legitimate government of Korea and therefore assumed that all Korean nationals were automatically its citizens and they were grouped in a pro-ROK residents' association (Mindan). However, there were many among the Koreans in Japan who saw themselves as belonging to the North, not only because of the geographical roots of their families, but also because of ideological allegiance. They belong to a pro-DPRK residents' association (Chongnyon) which, to all intents and purposes, is an affiliate of the dominant Korean Workers Party of North Korea.[37] Some Koreans refuse to be identified with either side and remain unaffiliated. The Japanese authorities only recognized the legitimacy of the Republic of Korea, but with a significant qualification. According to the text of Article III of the Treaty on Basic Relations of 1965, 'the Government of the Republic of Korea is the only lawful Government *in* Korea' and not *of* Korea (emphases added). They encouraged membership of Mindan, but in practice allowed membership of either association and in 1970 travel restrictions were relaxed to permit Koreans to visit the North for family reasons, a decision strongly opposed by the Republic of Korea. Local government bodies controlled by left-wing parties also allowed Korean residents to switch their citizenship from ROK to DPRK, although the practice was officially frowned upon.

A related factor is the amount of money which Korean residents in Japan send or carry with them on visits to North Korea. According to some estimates, these remittances may amount to some ¥60 billion a year; a very considerable sum for the impoverished economy of the DPRK. Restrictions on such transmissions might be difficult to apply, but they could constitute a bargaining chip for the Japanese in their dealings with the North.[38]

The question of the nationality of Korean residents in Japan and the ambivalent attitude of the authorities was symbolic of a Japanese unwillingness to commit themselves whole-heartedly to one side in the divided peninsula. Unofficial trade contacts with the North, the strong pro-Northern stand of the Japan Socialist Party (JSP – now renamed in English as the Social Democratic Party of Japan, SDPJ), which was the main opposition party, the efforts to modify the implications of the 'Korea clause' (see p. 64), and the policy of equi-distance in the early 1970s, underline these hesitations. They were, of course, a response to domestic economic and political pressures, but also to a longer-term though never clearly articulated policy of keeping options open for the time when the international environment might change. None the less, the official position was to support the South and to coordinate policy with the United States.

There was plenty of friction with the North, especially over periodic seizures of Japanese fishing boats and their crews on charges which varied from unauthorised fishing to espionage. However, the close relations with the United States and South Korea were of much greater importance as reasons why Japan's margin of diplomatic manoeuvre remained limited. Furthermore, strategic interests required support for the South in the face of the close ties between the North and its giant communist neighbours. The Sino-Soviet conflict of the 1960s and 1970s enabled the DPRK to play off one against the other and removed the threat from a communist bloc in East Asia. Nevertheless, for as long as the basic Cold War structures subsisted, Japan had no alternative but to keep in line, if not always in step, with the basic movement of American policy in the region.

The most dramatic manifestation at the end of the Cold War in East Asia was in the international environment of the Korean peninsula. Within less than three years the Republic of Korea had established diplomatic relations with Mongolia, the Soviet Union and China. Both Korean states had become members of the United Nations in September 1991. From September 1990 a series of meetings between the prime ministers of the two Koreas had been inaugurated, implying a mutual *de facto* recognition. There had been a tentative start to economic cooperation between North and South. A dialogue had begun between the United States and North Korea, and Japan had embarked on official negotiations for the establishment of diplomatic relations with the DPRK. Add to this Russia's policy of replacing the old DPRK–Soviet Treaty of 1961 with a new Friendship and Cooperation Treaty without a military clause, and we have clear evidence of the continuing interest of all the major external powers in preserving stability on the Korean peninsula.

Many dangers remain. At the time of writing, the one in the forefront of public attention is the question of a North Korean nuclear armament programme. The DPRK had signed the Nuclear Non-Proliferation Treaty (NPT) in December 1985, but it took another seven years before the North Koreans accepted the safeguards system of inspections operated by the International Atomic Energy Agency (IAEA). Although there had been six inspections since, Western intelligence agencies and the IAEA had become concerned that there were 'major inconsistencies' in the quantity and quality of nuclear materials held by North Korea. It was feared that the details of nuclear waste given by Pyongyang did not tally with the plutonium which was derived from it. This suggested that amounts of plutonium were being withheld for enrichment and the production of fission bombs. This was strenuously denied by the North Korean authorities. Controversy centred on the inspectors' right to monitor the sole nuclear reactor at Yongbyon, sixty kilometres south-west of Pyongyang, where it was suspected that a nuclear reprocessing plant was nearly completed.

Although Pyongyang insisted that it had no programme to produce nuclear weapons, its fierce resistance to the demands from IAEA and its accusations that the United States was using the international agency as a cover for spying on North Korea's military facilities, only strengthened suspicions. They were reinforced by reports that the North Koreans had developed a medium-range missile capable of carrying a nuclear warhead and of hitting targets in western Japan.

Matters came to a head when the DPRK announced its intention to withdraw from the NPT after the IAEA had set a deadline on 25 March 1993 for access by its inspectors to secret storage sites at Yongbyon. The date for withdrawal was fixed for 12 June 1993. Following negotiations between senior American and North Korean officials in New York, both sides announced in a joint statement on 11 June that North Korea 'has decided unilaterally to suspend as long as it considers necessary the effectuation of its withdrawal from the 1970 Treaty'. There was no indication of the length of the suspension. The IAEA announced on 3 August that the North Korean authorities had allowed three inspectors to enter the country for the first time since May. But in October Pyongyang announced that it would no longer deal with the IAEA and would only settle the crisis in direct talks with Washington. The dispute has continued to fester since then. It reached a new climax in June 1994 when the Americans threatened to ask for the imposition of sanctions by the Security Council of the United Nations. Once again, the crisis was at least temporarily defused by some gesture from the North Koreans and the resumption of talks between them and the Americans in July 1994. A complex agreement was reached in October, but serious difficulties remain at the time of writing.

North Korean behaviour and the reaction of the West, particularly the United States and Japan, suggest that these events had a wider significance than the nuclear issue. North Korean threats and their subsequent partial withdrawals, followed by the insistence that a solution can only be found through face-to-face negotiations with the United States, raises the question of its real motives. Did it reject the demands of the IAEA because it intended to acquire nuclear weapons or was it using the nuclear issue to break out of its increasing isolation and, the greatest prize of all, try to obtain diplomatic recognition from the United States? It could also be that heightened tensions served as a means to mobilize the population and distract attention from serious trouble in the domestic economy.

The evidence is ambiguous and defence analysts are divided in their assessments. Some think it was on the brink of acquiring a nuclear warhead and of developing an appropriate means of delivery. Others believe that it did not have a testable weapon and was some way from possessing a suitable means of delivery. Reports in the spring of 1993 that a medium-range missile had been test-fired over the Sea of Japan provoked alarm and provided the SDF with an opportunity to press for the acquisition of an anti-missile system such as the US Patriot. In contrast to the Japanese, the South Koreans seemed to be less perturbed, perhaps because the kind of missile the North is said to be developing would fly over their heads.

The Japanese position over the nuclear issue is a microcosm of Japanese policy towards Korea as a whole. The concerns of the defence establishment were not reflected in Japan's diplomatic response, which was more ambivalent and subject to the exigencies of domestic politics. Prime Minister Miyazawa's first reactions to the reports of the test-firing was to dismiss them as 'rumours', and was in keeping with a generally low-key approach to Pyongyang's nuclear programme.

The talks over the normalization of Japanese-North Korean relations were launched following a joint declaration issued in September 1990 by the North Korean Workers Party and a visiting delegation from the LDP and SDPJ. This event was significant for two reasons. The fact that leaders of the two principal parties in Japan acted in unison pointed to a blurring of the traditional left–right divide over issues of foreign policy and foreshadowed the changes in the political landscape of Japan a few years later. The other significant factor was that the declaration completely ignored the nuclear issue which was worrying the United States.

The question of a North Korean nuclear armament programme was raised, very much as a result of pressures from Washington, when official talks between Japan and the DPRK began in November 1990. During the first three meetings, the Japanese side made the acceptance of nuclear inspection a condition of continuing the negotiations, but it changed its position at the fourth round of talks in September 1991 and made acceptance a requirement before Japan would sign any agreement. The deadlock over this problem was therefore no longer regarded as an obstacle to the continuation of the negotiations as a whole.

The generally soft line pursued by Japan was in large measure due to the personal ambitions of Shin Kanemaru, a powerful politician who had led the LDP side in the three-party talks of September 1990. His initiative had been strongly criticized by officials in the Foreign Ministry and some members of the LDP, but even after his fall from grace two years later, following implication in a corruption scandal, Japan's policy continued to waver. If anything, the internal contradictions sharpened in the era of unstable coalition governments which began in 1993 (see below, pp. 137–40). Differences over policy on this issue, and in particular the possibility of United Nations sanctions against North Korea, were said to have been behind the difficulty in reaching agreement before the selection of Mr Hata as prime minister in April 1994.[39]

Following the end of the Cold War, a new and crucial item has appeared and is likely to dominate the agenda of intra-Korean and international relations: unification – how and when? This has become a *real* and not just a propaganda issue. In spite of the continued salience of the relationship with the United States in Japanese foreign policy, Japan has an opportunity for the first time since the Pacific War to take an independent position over Korea. None the less, apart from the negotiations for the establishment of official relations with the North, a process in which Japan seemed to be ahead of the US until the crisis over North Korea's nuclear intentions, the full thrust of a distinctive Japanese policy may be slow to show itself.[40]

The main reason for caution is uncertainty about developments in North Korea after the death of Kim Il-sung on 8 July 1994. The outlines of a post-Kim Il-sung regime are not yet clear and several scenarios present themselves. Continuation of the personality cult under his son Kim Jong-il and maintenance of a policy of semi-isolation is one possibility, though perhaps not the most likely, given doubts about the younger Kim's ability to impose himself on the country as well as North Korea's economic problems which cry for an opening to the world outside.

A trend towards reformist communism, which combines economic restructuring with political orthodoxy on the Chinese model, is another possibility, but cannot be taken for granted. Korea is not China and the regime has been able to exercise a much tighter control over all aspects of life in the country. A speedy collapse into revolutionary chaos might occur, but knowledgeable observers are not convinced that there is any basis for the kind of changes that occurred in eastern and central Europe with such startling rapidity. An alternative scenario would be a regime which felt itself to be threatened and therefore struck out aggressively towards the south in order to ward off the danger of domestic collapse. The military capability for such a desperate course is presumably there, but it would assume an absence of rationality among the policy-making élite which is difficult to imagine. The strain imposed by such an operation might trigger the very event it was designed to avoid and it would have the effect of drawing in the external powers with little likelihood that the Chinese, the traditional supporters of the North, would intervene on its behalf.

Unification on the German model, with the South absorbing the North in a bloodless revolution, is yet another prospect. The economic disparities between the two Koreas suggest a similar course of events, but the politcal dialogue and degree of contact between the two states are much less advanced to make it a similar, relatively smooth transition. After all, the two German states had been opening to each other gradually in the two decades before 1989. In Korea that process only began in the late 1980s. Moreover, the heavy economic cost of German unification is hardly an encouraging example for the South Korean economy.

The review of possible scenarios points to only one conclusion: progress towards unification and the manner in which it is attempted will be dictated by the Koreans themselves and the role of the external powers will be to ensure damage limitation. This would certainly be the objective of Japan. Though never publicly admitted, it would probably be quite content to see the peninsula remain divided indefinitely, provided the two entities could evolve a satisfactory and stable *modus vivendi.* A unified Korea would be a much more formidable neighbour, both economically and militarily, once the economic disparities between North and South had been ironed out and their complementarity realized, i.e. the highly developed market economy of the South and the natural resources of the North. With the legacy of its own tangled relations with Korea, Japan would hardly be in a position or want to exercise a dominant influence over the peninsula, even though it is the dominant economic power in the region. On the other hand, Japan would be anxious to prevent any other power from acquiring a hegemonic position in Korea. Both Russia and the United States seem unlikely to have such aspirations, let alone capabilities. China might pose a greater challenge in the long term. It has a long history of close involvement in Korean affairs, to which must be added an interest in tapping the financial and technical resources of the South.

Clearly, a balanced and stable division with a gradual lowering of the barriers would be the most desirable outcome. Japan shares the interest of the three other external powers in this and one can see a parallel here with the less than wholehearted enthusiasm with which the major European powers watched the process of German unification. Korea does not, of course, stir the same unhappy memories of aggressive expansionism among its neighbours as Germany. More to the point is the fact that the end of the Cold War makes it very probable that developments on the peninsula will depend primarily on the Koreans themselves and it is the possibility that things might get out of control which worries their neighbours.

Japanese policy is therefore closely attentive but remains cautious. A weakening of Russian and American involvement would leave Japan and China as the two external powers most affected by events in Korea. Thus, Japanese policy towards Korea in the future may be shaped increasingly by Japan's relations with China.

RELATIONS WITH CHINA/TAIWAN

From the beginning of the Cold War the flow of Sino-Japanese relations was narrowly confined within the limits set by Japan's close association with the United States. However, beneath the surface of events there were currents which shifted direction from time to time and which revealed the complexity of the relationship and the issues that would dominate the China policy of Japan once it was freed from Cold War constraints.

Romantic sentiment and the calculations of *Realpolitik* were intertwined in the Japanese approach to China throughout the past century. A concern to protect East Asian culture and civilization from the depredations of Western imperialism mingled with expansion in south China for the benefit of the coal industry in Kyūshū. Support for the revolutionary movement of Sun Yat-sen with its projects for liberal and radical reforms was combined with plans to exploit China under Japanese domination. Japanese pan-Asianism did not prevent collaboration with the imperialist powers in suppressing the Boxer Rebellion or an alliance with Britain to contain Russian expansion.

Similarly mixed motives were at work on the Chinese side. Sun Yat-sen and many of his followers had acquired an affection for Japan and the Japanese, among whom they had lived as exiles or students. They were ready to abandon traditional claims to superiority and to learn from what seemed to be Japan's example of the successful synthesis of Western methods and Eastern values. At the same time, Sun tried to use and manipulate Japanese ambitions and power against his enemies in China. Japanese imperialism was considered to be the lesser evil when compared with Western imperialism.[41]

The ambivalence of both sides continued during the worst period of their enmity in the 1930s and 1940s. Until his kidnapping and subsequent release at the end of 1936, Chiang Kai-shek had been more concerned to fight the Chinese communists than the Japanese invaders. There were many in China who were prepared to collaborate with the Japanese under the regime of Wang Ching-wei, which had been set up in Nanking. Their motives were a mixture of idealism and sheer self-interest. Throughout the war, Chiang Kai-shek, the symbol of anti-Japanese resistance, had left open lines of communication to the Japanese, among whom there was an active and influential 'peace party', clustered around Prince Konoe, which opposed the expansionist policies of the military. They included genuine sinophiles as well as idealists of the pan-Asian variety.[42]

The extraordinary post-surrender cooperation between the Chinese and Japanese military in their common stand against the communists as well as Chiang's 'magnanimity' over the issue of reparations continued the strand in the mutual relationship, which was directed at the alien intrusion of both the Western imperialist powers and communism.[43] Such attitudes had been articulated by Sun Yat-sen when he wrote in 1917:

> The relationship between China and Japan is one of common existence or extinction. Without Japan there would be no China; without China there would be no Japan.[44]

and again by Shigeru Yoshida in 1951:

> Red or White: China remains our next-door neighbour. Geography and economic laws will, I believe, prevail in the long run over any ideological differences and artificial trade barriers.[45]

Each statement combines the sentiment arising from cultural and historic ties and the imperatives of physical proximity, which brought with it material issues that have caused cooperation and conflict in the mutual relationship. Its historical dimension has been discussed in Chapter 2. The legacy of the bitter war years was carried over into the post-war era when the impulse of the Chinese Nationalist leadership towards reconciliation was restrained by popular anti-Japanese feelings. After 1949 all the major issues in the post-war relationship had crystallized. They included political, ideological and economic factors as well as the international and domestic environments in which policy was formulated.

The principal political issue until 1972 was the question of the recognition of the People's Republic of China. Under American pressure and also because of personal relations between some of the leaders of the LDP and the Kuomintang government in Taiwan, Japan signed a peace treaty with the Nationalist government of the Republic of China, which had established itself on Taiwan after defeat at the hands of the communists. The fact that Japan had no diplomatic relations with the government in Beijing severely restricted Japan's room for manoeuvre in its dealings with China. It also became an issue in domestic politics where not only the left-wing opposition parties but some influential members of the LDP and sections of the business community pressed the government to come to terms with the communist authorities and to adopt a more independent posture from the United States over this matter. The interests involved included those of industrial and commercial enterprises seeking entry into the potentially huge Chinese market, political groups sympathetic to communism, nationalists of various kinds driven by their 'Asianism' or eager to see Japan assert itself against American domination, and scholars with a deep knowledge and appreciation of Chinese civilization and culture.

The principles of the 'Yoshida Line' required adhesion to the American position over China. This was illustrated by Japanese voting behaviour in the United Nations over the issue of which government should occupy China's seat in the organization. On the procedural question whether the decision required a two thirds majority or a simple majority, Japan invariably voted with the United States to designate it as a substantive issue requiring a two thirds majority of members present and voting. On the main question, Japan always supported Taipei alongside the US. The Japanese were therefore surprised when President Nixon announced his forthcoming visit to China on 15 July 1971.

The few minutes' notice given to the government before the broadcast of this dramatic reversal in American policy was regarded as an insult and a poor recompense for Japan's loyalty over the previous twenty years. The historic encounter between the American President and the Chinese leaders in February 1972 marked the first stage in the lengthy process which culminated in the establishment of full diplomatic relations seven years later. The joint communiqué issued by Nixon and Zhou Enlai on 27 February 1972 reiterated the Chinese stand over Taiwan, but did not go much further than an assurance that the United States did not 'challenge' the claim that Taiwan was a part of China. It also included a statement that:

> Neither [side] should seek hegemony in the Asia–Pacific region and each is opposed to efforts by any other country or group of countries to establish such hegemony.

This was the origin of the celebrated 'anti-hegemony clause', which reappeared in the communiqué of 15 December 1978* announcing the establishment of diplomatic relations between the People's Republic of China and the US as from 1 January 1979. Opposition to hegemonism had been written into the preamble of the Chinese constitution of January 1975. Three years later it was repeated in the new constitution of March 1978, but more specifically directed against the hegemonism of 'socialist imperialism' (the USSR) and 'imperialism' (the US). However, it had been incorporated in the Nixon–Zhou communiqué on the initiative of the American side, as

* It added the phrase 'or any other region' after the words 'Asia–Pacific region'.

part of its search for a strategic relationship with China aimed at curbing Soviet power.

Japan followed the American lead over China, but 'retaliated' with a decision over the convertibility of the dollar in Okinawa without consulting the US authorities who still exercised administrative rights in the Ryūkyūs. Prime Minister Kakuei Tanaka visited China in September 1972 and he went further than Nixon in the subsequent joint statement. Beijing was recognised as 'the sole legal government of China', while Japan 'fully' understood and respected China's insistence that Taiwan was 'an inalienable part of the territory of the People's Republic of China'. Diplomatic relations were established on 29 September 1972. However, Taiwan continued to be an embarrassment to the Japanese government until the signature of the Treaty of Peace and Friendship between the two countries in August 1978 (see Appendix IV), not least because of the activities of pro-Kuomintang members of the LDP.

The anti-hegemony clause of the Nixon–Zhou communiqué reappeared verbatim in the statement issued at the end of Tanaka's visit. It was to cause considerable difficulties in the negotiations leading up to the Peace and Friendship Treaty, chiefly because the Chinese and Americans saw it as directed against the Soviet Union, whereas for Japan such an interpretation seemed to imply abandonment of its policy of even-handedness. Eventually, and in spite of Japanese reservations, the clause was embodied in Article 2 of the treaty as a result of Chinese and American pressures.[46]

A pattern soon established itself in which officially friendly relations and a substantial increase in trade and investment were periodically disturbed. Ever since the war the Chinese have exploited Japanese unease over the past to put pressure on the government and exercise a kind of moral blackmail. In addition, the territorial dispute over the Senkaku (Diaoyu) Islands also surfaced from time to time in incidents which coincided with a delicate phase in the bilateral relationship. One such crisis took place at a critical stage in the negotiations over the Treaty of Peace and Friendship, when a large number of Chinese fishing boats, some armed with machine-guns, operated around the islands in April 1978. A few of the boats displayed the slogan: 'We have the right to haul fish within Chinese territorial waters'. After two protests by the Japanese government, the incident was eventually closed with Chinese assurances that it had been an 'accident'.

However, China continues to remind Japan of its claim to sovereignty over what the Japanese insist belongs to them. When the Secretary-General of the CCP, Jiang Zemin, visited Japan in April 1992, Prime Minister Miyazawa raised the issue because the National People's Congress had enacted a law in February, which in effect declared Chinese sovereignty over the islands. As on previous occasions, the Chinese avoided a direct confrontation by falling back on Deng Xiaoping's statement in 1978 that the dispute would be shelved for some time because 'the people of our generation don't have enough wisdom. The people of the next generation may be wise enough to find a good solution'. Since it takes a long time in China for the next generation to come to the fore, this could be taken to mean that a settlement might have to wait until the end of the century or beyond. In the meantime, the problem remains to haunt bilateral relations.[47]

It is not easy to establish an exact correlation between these hiccups and the larger movements in Sino-Japanese relations, particularly as they were often related to domestic political manoeuvres. The events described above, and which took place in April 1978, may have reflected differences within the CCP over general policy towards Japan and have been used by one faction to sabotage the smooth progress of negotiations over the peace treaty. Similarly, anti-Japanese demonstrations in the 1980s were a cover for attacks on party Secretary-General Hu Yaobang. A parallel linkage of foreign policy issues and domestic politics can be observed in Japan. We have already noted the exploitation of relations with Taiwan by elements in the LDP in order to embarrass the pro-China elements in the Cabinet. Less than a year after the signature of the Peace and Friendship Treaty, there was a new clash over the Senkaku Islands. This time it arose out of a Japanese initiative to build a helicopter landing pad on one of the islands and revealed sharp differences between the Ministry of Transport, which supported the Maritime Safety Agency in this enterprise, and the Gaimushō which strongly opposed such a provocation. Again, sporadic attempts by nationalist-minded ministers and senior members of the LDP to justify Japanese behaviour during the war and to minimize atrocities like the Nanking massacre of 1937, embarrassed their colleagues and did nothing to improve relations with China.

The economic relationship, too, was not always smooth. Bouts of 'China fever' among Japanese firms, which had rushed into the China market, driven by competition with Western companies and their rivals at home, soon subsided in the face of disappointed expectations. Chinese inability to honour agreements and the general difficulties of operating in a tightly controlled command economy with its bureaucracy, red tape and corruption quickly dampened their ardour. The Chinese for their part complained that Japanese motives were purely exploitative, that they refused to transfer up-to-date technology and that they used the Chinese market to dump surplus and inferior goods. Nevertheless, the Japanese government encouraged the private sector to persevere, providing various forms of assistance to that effect, not least through the provision of substantial loans for the development of infrastructure (power generation, railways, ports, technological training).

The growth of Sino-Japanese trade and economic cooperation was underpinned by an ever-growing traffic of people between the two countries. They included officials, businessmen, delegations of all kinds, including veterans from the war, students – particularly Chinese students in Japan – and tourists. Familiarity can breed contempt and some of the more exalted ideas which had gained currency in the era when travel between the two countries was severely restricted and largely confined to those who held ideologically correct views, were soon replaced by more negative images of Chinese backwardness and inefficiency.

Japan's China policy underwent three transformations after 1945. The first was marked by virtual isolation from the mainland. It ended in 1972 when the second change began and led via the treaty of 1978 to a normalization of the relationship and a thickening network of ties between the two countries. The third transformation started in 1989 and is still underway. It is marked by the removal of Cold War constraints and an awareness that Japan is a free agent in its dealings with China. The 1990 Houston summit of the Group of Seven symbolized this freedom of action and Japanese assertiveness. Japan's partners did not oppose its intention to launch the US $5.2 billion (¥810 billion) loan which had been offered by Prime Minister Takeshita on his visit to China in August 1988. The loan, the third in a series designed to develop China's infrastructure and energy resources, was to be spread over five years from 1990 to 1995. All talks about its implementation came to a stop after the suppression of the pro-democracy movement in June 1989. Some disbursement of funds, earmarked mainly for food and medicines, had been made in the autumn of 1989 and talks were resumed in January 1990.

By the time the G-7 leaders met in Houston, consultations between Chinese and Japanese officials over a number of bilateral economic arrangements were in progress. In spite of the sanctions imposed at the previous summit in 1989 and the ban on contacts between senior officials from China and the G-7 countries, the United States and the other members of the summit did not make an issue of the fact that Japan was breaking ranks. Secretary of State James Baker said on television:

> The President of the United States is not in the business of opposing something that other countries do on a bilateral basis . . . The Japanese have certain commitments to the Chinese on something called a 'third yen-loan' and they want to go forward and keep those commitments. It's not up to the United States to tell them, 'No, you can't do this.'

The furthest the Americans were prepared to go to voice their displeasure were the words of an anonymous senior official in the administration:

> We can understand the Japanese wanting to proceed, because of their unique relationship with China. But we wish they would proceed in a more restricted form than they now envision.[48]

The Japanese had prepared a draft for the summit, which admitted modest changes in China since June 1989 and opened the way for loans from the World Bank for humanitarian and ecological projects. In the end the Summit Declaration stated that the members of the Group of Seven:

> acknowledge some of the recent developments in China, but believe that the prospects for closer cooperation will be enhanced by renewed political and economic reform, particularly in the field of human rights. We agree to maintain the measures put into place at last year's Summit, as modified over the course of this year. We will keep them under review for future adjustments to respond to further positive developments in China. For example, in addition to existing lending to meet basic human needs, we will explore whether there are other World Bank loans that would contribute to reform of the Chinese economy, especially loans that would address environmental concerns.[49]

The events of the summer of 1989 and their aftermath are a clear indication that Japan has set limits to its collaboration with the United States and its identification with the Western group of states. Ten years earlier it had exhibited a similar tendency to distance itself from the American position in the Iran-hostage and Afghan crises, but it was within the framework of a wider Western alliance 'in which Japanese and Europeans worked together to exercise a moderating influence in the context of the Cold War'.[50]

The brutal and bloody suppression of the pro-democracy movement in Tiananmen Square caused outrage in the West, and China was temporarily ostracized. Human rights were the central issue and both the United States and Western Europe were prepared to take specific measures at some cost to their economic interests, in order to underline their displeasure. Japan shared the outrage to a limited extent, but did not want it to interfere with the essentials of the bilateral relationship.

Its immediate and longer-term responses to the massacre of Tiananmen Square illustrate the priorities of Japan's China policy and provide some indication of the direction it is likely to pursue in relations with China.[51] The immediate reaction was characteristic: condemnation in moderate language, an emphasis on watching developments and collecting information, and an initial reluctance to impose sanctions. The primary concern was with the safety of Japanese nationals. Although the action of the Chinese authorities was described as 'intolerable' from a humanitarian point of view, the emphasis was on avoiding 'black-and-white judgement' and on non-interference. This 'soft' position was excused on the grounds of the special nature of Sino-Japanese relations, which were influenced by the legacy of the war. Japanese spokesmen also drew a distinction between China's 'political and social structures and values' and general humanitarian principles. This differentiation is important because it reveals the unideological and pragmatic approach which Japan brings to its external relations, in contrast to American and European tendencies towards universalism.

Ten days after the events of June 4–5, twenty Japanese businessmen returned to Beijing, eager to fill the vacuum created by the departure of foreign competitors. An embarrassed government urged them to exercise 'self-restraint'. By the autumn of 1989, delegations of politicians from both countries had exchanged visits, while other Western states maintained their boycott of China. Former foreign minister Masayoshi Itō played a leading role in these exchanges and remarked: 'We have much stronger ties with China than the United States or European nations.' At the Houston summit, the chief spokesman of the Foreign Ministry insisted: 'Our position is that no one has forgotten Tiananmen Square, but there is more to be gained in terms of reform from an open-door policy towards China.' By January 1991, Japan had lifted the last of its sanctions and in August Prime Minister Kaifu became the first Head of Government of the G-7 states to visit Beijing.

Several conclusions may be drawn from these reactions. First, it is the paramount interest of Japan to have a politically and socially stable China as its neighbour. There may have been sympathy for the aspirations of the pro-democracy student movement, but the extent of public outrage at its suppression was feeble when compared with the reactions in Europe and America. The massacre of June was 'regrettable', but order was seen as essential for the continued stability and economic development of China.

Second, Japanese policy was driven largely by economic interest. This has several aspects. Ever since 1972, the government has encouraged industrial enterprises and trading houses to persevere in their investment and trade and, as already noted, this encouragement was especially important during the periods of stagnation and frustration. Furthermore, enterprises themselves are repeatedly drawn into the China market because of anxieties that they may be left behind by their competitors at home or displaced by foreign firms. An example of the competition among Japanese companies was the scramble of motor manufacturers to set up joint ventures with the Chinese in 1985, a phenomenon aptly described as the 'pack instinct'. Fear that foreigners would pre-empt them in the market was an important motive behind Japan's readiness to resume discussions about the third yen-loan and the invitation to the Chinese minister of machinery and electronics to come to Tokyo in January 1990. In the previous month, President Bush had approved loans by the US Export–Import Bank to American firms doing business with China.

Behind the element of competition there lies a strategic calculation, which is the third conclusion to be drawn from the events of 1989–90. The more the Chinese economy becomes dependent on Japanese capital, technology and managerial skills, the greater the influence Japan hopes to be able to exercise over the general direction of its neighbour's policy. There have been several instances when Japan tried to exploit its economic strength in support of diplomatic and strategic objectives, ranging from Prime Minister Ōhira's attempt in 1979 to persuade the Chinese to exercise a restraining influence over North Korea to the recent pressure on China during the Gulf crisis in 1990 not to veto the authorization of war against Iraq by a coalition under the auspices of the United Nations. In the aftermath of the Tiananmen incident, Japan linked the promise of an early resumption of economic assistance to demands for a relaxation of political repression. The effectiveness of such attempts to influence policy is, of course, difficult to assess, but they illustrate Japan's intention to use its economic primacy in order to increase its political status and power in international politics.

Recent Japanese policy underlines the very strong economic ties between the two countries. In the early 1990s, Sino-Japanese economic relations were once again in a period of boom, largely as a consequence of Japanese retrenchment in the stagnant American and European markets. In contrast, the Chinese economy seemed set on a course of phenomenal growth which is expected to last until the end of the century. Japanese investment in 1992 reached US $1.5 billion, three times the level of 1990. It has become the third largest investor in China after Hong Kong and Taiwan. There are forecasts that the value of bilateral trade will have surpassed $30 billion in 1993. The content of trade has also changed. A decade ago, Japan imported mainly raw materials from China and exported machinery and capital goods. In 1990 more than sixty per cent of China's exports to Japan consisted of manufactured goods, including textiles and furniture.

The extraordinarily rapid growth of the Chinese economy, especially in the so-called China Economic Area (southern China, Hong Kong and Taiwan), has not only created a Chinese surplus in the bilateral trade balance, but raises the prospect of a more even economic relationship in which the attraction of Japanese finance and technology is equalled by the pull of a buoyant Chinese economy, based on a skilled but cheap labour force and plentiful supplies of raw materials. Mutual dependence might well weaken the political clout of Japan's economic superiority.

A fourth conclusion points to the importance of the cultural nexus in the Sino-Japanese relationship. In justifying their demand for an early restoration of normal relations, the Japanese tended to place great emphasis on this factor. This had been the essence of the argument used by the 'Asianists' in their debate with the 'Westerners' over Japan's fundamental orientation after the Meiji Revolution. Here, the Chinese also have some advantage, as in their repeated and quite successful exploitation of this sentiment and of the Japanese shame over past aggression in order to manipulate public opinion in their favour. However, with the passage of time this kind of appeal to the Japanese conscience is bound to weaken if not to disappear.

Finally, and as a fifth conclusion, the whole episode confirmed that while it is possible to see the shoots of an independent Japanese policy towards China, Japan still sees itself as a member of the group of industrialized democracies and as having a special relationship to their leader. Various utterances and measures in the immediate reaction to the events of June 1989 show that Japan was at pains to appear to be acting as a member of the Western alliance. The importance of remaining close to the United States still weighed heavily in its policy, particularly in the perspective of the Gaimushō. However, its wealth and the fact that the United States is also dependent on Japan, gave Japan more freedom to act independently than might have been possible in the past. It effectively exploited its strength to persuade the partners to accept the decision to restore economic ties with China.

The absence of the Taiwan factor is an interesting phenomenon in the discussion of contemporary Sino-Japanese relations. No consideration of Japan's China policy in the 1970s could have ignored the problem of Taiwan as a major issue, even though Japan had made its decision in favour of Beijing by 1972. The importance of the Taiwan factor declined in the 1980s, and in the 1990s one can question whether it remains an issue at all.

Relations between the mainland and Taiwan have still to be resolved. Economic interest pulls them together. Statistical evidence points in that direction. Between 1987 and 1991 some 2,300,000 visits were made to China by people from Taiwan and more than 200,000 mainlanders visited the island. In just over two years (June 1989–September 1991) more than 10,000,000 telephone, telex, fax, and telegram messages were exchanged between the mainland and Taiwan. China has become the fourth or fifth largest trading partner of Taiwan. In 1993 the value of two-way trade exceeded US $10 billion. Commerce via Hong Kong, the principal route for such exchanges, accounted for 3.82 per cent of Taiwan's total foreign trade and by 1991 about 3000 Taiwanese companies had invested about $2 billion in China, a figure estimated to have risen to more than $10 billion by 1993.[52]

At the political level, too, there has been an inching towards each other, furthered by the Taipei government's official declaration of 30 April 1991, ending the state of 'communist rebellion' and forty-three years of emergency rule. Official contact is still banned, but Taiwanese are allowed to go to the mainland to attend conferences organized by international bodies such as the World Bank, thereby allowing plenty of opportunity for informal and off-the-record contacts. Such encounters were considerably increased by an agreement in 1993 whereby nominally unofficial bodies in both countries, which oversee their economic relations, set up regular meetings of their secretaries general and working-level officials. The topics of consultation include cooperation in combating piracy and the repatriation of illegal immigrants in addition to measures of economic cooperation. Much will depend on the evolution of the situation in Hong Kong; the first test in applying Deng Xiaoping's 'one country – two systems' formula. This has two aspects. In view of Hong Kong's importance in Taiwan's economic relations with the mainland, will it continue to fulfil this role under Chinese sovereignty? If not, how might that affect the economic relationship? The answers to these questions will be affected by the second aspect. If the emerging democracy of Hong Kong can be preserved after 1997, then the prospect of an eventually peaceful accommodation between an increasingly democratic Taiwan and the People's Republic of China will be improved.

There remains the possibility that the government on the island will opt for a unilateral declaration of independence (UDI) as the Republic of Taiwan. The ruling élites who came from the mainland in 1949 are dying out and control is passing into the hands of those who were born in Taiwan. A native-born Taiwanese, Lien Chan, became prime minister for the first time in February 1993. A move towards UDI might gain the support of the United States and other Western countries, especially if there is no sign of democratic reforms in China.

The United States followed its principal Western allies in withdrawing official recognition from the Republic of China but, like them, retained flourishing economic and cultural relations with Taiwan. Moreover, it remained committed to its defence against any attempt by the People's Republic of China to seize the island by force. The most recent indication of this policy was the announcement by President Bush in September 1992 of the sale of 150 F-16 Fighter planes to Taiwan. The motives behind this provocative move were linked to the presidential campaign then in progress as well as to the need of boosting the American economy with a deal expected to net some $40 billion. It would also help to reduce an adverse balance of trade with Taiwan and prevent either France or Israel from becoming suppliers for the replacement of Taiwan's ageing fighters.

Japan accepts that Taiwan belongs to China and will want to remain aloof from any conflict over the island, in spite of its close relationship with the United States and strong economic links with Taiwan. The Japanese might prefer to see the emergence of an independent Taiwan, but certainly not if that brought them into confrontation with China. During some of the more tense moments in Sino-American relations over Taiwan under the Reagan and Bush administrations, it was generally understood that Japan would not and could not intervene in support of Taiwan, in spite of its preferences and a considerable stake in the island's economy.

Japan enjoys a substantial surplus in its trade with Taiwan, which was expected to reach US $16 billion in 1993 according to Taiwanese sources.[53] In the late 1980s about one half of Taiwan's foreign trade was handled by Japanese trading houses and Japan is the largest foreign investor on the island. Funds have been concentrated in labour-intensive industries that handle semi-finished products which are imported from Japan and then exported as finished goods to the United States and elsewhere. Taiwan makes the same complaints about Japanese practices as other countries in East Asia: trade imbalance, insufficient opening of the domestic market and a reluctance to transfer technology, all seeming to point to a policy of turning Taiwan into a workshop of sweated labour for the benefit of the Japanese economy.

Economic relations have been accompanied by much intervisitation, including officials whose visits are invariably described as 'unofficial'. One of the recent arrivals in Japan was Taiwan's Foreign Minister, Frederick Chien, in February 1993, the first such visit for twenty-one years. It evoked a vigorous protest from Beijing. Chien in turn criticized his hosts for not arranging informal meetings with government officials, though he met many influential politicians. The event illustrates two features of the Japan–Taiwan relationship. First, that a good deal can be achieved without official relations – an example of the East Asian tendency to bypass or ignore rules and regulations and thus avoid the trouble or danger of trying to change them. Second, that under pressure or threats from Beijing, Japan will take some action to appease its anger without necessarily affecting the substance of the matter under dispute.

Regardless of the Taiwan connection, relations with Beijing are at the centre of Japanese policy in North-East Asia. In 1978 I published a study from which I concluded that Japan was moving towards businesslike and friendly relations with China, but that a very close association was not the objective.[54] It was written before the signing of the Peace and Friendship Treaty and in the context of the Cold War. The intervening years have witnessed a steady development of the economic nexus between the two countries, despite several setbacks which were usually overcome by encouragement and material assistance from the government. There have been innumerable official visits as well and myriad expressions of friendship and good will. The climax was the visit of Emperor Akihito and his consort to China in October 1992, the first Japanese monarch to do so in the 2000-year history of relations between the two countries.[55]

It was a momentous event, accompanied by new developments in the bilateral economic relationship, but it also demonstrated the underlying difficulties on both sides. Within the LDP there had been considerable opposition to the imperial pilgrimage, chiefly because the Emperor would be expected to apologize for the past. Hence the original evasiveness of the Japanese Prime Minister in the face of repeated invitations from the Chinese side. Eventually he was able to establish a consensus which allowed arrangements to be made. The Emperor changed the official Gaimushō draft of the speech in which he expressed his contrition, by inserting a phrase which made specific reference to the suffering Japan had inflicted on the Chinese people. In thus strengthening his condemnation of the war, the Emperor spoke for many of the post-war generation to which he belongs. Even so, the Chinese were not wholly satisfied and the interpretation of the legacy of the past is likely to continue to trouble the bilateral relationship. In spite of the passing of the wartime generation, the issue will remain as anxiety increases over Japan's role and intentions in post-Cold War East Asia. It is often said that the Chinese have a long perspective which does not run to decades but to centuries. That view is not confined to the future but applies equally to the past.

The long-term stability of China is seen to be in Japan's best interests. This concern presently outweighs the potential threat from a unified, modernized and powerful China in the next century, extending its influence and attempting to establish its hegemony over the region with economic and military means. That prospect is not ignored, but Japan hopes to use its present economic and technological superiority to steer China into a constructive and cooperative engagement in regional politics and thereby indirectly to exercise its own power and influence.

SUMMARY

Throughout the post-war era until the end of the 1980s, Japan's relations with its neighbours in North-East Asia were conducted with reference to the central element in its external policy: the close association with the United States. There had been intimations of 'independence' in its approach to each of the neighbours. They included Hatoyama's readiness to go further in striking a deal with the Soviet Union in 1955–6 than was in the American interest at the time; the reluctance to recognize the Republic of Korea as the sole legitimate government of the peninisula and the probings to find ways in keeping open some lines of communication with the North; the subtleties of policy towards China between 1952 and 1972 and the unwillingness to accept the Kuomintang regime as the only legitimate government of China; and the increasing tendency in the latter half of the post-war period to pursue a more nationalistic economic policy which occasionally went against the interests of the West in the Cold War.

Notwithstanding such stirrings of a distinctive Japanese position in the international affairs of the region, it usually gave way to the overriding importance of the American connection. Hatoyama failed in his objective of signing a peace treaty with the Soviet Union, in part because of direct American pressure. Again, it was American pressure that pushed Japan into signing the agreements with South Korea in 1965. In spite of Japanese reservations, the Republic of China was accepted as the official representative of the whole of China and a full acceptance of political realities had to wait until President Nixon's historic visit to China in 1972. And whenever Japanese firms broke the rules of embargo on trade with the communist bloc, which had been established by the Co-ordinating Committee (COCOM) and the China Committee (CHINCOM), the Japanese authorities bowed to American demands.

Quite some time before the end of the Cold War, Japan was aware of the decline of American economic power and there was much discussion of its policy options in a world no longer dominated by the United States. The events of the 1990s have moved the debate from the hypothetical to the practical.

Whereas it is clear that one phase in the post-war relationship with the United States has come to an end, the same cannot be said about the legacy of the war itself. Half a century after Japan's surrender to the victorious allies, the consequences of Japanese aggression and military expansion continue to overshadow its relations with other countries in the region and they will influence the international politics of the new era. Among the unfinished business of the war are territorial disputes with Russia and Korea, the continued discrimination against the Korean minority in Japan, feelings of dislike and fear of Japan among the people of China and Korea, and the repeated exploitation by the Chinese and Korcans of Japan's 'guilt' as a means with which to manipulate Japanese opinion and to exert pressure on official policy. The legacy of the war is, of course, not one-sided. The Japanese also have their grievances. They include the circumstances under which the Russians seized the Northern Territories, the shameful treatment of prisoners-of-war in Siberia, the behaviour of the liberated Koreans in Japan under the occupation and, not least, the bombing of Hiroshima and Nagasaki.

The change of generations from wartime and post-war to recent has not removed the issues, but it has altered their impact. The Japanese want to close the militarist and wartime chapter in their history. This had been the declared intention of Mr Nakasone in the 1980s. The death of the Shōwa Emperor in January 1989 was the symbolic end of an era. Emperor Akihito represents the post-war generation – those who were children or students in 1945, who had some experience of the effects of the war but were educated in an atmosphere of total rejection of militarism. His generation want to close the chapter and are prepared to do so at some cost of self-abasement. Those who were born after the war have no such memories. For them it is history, a regretted episode no doubt, but one in which they had no part and for which they feel no personal responsibility. They, too, want to see the chapter closed and they are irritated by constant moral lectures and pressures from outside. The louder the protests from China and Korea, the greater the feelings of resentment in Japan.

Contemporary Japanese nationalism has two faces. There is the dwindling minority of nostalgics and unregenerates who yearn for past imperial glory. The other face of nationalism is that of the younger generation born after the war and which has no such sentiments, but which is proud of Japan's economic and technological achievements and wants to see it play a more prominent and assertive part in international politics. It resents the moral blackmail exercised by some countries and is in no mood meekly to accept lessons from outsiders about what Japan should do and how it should behave. Such attitudes are particularly noticeable among junior and middle-ranking officials in the ministries which handle Japan's external relations.

Their emergence coincides with the end of ideological confrontation between capitalism and communism. That confrontation had always been a veneer which was spread by the superpowers over the international relations of East Asia. Chinese, Korean and Vietnamese communism had been grafted on a more deep-rooted cultural nationalism in each country and as their ideological systems matured, they began to assume a distinctive 'national' colouring which made a nonsense of the international socialist brotherhood. The later phases of the Cold War in East Asia were dominated by Sino-Soviet and Sino-Vietnamese hostilities and by North Korean attempts to play off its two giant communist neighbours against each other.

The Asian members of the so-called 'Free World' were slow to adopt the kind of democratic institutions which are supposed to be the hallmark of that fraternity. Moreover, the ideology of liberal democracy is seen just as much as an alien importation into the East Asian cultural sphere as communism. This applies to Japan as much as to the other states, though it is the most 'Western' country in the region with the constitution and the institutions of a liberal democracy.

As in Europe, the constraints of the Cold War and its ideological context have given way to a revival of cultural and ethnocentric nationalism. There is a rising nationalist sentiment in all countries and this has affected their external policies. The dispute over the Northern Territories has ceased to be an issue of the rights or wrongs of Soviet action at the end of the Pacific War – something over which the Russians have largely accepted the Japanese point of view – or of their significance in the strategic balance of the Cold War. Instead, the central problem now concerns the presence and future of two generations of Russian settlers there; a question very similar to the issue over the Falkland/Malvinas Islands where the British population is of much older local descent.

At the beginning of the 1990s Japan recognized that it would be increasingly on its own in the region. The relationship with the United States is no longer the only point of reference as a guide to policy. It is not simply a matter of divergent interests, which have always been there in the background, but a question of how much longer it will be possible to rely on the American presence and involvement in East Asia. This is a disconcerting prospect for a country that has for so long and so successfully operated on the assumption that the United States could be relied upon to come to its support in a serious crisis. On the other hand, self-confidence and pride stemming from phenomenal economic success and the relative stability and social harmony of the country, when compared with the turmoil elsewhere in the world, has prepared the ground for a mood which is open to a more active participation in world affairs. Such an attitude may be strengthened by the demise of the 'catching up' mentality which has dominated Japanese élites ever since the Meiji Restoration. There are no models left for Japan to turn to. Indeed, it has become a model itself, not only in Asia but elsewhere as well.

The transformation of international politics has been accompanied by two conflicting pulls in Japan's regional policy. One moves it in the direction of traditional balance of power objectives. They would require policies that sought to retain an American presence in the region (similar to British policy in post-Cold War Europe), that sought to retain a balance on the Korean peninsula, and that calculated the comparative advantages of drawing closer to China or Russia with the aim of preventing the emergence of an alliance between them or the establishment of Chinese hegemony. The other moves it towards economic integration which cuts across the geo-political boundaries of North-East Asia, as in the development of a Japan Sea economic zone. It would also mean ever greater integration in a world economy in which Japan plays a leading role. In whichever direction Japan were to go, either could lead to an 'Asia first' position or a greater global orientation in its policies.

5 Regional interests and policy in South-East Asia

INTRODUCTION

The region includes the six member states of ASEAN (Brunei, Indonesia, Malaysia, the Philippines, Singapore, Thailand), the three states of Indochina (Cambodia, Laos, Vietnam), Myanmar/Burma, the south-eastern part of China, and Hong Kong as well as the oceans and waterways that link the vast expanse of landmass and islands which together constitute South-East Asia.

In the pre-modern era, Japan's main interest in the region lay in trade, piracy and as a passageway to south Asia and beyond. It was too distant to feature prominently in the political ambitions of Japanese rulers, though Hideyoshi is on record as having regarded the conquest of China as a stepping-stone in an advance on South-East Asia, India and Persia.[1] Such grandiose visions apart, the political focus was nearer home and centred on the Luchu (Ryūkyū) Islands, whose ports, especially Naha, became entrepôts for a triangular trade, where Japanese merchants purchased products from Indonesia and Malaya for shipment to Korea and China and from where Luchuan ships laden with Chinese and Japanese goods sailed down the Chinese coast as far as Sumatra, Java, Thailand and Burma. After the unification of the Luchus under one ruler in the early fifteenth century, he simultaneously sent envoys to the Ming court in Beijing and approached the military government (Bakufu) of Japan through the powerful Shimazu clan in Kyūshū.[2]

These were the roots of the tangled relationship of the Kingdom of the Ryūkyūs with China and Japan. It paid tribute to China, but occasionally also sent tribute to Japan. In 1590 Hideyoshi had proposed a special agreement with the king on the grounds that

Japan and the Ryūkyū Islands were members of one family. The unresolved dispute over the Senkaku Islands is an offshoot of the historic Sino-Japanese conflict over prime rights and sovereignty in this region.

Japanese pirates were active further to the south and west. The crews who manned the ships were a mixture of Japanese and Chinese, with the former serving as captains and navigators and the latter often providing the main complement. Moreover, the cause of the piracy lay as much in the efforts of the Ming dynasty to close Chinese ports to trade as in the predatory nature of the Japanese seafarers. Once the Chinese relaxed the trade embargo, the incentive for the illicit trade and smuggling was largely removed and piracy ceased to be a major problem.[3]

The penetration of the south seas by Japanese merchants came to an end with the onset of the exclusion policy in the seventeenth century, but by then the South-East Asian region had acquired a new strategic importance as the route to East Asia for the European powers. Portuguese, Spanish, Dutch, English and French ships soon made their appearance in the neighbourhood of Japan. In the closing years of the Tokugawa regime, the critics of the government accused it of neglecting the defence of the country against the encroaching West by failing to pursue a forward policy in Asia. Among other measures, they urged that South-East Asia should become an area for Japanese exploitation.[4]

While North-East Asia was the main focus of Japanese expansion in the Meiji and early Shōwa eras, it was the advance into South-East Asia, beginning with the occupation of French Indochina in July 1941, which led to the outbreak of the Pacific War.

BILATERAL RELATIONS

Although the Association of South-East Asian Nations (ASEAN) did not come into existence until 1967, Japanese interest in the region was revived soon after the end of the Pacific War. Following the outbreak of the war in Korea in 1950, the American occupation authorities took various measures to detach Japan from its preoccupation with China and sought to substitute the South-East Asian market for the China market.[5] Japan's return to the region was via the long drawn-out and difficult process of negotiating reparation agreements. The first was signed with Burma in 1954, with a supplementary agreement in 1963. Settlements were reached with the Philippines in 1956, Indonesia in 1958 and non-communist

South Vietnam in 1959. Laos and Cambodia received cash grants in the same year but not formal reparations. Malaya and Singapore were still British colonies at the end of the war and therefore did not have the right to claim reparations on their own account. That right lay with the British who did not, however, exercise it on their behalf. Following their independence, Japan concluded agreements with both countries on 21 September 1967, according to which Japan made a financial grant to each. The agreements also included identical articles stating that every problem that had arisen between the state and Japan as a result of the Second World War had been settled by the conclusion of the agreement.

Two features stand out from all these arrangements. One was the major role in the negotiations played by big business interests, commonly referred to as *zaikai* (financial circles), which often took the initiative and frequently represented the government in the talks. Individual leaders of economic organizations, such as the Japan Foreign Trade Association, the Chamber of Commerce and Industry, and the Federation of Economic Organizations (Keidanren), handled the negotiations concerning specific countries.

The other feature was the linkage between the policy of national economic recovery, part of the 'Yoshida Line', and the terms of the settlements. The basic position of the Japanese government was to make sure that payments would be in goods and services, that the products to be handed over were to be capital rather than consumer goods, and that payments would not impose additional foreign exchange burdens on Japan. The commercial and industrial interests were quick to grasp the connection between reparations and the revival of the economy and therefore pressed for settlements, even if on very favourable terms to the recipient country. The payment of indemnities in cash and kind served several purposes. They would compensate for the loss of markets as a result of the war; they would provide new outlets for Japanese industries following the decline in US procurements after the armistice in Korea; they would raise the level of the economies of South-East Asia and therefore create future markets for Japanese goods and investment; they would help to check the advance of communism in the region through the creation of a barrier of prosperity;[6] above all, Japanese enterprises would benefit directly through the supply of goods and services to the recipient countries. In other words, the sums disbursed in reparations by the Japanese government would find their way back into Japanese pockets.

The payment of reparations laid the groundwork for subsequent aid programmes and Japan's economic expansion in the region. The settlements are an illustration of the tendency of Japanese entrepreneurs to take a long-term view and to plan accordingly. Although the motivation was primarily economic and was to remain so in the following three decades, there was an undertone of political aspirations right from the start. In the context of the Cold War they included the objective of preventing the spread of communism, which was in step with American policy. But there was also an element of seeking to create a relationship of dependency between the recipients of reparations and Japan. Lastly, and most important, both business circles and government saw economic relations with South-East Asia as an important factor in the economic recovery of Japan, an essential prerequisite for its emergence as a leading power in East Asia.

Relations with the countries of the region began on a purely bilateral basis, but acquired a regional emphasis in the mid-sixties, especially after the formation of ASEAN. Henceforth Japanese policy pursued a twin-track approach, with the regional aspect acquiring greater salience as ASEAN developed its identity.

Once the Japanese had broken out of their American-dominated isolation in the first decade after 1945, economic relations with the countries of South-East Asia developed fairly rapidly on the back of the programme of reparations. Indonesia was potentially the most important partner in the region because of its reserves of oil and other natural resources. Japanese interest was summarized in the late 1960s by the representative of the North Sumatra Oil Development Company (NOSODECO), who listed four objectives of his enterprise, which he described as a 'pilot project'. The first was to secure a supply of oil. Next came the intention to increase the number of Japanese technicians in the field of oil extraction and refinement. The third and fourth aims were vague but revealing: to make Indonesia dependent on Japan to a certain extent and to expand Japan's political influence generally.[7] Japan was the last of the Western states to abandon President Sukarno and provided a yen credit a few months before the events in 1965 which led to his overthrow.[8] By the beginning of the 1970s Japan was well established as Indonesia's principal trading partner, accounting for nearly one third of its foreign trade. In addition, it provided more than one third of its foreign direct investment (FDI). At the end of the decade the dependence syndrome had reached the stage where more than half of Indonesia's revenue was derived from the export of oil, more than forty per cent of which went to Japan.[9] The pattern continued in the 1980s. Indonesia provided Japan with some thirteen per cent of its imports of crude oil and Japanese investment was by far the largest when compared with American and European FDI or with Japanese investments in any of the other countries of the region.[10]

Japan's relations with Indonesia are probably the closest of all with members of ASEAN. Although the economic motive is predominant, Indonesia's strategic importance has undoubtedly played a part in fostering Japanese interest. It is the largest of the ASEAN states in terms of geographical extent and size of population. It is the source of strategic raw materials, not only oil, and it straddles the sea routes to Australia, the Indian Ocean, the Middle East, Europe and Africa.[11] Japan has also developed close relations with each of the other members of ASEAN, though none is as important and has quite the same politico-strategic potential as Indonesia. The connection with each has distinctive characteristics.

Relations with Thailand are not burdened by the wartime experience and there was no call for reparations. The Thais are the region's great survivors. Throughout the era of European domination they had retained their political independence through skilful manoeuvring between the rival ambitions of Britain and France. Under the military dictator Phibul Songkhram they signed a treaty with Japan in 1940 and hitched their fortunes to the Japanese empire. At the outbreak of the Pacific War the Japanese occupied Bangkok and on 25 January 1942, Thailand declared war on the United States and Britain, and was duly rewarded with territory taken from French Indochina, Malaya and Burma. As the tide of war turned, so did Thailand change tack. A Free Siam movement under the leadership of the regent Pridit Phanomyong established contact with the allies, whose agents began to move freely around Bangkok before the end of the war. It is a mark of the diplomatic finesse of the Thai government that this former 'enemy' was admitted to the United Nations in 1946. After the war Thailand became a source of rubber, sugar and other primary materials, and an important field for investment. Japan is the largest single investor, though the annual rate declined at the beginning of the 1990s.

Japanese economic and political interest in Malaysia and Singapore is somewhat greater than it is in Thailand. Both countries suffered under Japanese occupation during the war, and Malaysia, in particular, has been wary of any suggestion that Japan might relieve the United States of some of its responsibility as guardian of the region's security. The effective ruler of Singapore, Lee Kuan Yew, has been less worried about the prospect of a revived Japanese militarism. Both Malaysia and Singapore have turned to Japan and South Korea as models for their economic and social development in the 1980s, an approach encapsulated in the 'look east policy' advocated by Malaysia's Prime Minister Dr Mahathir Mohamad in 1981.

Nevertheless, there were marked differences in the economic relationships right from the start. A joint venture between the Economic Development Board of the Government of Singapore and Ishikawajima Harima Industries for the development of Jurong Shipyard in the early 1960s was a first step in making Singapore the most important ship-repair and servicing centre between Yokohama and the Gulf. It was a long-range enterprise which gave Japan a significant stake in the future of Singapore and was a recognition of its strategic importance along the Straits of Malacca and Singapore.

Whereas Singapore is the source of manufactured goods and petroleum products, Malaysia remains an important supplier of raw materials, especially rubber, timber, bauxite and tin metal, providing Japan with slightly less than one third of its total requirement of the last mentioned in 1991. A project for a steel mill in Prai, opposite Penang, was launched in 1967 with a thirty-nine per cent stake held by Japanese companies, more than half of which came from Yawata Steel. As in Indonesia, this development was seen as a long-term investment with the objective of establishing a base in the Malaysian economy and as part of a general expansion of Japanese influence in the South-East Asian region.

Relations with the Philippines were overshadowed from the start by bitter feelings aroused by the memories of Japanese military occupation. They were also influenced by the special position of the United States in that country. While the Philippines, too, are an important source of raw materials (copper and zinc ores), the bilateral relationship has had a stronger politico-strategic component than with any other country in the region, apart from Indonesia. The Republic of the Philippines has been plagued by communist and muslim insurgencies since its emergence as an independent state. At Subic Bay it was host until 1992 to the largest American naval base in the East Asian region and, alongside Clark airbase, it has occupied the same pivotal position in South-East Asia with regard to American strategic deployment as the string of

Japanese bases in North-East Asia. The archipelago lies astride the route to the south and Japan is concerned that it should remain under the control of a friendly government. For all these reasons Japan has given priority to its aid programme in the Philippines. By the end of the 1980s it had become the largest aid donor and the largest foreign investor.[12] None the less, the Filipino government has always been reserved over any suggestion that Japan should guarantee the security of the region. This was especially noticeable at the time when Japan bowed to American pressure to extend its defence perimeter to include sealanes up to 1000 nautical miles from the national territory, which would bring ships of the Maritime Self-Defence Force (MSDF) to the north of the Philippines.[13]

Brunei, the sixth and newest member, joined ASEAN in 1984. It exports some thirty per cent of its oil and all of its natural gas to Japan. It is therefore in what is officially described as an 'interdependent relationship' with Japan.[14] In fact, its economy relies exclusively on the production of crude and of natural gas, with Japan accounting for more than half the total exports and South Korea taking a further fifteen per cent. However, most of its imports come from Singapore.

Taken as a whole, Japan's bilateral relationships with the non-communist states of the region have been defined by certain characteristics. Apart from Singapore, each one of the countries provides Japan with important sources of energy or industrial raw materials, both in some cases, and a pattern emerged in which they depended on the import of manufactures and capital goods in exchange. The reparations paid to some laid the foundations of economic development, which was later supported by substantial amounts of Official Development Assistance (ODA). Over time and partly due to the structural changes in Japan's economy following the 'oil shocks' of the 1970s, the nature of bilateral relationships changed with the increasing role of Japanese FDI. This meant in effect the relocation of heavy industry from Japan nearer to the sources of essential raw materials and to take advantage of cheap labour. It was also a form of pollution export, promoted by the pressures from an environmentally conscious public in Japan. Of course, the relationships varied from country to country, with a particularly heavy dependence on Indonesia and Brunei and much less in the way of economic stakes in Thailand, which has a large adverse balance of trade with Japan. One other general feature is noteworthy: the extensive cooperation between Japanese and

Chinese entrepreneurs in South- East Asian projects. This collaboration has aroused apprehension in some countries, particularly those with Malay majorities and large Chinese minorities, which has increased substantially since the end of the Cold War and the rapid economic development of China.

While political relations with all the countries have been generally good, there are differences, especially over the question of the potential for Japanese involvement in the security of the South-East Asian region. The wartime experience of each plays a part here, but it is fading as a factor in local attitudes. On the other hand, the nearer a country is to Japan or the more likely to be affected by the projection of Japanese power, the more apprehensive its government. States like Thailand or Singapore, which have less to fear, are inclined to view a certain Japanese presence as a welcome reinforcement in the face of a likely decline of American involvement.

In the 1970s Japan's focus began to shift from preoccupation with bilateral relations to the issues raised by the question of links with ASEAN as a whole. Before turning to this subject it is necessary to refer briefly to Japanese relations with Burma.[15]

Burma or Myanmar, as it is now called, is the poorest state in South-East Asia and the most inaccessible. It has followed a policy of deliberate isolation; a policy that led it to withdraw temporarily from the Non-Aligned Movement in 1979. Though a natural recruit for ASEAN, it shunned any association with that body, not even sending observers to its meetings until 1994, when its foreign minister was invited as a guest to the meeting of ASEAN at Bangkok in July, largely on the initiative of Thailand. The country has been in a state of chronic disorder since the 1960s. One of the six Secretaries-General of the United Nations was a Burmese, but his nation has been almost unnoticed in the world community, except as a violator of human rights.

It is all the more curious, therefore, that Japan has had a remarkably close relationship with Burma. It was the first country with which it concluded a reparations settlement, later extended by a supplementary agreement in 1963. Nobusuke Kishi was the first post-war prime minister to make a tour of Asian countries before going to Washington, and Rangoon was his first port of call. His successors, Hayato Ikeda and Eisaku Satō, also visited Burma on their tours of South-East Asia. Moreover, in 1987 Myanmar received more than seventy one per cent of its ODA from Japan, which covered some twenty per cent of expenditures in the national budget. After the brutal military suppression of the uprising of students and monks in 1988, Japan and other donor countries suspended aid in protest against the violation of human rights by the regime. Less than half a year later, Japan abruptly and unilaterally restored its aid programme in March 1989. The reasons for the reversal can be traced to bureaucratic in-fighting in Tokyo. It also reflected the substantial Japanese stake in the economy, especially the risk that the Burmese might default on a huge debt.[16]

Japan's special relationship with Myanmar continues. It is based more on the economic potential of the country than on its actual performance. The Japanese have an interest in some large-scale projects such as the expansion of Rangoon airport, a sugar mill and a power station. Furthermore, they have retained a privileged position in the country as against other countries and aid donors. Part of the explanation of the relationship lies in sentiment. Initially, Burmese independence fighters had supported the Japanese during the war, welcomed them as liberators and enthusiastically embraced the Greater East Asia Co-prosperity Sphere. Many were to be disillusioned by the Japanese occupation. None the less, friendly ties were restored after the war and strongly reinforced by economic largesse. On the Japanese side there lingered a sentimental attachment, symbolized by Michio Takeyama's novel *Harp of Burma*, which became a best-seller and was turned into a film.[17]

RELATIONS WITH ASEAN

The emotions which colour Japanese attitudes towards other Asian countries should not be ignored as an element in the 'Asianism' of many Japanese. They are certainly present and frequently articulated in the approach to ASEAN as a whole. Japan's relations with the Association have tended to follow its evolution and there is little evidence of any positive encouragement in its formation and initial development. Indeed, the Gaimushō was not inclined to take it very seriously at the beginning and MITI was worried that it would undermine the generally favourable bilateral relationships which Japan enjoyed with the member states. The authorities were also uneasy about ASEAN's declared intention in 1971 to establish a Zone of Peace, Freedom and Neutrality (ZOPFAN) in the region, for it might have had the indirect effect of reviving domestic opposition to the Mutual Security Treaty with the United States.[18]

Before the founding of ASEAN in August 1967, the Japanese government itself had convened a ministerial conference for the economic development of South-East Asia (MEDSEA) in Tokyo in

April 1966. It had a wider scope than ASEAN was to have and the invitations included Burma and the countries of Indochina. Not all those invited came and some attended as observers. However, the significance of the initiative lay in the fact that this was the first time since the war that Japan had called together an international conference and that no prior notice had been given to the United States, which was not included.

MEDSEA was followed by further meetings in 1967 and 1968. The objective was economic and practical, focusing on agricultural development, the promotion of tourism, the marketing of new products, and regional programmes to develop transport and communications. The original purpose had been to set up an informal forum, but it acquired greater standing through the subsequent ministerial conferences. Essentially it symbolized Japanese commitment to the economic progress of South-East Asia. Many of the proposals which were considered at the meetings of MEDSEA depended on Japanese financial and technical participation.[19]

Japanese attitudes towards the South-East Asian region were ambivalent. On the one hand, Japan was primarily interested in economic ties with individual countries, especially those which could supply it with sources of energy and raw materials, and it was suspicious of any attempt by the South-East Asian nations to form a bloc which might improve their collective economic bargaining power. On the other hand, Japan sought to establish a forum in which it would have a major voice. It became clear that in their search for a distinctive international role, successive Japanese governments saw an opportunity in cultivating relations with South-East Asia. Such a policy was reinforced by the personal ambitions of successive prime and foreign ministers. We have already noted Prime Minister Kishi's Asian tour in 1957, prior to his first official visit to Washington. He sought to exploit Japan's Asian connection to establish a more equal partnership with the United States and eventually to create a triangular relationship in which no doubt he envisaged a pivotal role for Japan.[20]

As it turned out, the formation of ASEAN did not pose an 'economic threat' to Japan. Its original purpose, and the one which dominated the first decade of its existence, was to ensure internal collective security through the management and mitigation of the conflicting interests of its members. The military confrontation between Indonesia and Malaysia had only ceased in 1966 after a change of regime in Indonesia. There were other troublesome and potentially explosive disputes between the member states and at the back of it all loomed the prospect of Indonesian domination of the region. ASEAN provided an instrument for containing such threats to peace and stability through the medium of regular ministerial meetings and a common secretariat.

There had been much emphasis on economic, technical and educational collaboration among the member states in the original Bangkok Declaration of August 1967,[21] but the economic nexus remained weak. Each country retained its special relationship with partners in the industrialized world, whether they were the former European colonial powers, Japan or the United States. With the exception of Singapore, the ASEAN states were rich in primary products and in need of the capital goods, investment and technology which only the advanced economies of the West could provide. Japan, therefore, continued its economic exchanges with the individual members largely as before. The lack of mutual economic interest and of an incentive to develop an internal market meant that there was an absence of the kind of pressures which were pushing the European Communities towards integration and the development of supra-national institutions.

It is fair to say that when it came to ASEAN, Japan was long on rhetoric and short on action. This was especially noticeable when Prime Minister Fukuda delivered his celebrated speech in Manila on 18 August, 1977. The so-called 'Fukuda Doctrine' spelled out the basic groundlines of policy towards ASEAN. It included the ritual promise that Japan would not become a military power, the equally ritual emphasis on the shared Asian heritage with the promise to promote 'heart-to-heart' understanding with the ASEAN countries, the determination to deal with ASEAN as an equal partner, and the intention to help in bringing about stable relations between ASEAN and the states of Indochina.[22] In each of the five member states he promised substantial assistance for the development of a major industrial project. However, not all of them were realized.[23]

The Vietnamese occupation of Cambodia from December 1978 ushered in the second stage of ASEAN's evolution. It revealed both its strengths and weaknesses as a regional organization. In spite of differing strategic appreciations, with Thailand and Singapore seeing Vietnamese expansionism as the greatest threat, while Indonesia and Malaysia were inclined to view Vietnam as the stopper in the bottle which prevented China from spilling all over the region, shared political and economic values and the common interest were sufficiently strong to prevent opposed strategic perspectives from undermining ASEAN's unified diplomatic stance over the Kampuchean crisis. However, ASEAN could do little more than secure recognition as a diplomatic entity. It depended on the external powers for a solution to the conflict and that did not become possible until the end of the Cold War. As one of the external powers, Japan played only a minor part in the process, seeking to keep open lines of communication to Vietnam and trying with little success to use its economic power to influence Vietnamese and Chinese policies. Its public stance was one of support for ASEAN and during this period it raised the claim to act as spokesman for the Association in the councils of the industrialized nations, notably at their annual summits. At the Bonn meeting of the Group of Seven in 1978, Japan sought to represent the interests of ASEAN in economic cooperation with the West. In Ottawa, three years later, the Japanese succeeded in having the need for a solution to the problem of Kampuchea included in Prime Minister Trudeau's political report of the summit.[24]

The decade of the 1980s was dominated by the political and security issues arising from the war in Kampuchea and saw little progress in the economic development of ASEAN as an entity. However, it gave the Association a clearer profile in international politics, especially at the UN, and the world began to think of it as a whole and less as five separate states. Although Japan became more closely identified with the Western powers through the politicization of the annual summits of the Group of Seven, the link was expressed very largely in terms of the East–West confrontation. At the regional level, its relations with ASEAN were still dominated by their economic dimension, but with some political undertones.

The main anxiety of ASEAN, particularly those countries which looked upon Chinese influence in the region with apprehension, not least because they harboured large and wealthy Chinese communities in their midst, focused on the extent of Sino-Japanese cooperation. Would Japan neglect ASEAN and transfer most of its aid effort to China? This worry surfaced when Japan negotiated its first large aid package for China in 1979, and has continued ever since. Japanese leaders have spent much effort in reassuring ASEAN that this was not so and point to the comparative statistics of the aid programmes to prove their case (see Table 5.1).

Another concern was over the links between Japanese businesses and the Chinese merchants and financiers of South-East Asia, Hong Kong and Taiwan, who became increasingly involved in the rapidly developing Chinese economy, particularly in the south-

TABLE 5.1 Comparative ODA[1] flows to ASEAN and China ($ million, net disbursement)

	1985	*1986*	*1987*	*1988*	*1989*	*1990*
ASEAN	800(31.3[2])	914(23.8)	1680(32.0)	1920(29.9)	2132(31.5)	2299(33.1)
China[3]	288(15.2)	497(12.9)	553(10.5)	674(10.5)	832(12.3)	723(10.4)

Note: Between 1982 and 1986, China was first in the list of the top ten countries receiving aid from Japan. It was replaced by Indonesia in 1987 and thereafter remained in second place

1 ODA includes grant assistance, technical cooperation, loans
2 Figures in parentheses: percentage of Japan's global ODA
3 Figures rounded to nearest $ million

Sources: *Japan's ODA 1989*, pp. 59, 62; *Japan's ODA 1990*, pp. 42, 44; *Japan's ODA 1991*, pp. 63–5 (Tokyo, Ministry of Foreign Affairs)

eastern corner of China. The complementarity of the Chinese and Japanese economies: the primary resources, cheap labour and potential market of the one matched with the high technology, managerial skills and capital of the other, could overwhelm the developing industries of the region. Official Japanese policy, in fact, has sought to maintain a balance of economic interest between China and South-East Asia, but the linkages between Japanese and Chinese enterprises in the region indicate developments which could cut across the political boundaries of South-East Asia.

With the Vietnamese withdrawal from Cambodia in 1989 and the end of Soviet-American and Sino-Soviet antagonism in the region, ASEAN has entered a third stage in its evolution. The circumstances of the war in Cambodia had led to a coordination of diplomacy among the members, but not to an effective security policy. Until now, the Association had been an instrument of reconciliation among its members and of political defence of the common interest in the world outside. It had yet to develop an integrated and positive policy beyond its boundaries. ASEAN has so far lacked both the economic infrastructure and the political institutions which could make it a major force within the region and beyond. Some indications of a move towards a more coherent ASEAN presence are emerging, notably since its fourth summit in Singapore in January 1992.[25]

In Singapore the leaders of the six members began a process of trying to establish a common political and security policy. This had two prongs. One concerned the strengthening of intra-mural structures through organizational change, first steps towards establishing a free trade area, and the promotion of consultation among member states on security cooperation. The other prong pointed towards relations with the world outside. One of the measures included a decision to intensify the dialogue over political and security matters with the countries attending ASEAN's post-ministerial conferences (PMC). The original dialogue partners were Japan, the United States, Australia, New Zealand, Canada and the European Community. South Korea became the seventh at the twenty-fifth meeting of ASEAN foreign ministers in Manila in July of the same year. The Singapore summit had also agreed in principle to appoint China and India as dialogue partners.

Another indication of change in post-Cold War South-East Asia was the extension of the hand of 'friendship and cooperation' to the states of Indochina and an open invitation to all countries in the region to accede to the Treaty of Amity and Cooperation, which had been signed on 24 February 1976.[26] Vietnam adhered to the treaty at the Manila meeting in July 1992, to which the Chinese and Russian foreign ministers had also been invited for the first time.

In Singapore, ASEAN accepted a plan to establish an East Asian Economic Caucus (EAEC), which Japan was invited to join on an *ad hoc* basis for consultations on issues of common concern. Malaysia had tried to turn it into something more defined and regular, designed to counter the emergence of protectionist blocs in Europe and North America, but its partners in ASEAN diluted the proposal. Japan was reluctant to endorse it because the United States had not been included and also because it was afraid of anything that smacked of trading blocs and a breakup of the global free trading system, which Japan strongly supported abroad but was more reluctant to put into practice at home. Its emphasis on world-wide trade was reinforced by changes in the pattern of regional economic relations during the 1980s. The differentiation between the newly industrialized countries (NICs) of East Asia and the remaining members of ASEAN had brought a change in the structure of intra-regional trade.

The importance of Japan's commerce with ASEAN was declining in comparison with the growing importance of its trade with the NICs. Of course, the Japanese economy remained dependent on ASEAN countries for some raw materials such as rubber, wood, crude oil and copper. But the most significant increase was in imports of manufactured goods from the NICs as a result of the appreciation of the yen. These shifts followed the basic restructuring of the Japanese economy as it moved away from heavy and capital goods industries towards high technology and high value-added industries, which were dependent on very skilled and well paid labour. Trade with the region as a whole, including China, remains less important than trade with the United States. Statistical data in the early 1990s pointed to an increase in global interdependence rather than to a rise in regional interdependence.

While the principal Japanese interest in South-East Asia remains economic and is shaped by the interplay of commercial and industrial enterprises, on the one hand, and the 'economic' ministries (Ministry of Finance, MITI, and the Economic Planning Agency (EPA)), on the other, the political and security dimensions of relations with ASEAN have come to the fore gradually in the public statements of Japanese ministers. In this they are responding to developments within ASEAN. In spite of the economic objectives which were articulated in its official documents from the day of its foundation, the Association has been preoccupied right from the start by the issue of security; first with the idea of establishing ZOPFAN,[27] then with the containment of Vietnam, and since the end of the Cold War with the definition of a common security policy in a rapidly changing international environment.

As elsewhere in the East Asian region, the countries of South-East Asia have in the past looked to Japan primarily if not solely for financial and technical assistance in helping the process of modernization. In the 1980s there emerged signs that at least some of the members of ASEAN were beginning to think in terms of Japanese involvement in the security of the region. The Japanese response took the form of a series of balancing acts: keeping in step with the United States and the West while insisting on its distinctive 'Asian' ties with the countries of South-East Asia; siding with ASEAN while keeping the door open for economic relations with Vietnam; making sure that ASEAN is not neglected while pursuing a forward economic policy in China; supporting the Chinese position over the Vietnamese invasion of Cambodia while trying to restrain China's punitive policies against Vietnam.

Some of the requirements of balancing have disappeared with the Cold War and the Vietnamese withdrawal from Cambodia. None the less, Japan continues to resist any temptation to become identified with ASEAN – at least in public utterances – whatever the policy debate behind closed doors in the economic and political circles and among the bureaucrats. The proposal of the Malaysian Prime Minister for the establishment of some sort of regional bloc which would include Japan was rejected for two reasons. The reason given in public, as already noted, is opposition to anything that smacks of protectionism and undermines a global free trade system. The private reason is the inconclusive and ongoing debate among the policy-making élites between the 'Westernizers' and 'Asianists'.

Differences within the leadership over where to place the emphasis were reflected in a speech made by Prime Minister Miyazawa in Bangkok on 16 January 1993.[28] It contained both old and new elements in Japan's balancing act and seemed to point in various directions simultaneously. He suggested that bilateral security arrangements were preferable and that conflicts like those in Cambodia and the South China Sea (the dispute over the Spratly Islands between Vietnam and China) were most effectively dealt with 'through such frameworks as are best suited to the individual circumstances'.[29] On the other hand, the Prime Minister drew attention to the significance of 'the [multilateral] political and security dialogue which has been actively underway' since the annual PMC held at Manila in July 1992. This dialogue was conducted on two levels. The first level was that of the PMC, whose agenda at the Manila meeting included political and security issues for the first time as the result of a proposal made by the Japanese foreign minister at the previous PMC in 1991. The other level consisted of bilateral meetings between senior officials from ASEAN and Japan.

In his speech of January 1993, Miyazawa called upon the countries of the Asia–Pacific region:

> to develop a long-term vision regarding the future order of peace and security for their region. For this, various ideas should be thrashed out through political and security dialogue . . .

He hoped:

> that some picture of the future of this region's security will be gradually distilled through such a process, based on shared perceptions and concerns. Japan will actively take part in such discussions.[30]

Although Japanese participation was predicated on the continued existence of its bilateral security arrangements with the United States, these remarks could be interpreted as the go ahead for the establishment of the ASEAN Regional Forum for security (ARF).

In May 1993 there was a first meeting of senior officials (SOM) from ASEAN and its dialogue partners of the PMC, to discuss security issues on a multilateral level. It was then decided that such meetings should take place at least once a year. The formal inauguration of ARF took place in Bangkok in July 1994. It involved the members of ASEAN and their seven dialogue partners as well as two 'guests', China and Russia, and observers from Vietnam, Laos and Papua New Guinea.

Miyazawa also sought to reassure his audience that ASEAN was not being neglected at the expense of aid to other Asian countries. He stressed the strong economic ties between ASEAN and Japan. Their mutual trade had expanded at an annual rate of twenty per cent on average over the past few years. ODA to the ASEAN countries had accounted for between one quarter and one third of Japan's total bilateral ODA over the previous decade.[31] An example of Japan's ambivalent approach to the region emerged in the contrast between promises to develop the dialogue with Asia and the passage where he made clear 'that there is a need to expand further the activities of APEC (Asia–Pacific Economic Cooperation) whose basic goal is open cooperation and which now has its own secretariat and budget'.[32] This juxtaposition of Asian and Asian/Pacific regionalism can be interpreted as the old Asia versus the West dichotomy in a new garb. However, in two places the speech conveyed a more definite tilt towards Asia. First, in the remark that 'Japan will continue to regard Asia, including the ASEAN countries, as a priority region for its ODA',[33] and then in the proposal for an 'international conference of experts to discuss the means to preserve this region's invaluable traditional culture'.[34]

He concluded with a reference to Japan's policy over Indochina and with another proposal: to set up a 'Forum for Comprehensive Development of Indochina', with a preparatory meeting to be held in Tokyo in the autumn of 1993;[35] a further reflection on the need to balance, this time between ASEAN and Indochina. Alongside the accommodation of different and competing elements in Japanese interests and policy, there exists another aim: the ambition to act as a bridge or mediator. Miyazawa's promise 'to take care so that the importance of the dynamism of the Asia–Pacific countries, including ASEAN, be fully taken into account' at the Tokyo summit of the Group of Seven in July 1993,[36] stakes out a claim to be the bridge between Asia and the West. His emphasis on Indochina points to the role of mediator or conciliator.

RELATIONS WITH VIETNAM AND INDOCHINA

French Indochina assumed strategic importance for Japan shortly before the outbreak of the Pacific War. The port of Haiphong in northern Vietnam had been a conduit for the supply of war *matériel* to the Nationalist government of China, which had moved to Chungking in 1938. Taking advantage of the collapse of France in June 1940, the Japanese made their first incursion into the French colony with the demand that the port should be closed to imports destined for China. As relations with the United States and some of the European powers deteriorated, plans for an advance into South-East Asia made the harbours and airfields of Indochina essential staging posts for the attack on Malaya, Singapore and the Dutch East Indies. By the end of 1941, the French possessions were virtually under Japanese military control, which remained unshaken until the surrender in August 1945.[37]

A French resistance movement had developed in the later years of the war and the communist-led League for the Independence of Vietnam (Viet Minh) had come into being with the encouragement of the Chinese Nationalist authorities in south China. The activities of the Viet Minh were directed principally against the French, culminating in the proclamation of the Democratic Republic of Vietnam before the French could return in force to reassert their authority.

The legacy of the past, therefore, did not bring with it the fear and suspicion of the Japanese that is evident among the populations of other countries in South-East Asia. Although the Japanese had relied on the pro-Vichy administration and had not encouraged anti-colonial nationalism as they had done elsewhere in the region, the ordinary Vietnamese had been little affected by the Japanese presence and entertained no particular bitterness towards Japan. Indeed, ever since its victory over the Russian empire in the war of 1904–5, Vietnamese nationalists had looked to Japan for inspiration in their struggle against French imperialism.[38]

As an Associated State within the French Union, Vietnam, along with Cambodia and Laos, was a signatory of the Treaty of Peace with Japan in 1951. After partition in 1954, the non-communist Republic of (South) Vietnam concluded a reparations agreement on 13 May 1959, which provided for the payment of US$39 million, spread over five years, in the form of Japanese goods and services, in addition to loans tied to further purchases from Japan. Henceforth, the relations between Japan and Vietnam were dominated entirely by the war in Indochina.

Two considerations affected Japanese policy towards Vietnam: the need to support the United States for diplomatic and security reasons and the determination to avoid becoming embroiled in the war, which meant maintaining some sort of relationship with the communist North. The South had a much greater share of Japanese aid and trade, but even at the height of the war in the late 1960s, Japan retained a trading relationship with the North. The decision to pay reparations to the South did not stop commercial relations with the North. In the year in which the agreement with South Vietnam was reached, bilateral trade with the North amounted to some US$10 million. Within three years it had quadrupled in value. The Japanese exported chemicals, machinery and cargo ships in return for imports of raw materials, mainly coal, some of which may have been re-exported to the South.[39] In addition, there had been continual semi-official contacts with Hanoi through economic missions in both directions.

In the two years between the cease-fire in Vietnam and the final conquest of the South by the North in 1975, Japanese enterprises pressed for entry into North Vietnam while the government began to adopt an even-handed approach, which included the dispatch of officials from the Gaimushō, a retreat from the policy of recognizing the South Vietnamese authorities as the sole legitimate government in Vietnam, and the establishment of diplomatic relations with the Northern regime in September 1973.[40]

The overall Japanese approach to the war in Vietnam in the decade between 1965 and 1975 had been ambivalent and deliberately open-ended. Prime Minister Satō, whose term of office straddled most of this period, and the leadership of the LDP generally, supported the United States because they opposed any expansion of communism and because there was no doubt in their minds that the security relationship with the United States had top priority in Japanese foreign policy. Hence Satō's unreserved support for the American decision in 1965 to bomb North Vietnam.[41] The official position was without doubt influenced by the incidental benefit which Japan derived from the war. Once again, as in the Korean War, it had become an American logistics and resource base. The economic gains were not as substantial as those of the early 1950s, but they were sizeable none the less. The cumulative profits from the war were estimated to have been US$5 billion. They were derived from American military spending in Japan, the purchase of goods for US Army retail stores, and exports to other Asian countries as well as to the United States arising directly from the war. In addition, Japanese firms benefited from South Vietnamese purchases of consumer goods, which were subsidized by US aid.[42]

The Japanese government tried at the same time to keep some distance from the war and occasionally, especially in its later stages, expressed reservations about the wisdom of American policy. There were several reasons for this. Memories of anti-American demonstrations in the 1950s and of the political upheaval over the revision of the Mutual Security Treaty in 1960 were still fresh in the mind. The influence of the ideological left was declining, but opposition to the Vietnam War was strong among certain groups of the population, notably students and intellectuals; a sentiment reinforced by a fellow-feeling for Asians who were being hammered by the greatest military power in the world.

The Japanese also had their doubts about the efficiency of American military operations, drawing on their own experience of fighting against guerrilla forces in the difficult and hostile environment of wartime China. They did not share the simplistic ideological notions of their allies, knowing better the subtleties and complexities of the politics of Asian communism, especially its strong appeal to nationalist sentiment.[43] Finally, and most important, Japan, particularly its commercial and industrial entrepreneurs, was inclined to take a long-term view in which not only the anti-communist countries of ASEAN but the three states of Indochina had their place. Aware of the potential of Vietnam as a source of raw materials with an industrious and skilled labour force and as an important market for Japanese goods, its policy sought harmony and cooperation rather than conflict and confrontation in the region.

These last motives were uppermost in driving Japanese policy during the third war in Indochina and its aftermath. The initial Japanese response to the Vietnamese invasion of Cambodia was cautious and ambivalent. China, invoking Article 2 of the Sino-Japanese Peace and Friendship Treaty of 1978 (the so-called anti-hegemony clause), had called for a strong stand against Vietnamese aggression, including the severance of diplomatic relations with Hanoi and joint action in accordance with the treaty of 1978. Foreign Minister Sunao Sonoda pointed out that the terms of the treaty did not commit the two countries to take joint action to oppose hegemonism. On the contrary, Article 4 of the treaty stipulated that 'the present Treaty shall not affect the position of either contracting party regarding its relations with third countries'. He reminded the Chinese that Japan was one of a small number of countries which maintained friendly relations with Vietnam and that it intended to use this *entrée* to persuade the Vietnamese not to aggravate the situation in Indochina further. Japan did, however, suspend its economic assistance to Vietnam and swung in full support behind ASEAN's position over the crisis in January 1979.[44]

The polite rebuff of China and the endorsement of ASEAN policy set the tone of Japanese activity throughout the ten years of warfare and diplomatic manoeuvring around the Cambodian issue. As one of the major powers in the East Asian region, Japan had to be seen to be engaged and yet the opportunity for intervention was severely circumscribed. The key players were the Soviet Union, China and the United States. Gorbachev broke the *impasse*, chiefly because he wanted to restore relations with China. That was the paramount reason for the shift in Soviet policy over Cambodia. Undoubtedly it helped to persuade the Vietnamese to withdraw, but they themselves were ready for such a move because of the urgent need to reform their ailing economy.[45] The decision of the United States to withdraw recognition from the three-party coalition in Cambodia, which had fought the war against the Vietnamese-backed Heng Samrin regime, and to talk with the Vietnamese over the issue of free elections in Cambodia without, however, normalizing its relations with Hanoi,[46] was the catalyst which brought about acceptance of the UN peace plan by all the parties.

Vietnam's economic needs were Japan's window of opportunity. True to their general policy of using economic means as the chief instrument of deterrence or persuasion, the Japanese government sought to influence events in Indochina. The freezing of aid to Vietnam was intended to put pressure on the Vietnamese to abandon their Cambodian adventure. It did not work, but served as Japan's contribution to the Western stand and as symbol of its solidarity with ASEAN. It was also intended to persuade the Vietnamese not to rely too much on Soviet support – an objective in line with the general policy of containing Soviet influence in the region.

Public condemnation of Vietnamese aggression and specific measures to indicate displeasure were one strand of Japanese policy. The other strand consisted of retaining official relations with Hanoi and of continuing economic exchanges with it. This line of conduct was not only in the pursuit of commercial interests, but also, so it was hoped, designed to help in preparing the way for Japan to act as honest broker.

Immediately after the invasion of Cambodia, Japan froze US$135 million in grants and concessionary loans. Exports to Vietnam fell by almost one half. However, three years into the occupation of

Cambodia and Japan's trading relations with Vietnam began to revive. In 1987 a considerable number of initiatives to promote economic cooperation were underway. They included among others the formation of a Japan–Vietnam Trade Association (JVTA) to extend external assistance and long-term credit facilities, the establishment of a Japan–Vietnam Economic and Technical Joint Committee to further the production of commodity and consumer goods and to expand exports, and the rescheduling of Vietnamese debts by Japanese banks. In addition, individual Japanese corporations such as Nisshō Iwai and Honda had concluded deals with Vietnamese enterprises.[47]

Japan's role as intermediary was less outstanding. In a speech to ASEAN Foreign Ministers in Manila on 20 June 1981, Sonoda had outlined proposals for a resolution of the conflict, which bore remarkable similarities to the agreement reached eventually under UN sponsorship, including the introduction of peace-keeping forces, a phased withdrawal of the Vietnamese army, a UN election control team, and the establishment of a joint commission of all the factions in Cambodia.[48] However, in the tortuous process of negotiations leading to a cease-fire and the setting up of the United Nations Transitional Authority in Cambodia (UNTAC), Japan played a marginal role, except in one respect. It made the largest single financial contribution to UNTAC and to the work of the United Nations High Commission for Refugees (UNHCR) in its work of repatriating some 370,000 Cambodian refugees. At an international conference on the reconstruction and rehabilitation of Cambodia, held in June 1992 and chaired by Japan, about US$880 million in aid was pledged by the participants, with Japan offering between one fifth and one quarter of the sum.[49]

The significance of Japan's contribution to and participation in UNTAC will be discussed in the next chapter. It is an area where its global and Asian policies intersect. Relations with Vietnam, on the other hand, are an example of the pursuit of a national interest which is still primarily affected by the search for economic advantage and by balance of power concepts. In this respect, the government was prepared to break ranks with its principal ally and its friends in the region. In so doing, Japan was staking out a distinctive and autonomous role in Asia. When Japan established diplomatic relations with North Vietnam in September 1973, only a few months after the cease-fire, it was a gesture which compensated for the feeling that it had been cold-shouldered by the Americans in the negotiations for a post-war settlement in Vietnam.[50]

Such slights, real or imagined, are not quickly forgotten. Again, in August and September 1975 Japan voted for the admission of the two communist states of North and South Vietnam to the United Nations in spite of American opposition.

Underlying the friction with the United States was the element of economic rivalry, which came to the fore ten years later with the adoption of the Kasten Resolution by the US Senate in September 1987, which condemned Japanese trade with Vietnam. It had become Vietnam's second biggest trading partner, though a long way behind the Soviet Union, which accounted for 77.8 per cent of Vietnam's total trade compared with Japan's share of eight per cent. The displeasure of the United States had an immediate effect in forcing Honda to abandon its plans for a motorcycle assembly plant in Ho Chi Minh City (Saigon) for fear of jeopardizing its lucrative market in the US.[51]

Relations with a unified communist Vietnam were greatly favoured by the emergence of a young Japan-orientated technocratic leadership in Hanoi, some of whom had made several discreet visits to Tokyo. A closed-door seminar of experts from party, government and the media, to study the Japanese model of economic development, was reported to have been held in the autumn of 1984.[52] The leader of the reformers, Vo Van Kiet, became prime minister on 9 August 1991. Two months earlier, Tarō Nakayama became the first Japanese Foreign Minister to visit united Vietnam, ostensibly to discuss the Cambodian peace process, but also to advance Japanese interests in the gradually opening Vietnamese economy. He held out the prospect of substantial sums to assist in its reconstruction, but not until peace had been restored in Cambodia. Bilateral trade was flourishing, having more than doubled between 1988 and 1990. Eight Japanese trading companies had opened offices in Vietnam and thousands of Japanese businessmen visited the country. Investment remained low. There were twenty-one projects, but of the total of US$100 million disbursed in 1990, $70 million had gone into the construction of a floating hotel in Ho Chi Minh City. Japanese investors lagged far behind those from Taiwan, Australia, Canada, Hong Kong and several European countries led by France.[53] In November 1992 the Japanese planned the resumption of official yen loans to Vietnam and this was accompanied by a large commodity loan. A consortium of Japanese commercial banks also arranged to provide bridging finance for the repayment of Hanoi's substantial arrears of debt.[54]

The new relationship was celebrated by Premier Vo Van Kiet's visit to Japan in late March 1993; the first such trip by any Vietnamese leader since 1975. Little of material importance emerged from it, but there was some progress in the development of cultural relations between the two countries.[55] A major joint economic conference was held in Hanoi in early 1993.[56] The Japanese delegation included 130 businessmen from Keidanren as well as several government officials. Many difficulties remained over mutual understanding and over more specific problems such as investment. But it was the first of a planned series and it was symbolic of the emergence of Vietnam on Japan's horizon. Compared to economic ties with the ASEAN states or China, the actual economic content of the relationship with Vietnam was a mere trifle. Moreover, the country was still suffering from the aftermath of forty-five years of almost continuous warfare which had left the national infrastructure in a very poor state. However, a new phase has emerged in Japan's policy towards the region as the old dichotomy of ASEAN versus Indochina is fast disappearing.

The Japanese perception of the content and future of the relationship with Vietnam was summarized in the *Diplomatic Bluebook 1991*:

> it is very important for Japan's Southeast Asian policy as a whole to consider the medium- and long-term relations with Vietnam, which takes an important position both geographically and historically in Indochina and has great potential for economic development against the background of its abundant natural resources and high quality labour. . . . Trade relations between Japan and Vietnam have been dramatically expanding with increased exports of crude oil to Japan. Year by year, Japanese enterprises' interest in Vietnam is increasing.[57]

SUMMARY

Japan has had a long historical association with South-East Asia through the activities of its seamen, merchants and adventurers. The political ramifications of their penetration of the region mainly affected relations with China and centred on the Kingdom of the Luchu (Ryūkyū) Islands. A more direct politico-strategic concern emerged in the later years of the Tokugawa shogunate, but the roots of contemporary policy towards South-East Asia lie in the experience of the Pacific War.

The countries of this vast area have different memories of the Japanese advance and occupation. Apart from Thailand, all the members of ASEAN suffered varying degrees of exploitation and despoliation. None of the states of Indochina was seriously affected and the Japanese military presence in Vietnam was essentially to provide bases and ensure a passage towards the theatres of war in the south and west. Both the Vietnamese and Burmese took advantage of the Japanese onslaught to throw off French and British rule, though the Burmese soon discovered that they had exchanged one colonial master for another.

The legacy of the war influenced South-East Asian and Japanese views of each other. The experience of an arrogant and brutal Japanese army of occupation lies at the root of contemporary suspicions and fears in many of the region's countries. Opinion surveys among the members of ASEAN (excluding Brunei), which were conducted by the Gaimushō in 1983, 1987 and 1992,[58] revealed that memories of the past are fading slowly in popular perceptions. Indonesia and Thailand are the countries where the majority of the respondents thought that Japan would maintain its peace-loving stance and not become a major military power. The figures for those who thought it would become militarily threatening, combined with those who professed not to be sure, were in the clear majority elsewhere. In all countries those who were unequivocal in thinking of Japan as a 'trustworthy ally' were in the minority, most preferring to qualify their answer with a 'somewhat'. As for Japan's actions during the Second World War, sizeable minorities in 1992, ranging from forty per cent in Malaysia to twenty-nine per cent in Indonesia, said that they could not forget 'its wrong actions'. Thailand had the lowest score at eighteen per cent. The only clear majority (fifty-two per cent) who believed that wrong actions had been committed but should not be dwelt on now was to be found in Indonesia, and the largest percentage of those who had never considered this to have been an issue (twenty-seven per cent) was not surprisingly among the Thai people.

What is interesting about the comparative figures for the three years is that the percentages fluctuated in an unexpected direction. One should have thought that the further the events of the war receded into the past, the lower the percentage of those who recalled its war crimes and thought of Japan as a potential threat. Not so, and in some countries there was an actual increase in 1992 of the proportion of those who took this line. Too much should not be read into such polls, but they point to two features of the post-war relationship as seen by the public of ASEAN. The first is the continued existence of some anxiety about Japan's future role in the region. The second is that those anxieties seemed to grow in the course of time, at least in some countries, rather than decrease. Popular attitudes may also have been influenced by the realization that, with the unravelling of Cold War structures, the region might be more exposed to an aggressive Japanese policy without the restraining hand of the United States.

The Japanese are inveterate pollsters, which reflects a compulsion constantly to test the degree to which they and their policies are perceived by others. The results of such surveys are carefully studied and have some influence on the policy-making process in Tokyo. The disastrous consequences of the war and the dismal failure of the Greater East Asia Co-prosperity Sphere have been digested. Those lessons, combined with the conviction that the future well-being and safety of Japan will depend on economic and technological rather than military strength, have set the parameters of Japan's relations with South-East Asia.

The economic motive has been and still is uppermost in Japanese policy. At first it was directed to the recovery of Japanese industry, which was skilfully linked to the reparations programme in some countries and to the practice of providing tied loans. Later, especially after the oil 'shocks' and currency realignments of the 1970s, the restructuring of the Japanese economy led to a massive outflow of capital and a transfer of much of the industrial base of the electric and automobile industries to the countries of the region.

In spite of great caution over direct political involvement, the government could not avoid it entirely during the long Cold War period. This was due to the consequences of Japanese financial and industrial penetration and its contribution to the rapid industrialization of some of the recipients of Japanese aid and investment. Economic interest led the government to take stands which created tension with the United States, China and the South-East Asia countries themselves. Trade relations with North Vietnam during the second Indochina war became a kind of political statement that irritated the United States. The great expansion and official encouragement of economic ties with China after 1978 became a source of anxiety for ASEAN. The United States, China and ASEAN to varying degrees resented Japanese relations with Vietnam throughout the ten years of war in Cambodia. Whatever the measures that Japanese governments took, they could not avoid some suspicion or hostility from other countries, however hard they tried not to arouse them.

There is no real evidence of a very coherent or machiavellian design in Japanese policy towards the region during the post-war era. The objective was to further Japanese economic interests and to avoid trouble which would have been bad for trade and bad for Japan's image. It is true that Japan was publicly identified with and committed to the Western anti-communist cause. But at the back of the minds of those responsible for steering Japanese policy was a conviction that Asian thinking and conduct had their own roots and that beneath an ideological veneer which was Western in origin, whether it was Marxism or liberal democracy, there was an Asian 'logic' of behaviour and thought which would remain after the end of the Cold War and after the non-Asian powers (including the Soviet Union) had departed from the scene.

And that is precisely what happened, though it happened gradually, almost imperceptibly, in the late 1980s. A whole series of developments: the dissolution of the Soviet empire, the economic difficulties of the United States, the emergence of ASEAN as a diplomatic entity, the economic reforms in China, and the slow opening of Vietnam, made it impossible for Japan to avoid taking political decisions.

True to its long and very successful stance since 1952, which combined vigorous economic activity with a low, almost invisible profile in international politics, Japan has entered the present very uncertain era in world affairs stressing the inoffensive character of its position while seeking to exploit the course of events according to its perceived interests, the most important of which is to retain free access to the world's markets. But the dynamics of economic and political developments in South-East Asia are such that Japan can no longer wait upon the policies of other major powers and then decide how best to adjust. It must try to anticipate events and impose its own direction on them. In so doing it faces a number of difficult choices.

Should it pursue a close political alignment with ASEAN, with the objective of bringing Indochina into the fold and thus creating a barrier and balance *vis-à-vis* China? Participation in the ASEAN Regional Forum and bilateral talks with ASEAN on security would seem to indicate that Japan has embarked on such a policy, and influential voices are urging this course.[59] But that has its problems. China has shown a distinct lack of enthusiasm for ARF and Japan's stake in China is as important as its stake in ASEAN. Confrontation with China is hardly an attractive scenario as a successor to the confrontations of the Cold War. And would Japan be able to count on the support of the United States as it has done in the past? Would not the Americans, whose strategic interest in South-East Asia is waning, be more likely to side with China against a resurgent Japan which is already seen as a very threatening economic rival? Furthermore, Japan would not wish to antagonize the important Chinese communities of South-East Asia with which it is in such profitable partnership and which have such close links with China. Finally, the stability of the region cannot be taken for granted and nothing would be further from Japanese interests than involvement in local quarrels, whether between Vietnam and China over the islands in the South China Sea or between Vietnam and Thailand over Cambodia and Laos or among some of the other ASEAN states themselves.

The alliance with the United States remains paramount, yet American forces are being withdrawn from the region. The closure of Subic Bay naval base in the Philippines in 1992 is symbolic of the declining US presence. The transfer of some limited facilities to Singapore does not fully replace the function of Subic Bay. Talk of substituting a Japanese presence for that of the United States is decidedly premature if not unrealistic. Unease in South-East Asia over such a deployment, the danger of a collision with China, and strong resistance to it at home are overwhelming arguments for avoiding this course. The only acceptable justification for a further extension of the reach of the SDF would be in the context of close collaboration with the United States – as has been the case in previous moves of this kind – or as part of United Nations or some other internationally sponsored operations.

In a wider sense, these inhibitions would also apply to a more visible political and diplomatic posture. At present the Japanese government would only consider taking international initiatives within the framework of its association with the United States. Hence the tendency to lay stress on a Japanese role in the Asia–Pacific region, which envisages a vast and rather ill-defined zone of economic cooperation under an informal American-Japanese leadership. This alternative to the formation of a more pronounced Japanese/South-East Asian bloc is another aspect of the tension between Asianism and globalism in Japanese policy.

6 Regional policy in the global context

INTRODUCTION

The post-war histories of Britain and Japan present striking contrasts. Both are island states on the opposite sides of a huge continental landmass. Britain, a world empire in the nineteenth and early twentieth centuries, has seen its horizon contract steadily since 1945. Circumstances have compelled it to draw closer to Europe and to assume a European identity, in spite of some lingering pretensions of global status. Japan emerged from early post-war isolation to become an economic superpower with global interests and reach. Geography identifies it with the East Asian region, but the experience of the past and the economic realities of today are important restraints on a deeper involvement in the politics of the neighbouring mainland.

Another striking contrast between the two countries is the evolution of their post-war relationship with the United States. With its strong historical, linguistic and cultural links to North America, Britain has sought to involve the United States in the European balance of power throughout the century. The intensity of the British commitment to the 'special relationship' has grown in inverse proportion to the decline of British power and is still clung to as the country is pulled ever deeper into Europe. Lacking the same natural affinity, Japanese-American relations have passed through several stages in the post-war era, from conquered and conqueror to pupil and mentor to junior and senior partner to more or less equal partners. But whereas Britain has sought to use its alliance with the United States as a last, desperate means to salvage its status as a great power, Japan has used the American alliance as a means to facilitate its progress towards achieving global economic power.

The end of the Cold War saw Britain inextricably enmeshed in a Europe whose future political shape and character remain uncertain. It saw Japan entrenched in the global economy as a leading (some would say *the* leading) power, but not as a traditional hegemon. Its foreign policy has been described by Bill Emmott '. . . as a means of removing obstacles, or defusing possible minefields, in the path of Japan's economic interests'.[1] He went on to say:

> Although it might seem that Asia would inevitably be a major Japanese foreign policy concern, it is unlikely to prove to be so in the near term, except as a sub-set of general global concerns about trade and burden-sharing.[2]

Further on, he did however make a prognostication which suggests otherwise:

> the key issues will remain the political developments in China and North Korea. Events in those two countries will do more to shape Japanese foreign policy and attitudes than Japan's own directives.[3]

The contradiction between Emmott's near- and long-term prognostications underlines the predicament of Japan's pushmi-pullyu condition. The pushmi-pullyu was an intriguing creature which 'had no tail, but a head at each end'. When it was introduced to Doctor Dolittle's entourage, the duck exclaimed: 'Lord save us. How does it make up its mind?' To which the dog replied: 'It doesn't look to me as though it had any.' But appearances were deceptive. Apart from being very polite, it was perfectly capable of making up its own mind and had the added advantage that no matter from where it was approached, it was always able to face in that direction.[4]

Japan belongs to Asia and since the mid-nineteenth century the Japanese have stressed their Asian identity to distinguish themselves from the other great powers, which they sought to emulate and with which they competed for dominance in East Asia. However, the aftermath of the Pacific War, the geopolitics of the Cold War, and Japan's phenomenal economic success created a political and psychological distance between the Japanese and their Asian neighbours. Today they seek to reconcile a policy leading to renewed ties with Asia and a policy which attempts to give a political coherence to their global economic strength. Before turning to a closer examination of the options facing Japan, it is necessary to consider briefly the domestic dimensions of the debate over foreign and security policy.

THE SHIFTING FOREIGN POLICY DEBATE

The events of the 1970s – Soviet achievement of nuclear strategic parity with the United States and the *détente* of the early years of the decade, which raised the prospect of a joint superpower hegemony; the formal recognition of China as an independent actor in East Asian power politics; and the breakdown of the American-managed global economic system – led to the early debates over the purpose and direction of Japan's foreign and security policies. The debate (as described in Chapter 2, pp. 33–6) marked the rise of a new generation of bureaucrats, politicians and business leaders who were more detached from the traumas of the war and its aftermath. Many of them had spent years as students or residents in the United States and had become thoroughly acquainted with the kind of strategic thinking that dominated discussion of international politics in the Cold War era.[5]

The push towards a reassessment of Japanese policy took place against the background of altered perceptions of the United States. For a long time Japan had been dependent on a largely American-financed international system. The construction of the bullet train (Shinkansen) had been financed by a loan from the World Bank and Japan was still in receipt of substantial foreign aid at the time of the Tokyo Olympics of 1964, which had drawn the attention of the world to the Japanese 'economic miracle'. It finally ceased to be a debtor in 1990, when it repaid the last of the loans from the World Bank.[6] Nevertheless, by the end of the 1970s it began to look as if the roles were being reversed. The United States was becoming dependent on investment from Japan for industrial regeneration and on increased funding to retain its military presence in East Asia and to cover the growing budget deficit. American financial weakness raised demands for a greater equality in the Japanese-American partnership, although it was accepted that Japan would continue to play a strategically and militarily subordinate role. Meanwhile, Japan had achieved prominence on the world stage through its membership of international organizations and had gained equal status with the leading West European states through the annual summits of the industrialized nations. It was regarded as the third pillar in an unofficial tripartite alliance with the United States and Western Europe.

By itself, the reversal of economic relations might not have had a serious impact on the general stability of the alliance with the United States. Japan would have shouldered a greater share of the financial burden, leaving the United States to take care of military security. Indeed, until 1990, the equation: Japanese economic strength + American military strength = Asian/Pacific stability and security, was the officially accepted version of the optimum operation of the mutual security system. Within it both governments sought to contain the friction caused by trade imbalances and the fear and hostility which they aroused among the American public. What really stimulated a more profound debate over the future direction of Japanese policy, in which there has been a revival of some of the themes of the 'Asia versus the West' argument of the past, was the perceived decline of American power.

Strategic parity between the superpowers raised anxieties about security guarantees and the reliability of the American deterrent. They were the backcloth to more specific worries which arose from the events of the 1970s and 1980s. They included the American failure in Vietnam, wobbles over a continued United States presence in Korea, and the propensity to seek deals with the Soviet Union over the heads of the allies, as in the INF (Intermediate-range Nuclear Forces) negotiations, which threatened to decouple European from East Asian security. Another nagging though not immediate fear was the possibility that the United States might transfer its preference from the alliance with Japan to an alliance with China. American insistence on greater burden-sharing began to look more and more like a demand that Japan should pay for American operations designed to serve primarily the American interest. All these considerations raised doubts about the viability and the durability of the American connection.

The NATO Declaration at the London summit in July 1990, which included a proposal for a joint declaration with the Warsaw Pact countries that 'we are no longer adversaries', could be taken as the formal conclusion of the Cold War. But the process which forced Japan to reconsider its fundamental policies came in two stages. The first began with the US–Soviet Treaty of 8 December 1987, to remove and destroy their INF, which was followed by a cascade of arms control and disarmament agreements as well as unilateral initiatives. It raised the question whether the new phase of *détente* was really the end of the Cold War or, like previous *détentes*, merely an interlude before the resumption of superpower antagonism with its accompanying acceleration of the arms race. Japan was reluctant to acknowledge any diminution of the 'threat' in the late 1980s. There was little concrete evidence that the Soviet Union was preparing to reduce its military power in East Asia, where there had been no dramatic event like the breach of the

Berlin Wall in November 1989. On the contrary, the military situation in Korea remained tense and the war in Cambodia continued. Furthermore, the crushing of the pro-democracy demonstrations in Tiananmen Square in June 1989 seemed to indicate that economic reform in China would be pursued without political reform and that the Chinese Communist Party was determined to exercise its power as ruthlessly as before.

Since the build-up of the SDF and Japan's rearmament had been justified as necessary in the face of the threat from the north, it was hardly to be expected that the Japan Defence Agency and the military lobby generally would be easily persuaded to give up the main argument for this policy and acknowledge a diminution of the threat posed by the Soviet Union. Prime Minister Kaifu insisted that the JDA should omit the ritual reference to the Soviet threat from the Defence White Paper of 1990, although it contained a statement about pressure from the Soviet Union on its neighbours and that there was still no change in the tense military situation around Japan.[7] The White Paper of 1991 referred to the 'Military Posture of Soviet Armed Forces in the Far East' in the following terms:

> Although the recent domestic and international environments of the Soviet Union apparently make it more difficult than before for the Soviet Union to conduct aggressive behavior against another country, it remains unchanged that the above-mentioned situation of the Soviet forces in the Far East makes severe military environment [sic] around Japan.[8]

Right up to the demise of the Soviet Union, the main focus was on the military capabilities of Japan's giant neighbour in the north. However, there was a growing awareness of the complexity of the military situation around Japan, which was regarded as more complicated than that in Europe and as 'unforeseeable'.[9]

The second stage in the policy review process began with the collapse of the Soviet Union at the end of 1991 and the strong American support for President Boris Yeltsin. It undermined the principal purpose of Japan's politico-strategic alliance with the United States and upset the balance between the cooperative security aspect of the bilateral relationship and its competitive economic aspect, leading to the prospect of a rapid politicization of the economic friction between the two countries. This element had already become apparent in the 1980s, especially on the American side, with a spate of books and articles seeking to explain the Japanese challenge. Their main focus was an examination of the causes of Japanese success in contrast to American decline. Their prescriptions for the recovery of American economic competitiveness concentrated largely on how to remedy structural weaknesses in the US economy and what lessons might be learnt from the Japanese example.[10] In general, their authors did not doubt that the two countries should remain allies with common political and strategic interests.

The tone of such writings sharpened in the 1990s amid a growing perception among the general public that Japan was destined to become adversary number one. Books appeared under sensational titles, propounding a variety of conspiracy theories which responded to a mood of frustration and anxiety, fuelled by the effects of the recession.[11] There were, of course, more objective appraisals by academics and others who were sympathetic towards Japan. The main thrust of their argument pointed to the danger that economic competition might get out of hand and lead to political confrontation. Such studies were based on the assumption that it was necessary to retain the essence of the partnership, not only for the mutual advantage of the two countries, but also for the sake of stability and order in the Asia–Pacific region.[12] The more balanced and scholarly works had less impact on the mass media which were more interested in the theories of the polemicists. The latter inevitably evoked responses from the Japanese side. The burden of their message was to explain American weaknesses, in which one could occasionally detect racist undertones, and to suggest that it was high time for a successful Japan to discard its subservience to the United States.[13] Those were, of course, extreme reactions, but they reflected a rising acrimony on both sides of the Pacific; a direct result of the crumbling ideological cement which had been so important in the confrontation with the Soviet Union.

Another consequence of the revolutionary changes in the former Soviet empire was an acute awareness in Japan that the security of the Cold War system and its fixed points of reference had disappeared, leaving it to face an uncertain and unpredictable environment. Many of the old problems of the East Asian region continued as before: the division of Korea, the uncertainties over China's development, the issue of Taiwan, the civil war in Cambodia. But the context was different, and in shaping its responses to existing problems and to new problems as they might arise, Japan would have to operate on the assumption that policy could no longer be automatically adjusted with reference to the American position over the issue in question.

THE DOMESTIC DIMENSIONS

Post-war Japan has been able to draw on substantial assets in steering its way through world affairs. Its financial, technological and managerial strengths have placed it in the front rank of the powers. The governmental and administrative machine has been more adaptable than one would have thought possible, perhaps because of its 'flexible rigidity', to adopt the phrase of Professor Ronald Dore.[14] Last, but not least, Japanese society has been one of the most cohesive and stable polities in the world. Policy-making in this setting has been a mixture of political indecision, vacillation, great caution, and bold and purposeful planning. The upshot was a Japan which presented a hesitant and timid face to the world outside, while systematically laying foundations for the opportunity to take up various options as might be required by circumstances in the future.

This kind of preparedness is illustrated by the development of the nuclear power industry. It arose from a far-sighted policy of trying to reduce the country's dependence on imported sources of energy for power generation. Efforts in this field, combined with determined measures aimed at energy conservation after the oil shocks of the 1970s, have begun to yield results.

Table 6.1 Sources of primary energy (percentage share of total)

Source	*1978*[1]	*1983*[2]	*1990*[3]
Petroleum	73.0	60.9	58.3
Natural Gas and LNG	4.8	7.8	10.1
Coal	13.8	18.2	16.6
Nuclear Power	3.6	7.4	9.4
Hydropower	4.8	5.7	4.2
Others	–	–	1.4

Notes: 1 *Statistical Handbook of Japan 1980* (Tokyo, Statistics Bureau, Prime Minister's Office, 1980) p. 43

2 *Statistical Handbook of Japan 1985* (Tokyo, Statistics Bureau, Management Coordination Agency, 1985) p. 42

3 *Statistical Handbook of Japan 1993* (Tokyo, Statistics Bureau, Management Coordination Agency, 1993) p. 55

But the policy also created the potential for a military option in the future. The nuclear programme has now reached the stage where Japan has a theoretical capability to produce an explosive device within a relatively short space of time, should the government so decide. The technical problems remain formidable in spite of the construction of fast breeder reactors which reduces somewhat Japan's dependence on the import of uranium supplies. In addition, there is a uranium enrichment plant, operating on the centrifugal method, which became operational in April 1988 and was followed by a larger plant for commercial purposes in 1991. Japan now has a nuclear fuel cycle, though much of it is still at the experimental level and its potential for military application remains circumscribed until the full development of a controlled nuclear fusion process would create the prospect of complete self-sufficiency, both in power generation and military production.[15] With its advanced technology and achievement in placing satellites into orbit, there can be little doubt that it could develop a capability to launch ICBMs (Intercontinental Ballistic Missiles). This is not to say that Japan is about to or intends to become a nuclear weapon state. But it is an indication that, should it so decide, a Japanese government could eventually acquire such armament. The option remains open.

The same applies to other military spheres. Japan is self-sufficient in the production of so-called conventional weapons except aircraft, which it has developed in cooperation with the United States or under licence agreements. In the latest instance of aircraft procurement, the FS-X (Fighter Support Experimental) to replace the F-1 Fighter, the Defence Agency would have been able to develop the plane without foreign assistance, except for the engine. However, it was decided to make this a joint venture based on the American F-16 produced by the General Dynamics Corporation. The debate over the choice between a domestically produced aircraft and one that was jointly developed was complex. It divided the bureaucracy, with the JDA and MITI in favour of a nationally produced fighter and the Gaimushō and Ministry of Finance supporting the joint venture. Eventually, the second option was taken in November 1988 on financial, strategic and diplomatic grounds and under some pressure from the United States. It is a deal in which the benefits do not flow in one direction only. The JDA shoulders all the development costs, with the United States providing all the technological information on the F-16 which is relevant to the development of the FS-X. The Americans also have access to technology in areas where the Japanese are more advanced.

The lengthy negotiations, which began in 1986 within the Cold War era, and the intensive debate in both countries revealed the extent to which Japan had become largely self-sufficient and was to all intents and purposes an equal of the United States.[16] What is particularly interesting in the case of aircraft production, where Japan had remained most dependent on the United States throughout the post-war era, is the deliberate policy which sought to retain the services of the military technicians who had built Japanese aircraft during the war, to form the nucleus of the post-war teams that began to produce those weapon systems under American licence. This enabled them to understand the key technologies involved, though they were not specifically made available under the licensing agreements.[17]

The military potential of the research and development effort of both government and private industry is enhanced by the existence of dual-purpose technology which makes it impossible to draw a clear distinction between its civilian and military application. Under the FS-X agreement, for instance, the Americans will be able to incorporate Japanese technologies in the aircraft, which had been developed for purely civilian purposes. Thus, while claiming to abide by the spirit of the 'Peace Constitution', Japan has acquired the potential to become a military power of the first rank, where the quality and sophistication of the weapons is more important than the numerical strength of the armed forces. The constantly evolving technical capacity without the actual production of weapons gives Japan a 'High Technology Deterrent',[18] a concept that fits well with the often repeated assertion that in the future the techno-industrial capacity of a state and not the possession of large military forces will be the true gauge of national power.

What is not at all clear is whether and how Japan will exploit its potential in high technology in the long run. It may, of course, leave it in the background and seek to continue to play an inoffensive political role in regional affairs. One line of argument, however, points to the inevitability of an emphasis on military development on the grounds that 'the propagation of information is intangible'. It suggests that knowledge of the development of some new military technology in one country will automatically stimulate similar developments and counter-measures in countries of equivalent industrial and technological strength. For example, during the Cold War the two superpowers developed ICBMs, SLBMs (Submarine-launched Ballistic Missiles), and MIRVs (Multiple Independently-targetable Re-entry Vehicles) without any direct technology transfer between them. It follows that, once embarked on this course, Japan will be sucked into a spiralling high technology arms race with potential rivals, regardless of whether it wants to continue with a low profile, purely defensive military posture or not.[19]

Against such determinism, it is possible to advance another point of view which suggests that perhaps there may be other and more effective means with which to further the national interest and influence the world. Japan may wish to continue to exploit the appeal of a rich and exotic culture, underpinned by great wealth and a manifestly successful style of management. Translated into policy, it would be pursued through two channels: economic largesse and cultural attraction. The first includes ODA, investment abroad, the transplant of factories and other enterprises, and the training of engineers, scientists, technologists, managers and other professionals, especially from Asian countries. The second involves extensive language teaching which reaches down to senior students in secondary schools in some countries, exhibitions, tours by artists, theatrical and musical performers, the organization of cultural festivals, the export of traditional sports such as the martial arts, educational exchanges and the subsidy of scholarship in things Japanese.

Both the economic and cultural efforts are supported by a substantial outflow of capital, not merely in FDI but also in aid and cultural programmes which are financed by a multitude of official, semi-official, and private agencies. They include the Overseas Economic Cooperation Fund (OECF) which is responsible for yen loans, the Japan International Cooperation Agency (JICA) which is responsible for technical assistance, training, and the sending of Japanese Overseas Volunteers, the Japan Foundation which handles educational and cultural exchanges, and a growing number of independent trusts and foundations, often tied to large companies, which disburse funds for a variety of purposes. In addition, several ministries, especially those of Foreign Affairs and Education, run schemes such as the Japan English Teaching programme (JET) under which hundreds of young graduates from English-speaking countries, France and Germany are brought to Japan every year as language assistants in schools, colleges and businesses.

The net effect of all these activities is difficult to assess. Their purpose is clear: to promote greater knowledge and sympathetic understanding of Japan and to win friends for the country and thus to extend Japanese influence in the world at large. It is too early to say whether the much greater interest in Japan than ever before will become deep-rooted or has been largely stimulated because the Japanese have money to disburse. At least, Japan is 'important' if judged by the number of research institutes and universities which have discovered urgent reasons for promoting Japanese studies. Importance in terms of status ranks high in the list of Japanese values and in this regard the economic, educational and cultural diplomacy of Japan can certainly claim results.

These measures, combined with a military strategy which sought to ensure basic initial defence in the event of an attack on the national territory and to hold an enemy until the power of the United States could be brought into play, became known as the doctrine of 'Comprehensive Security' (Sōgō Anzen Hoshō). It evolved in the course of the 1970s and was formally enshrined in government policy in the early 1980s. Very briefly, the term 'comprehensive security' postulated an all-embracing policy based on economic power, information, diplomacy and a defensive posture closely linked to the American military presence in the region. As is the case with generalized concepts of this kind, it was ambiguous and open to varying interpretations. Some saw it as a cover for an accelerating military build-up, others maintained that it moved Japan away from an excessive reliance on the military instrument.[20]

The breakup of the Cold War system has placed a question mark over the future of the security treaty with the United States and by implication over the basic military posture of Japan. Another doubt has arisen independently of these events: will Japan's economic success story continue? The answer to that question will determine whether the Japanese will be able to continue relying on their economic muscle as the principal instrument of persuasion or pressure in their external relations as they have done in the past, especially in Asia. The question has, of course, been asked ever since their economic success became apparent. A series of 'shocks' to the economy during periods of recession and in the oil crises of the 1970s slowed down its rate of growth and brought about structural readjustments. Every time Japan emerged stronger than before in comparison with its partners and rivals in the industrialized world. During the latest and most severe post-war recession in the early 1990s, it continued to pile up huge balance of payment surpluses.

None the less, certain underlying trends point to changes which might have the effect of undermining those elements which have helped to make Japan pre-eminent within the East Asian region. One is the slowing down of the rate of growth in comparison with its acceleration in South Korea, Taiwan, the countries of South-East Asia, and the coastal regions of China. Another is the labour shortage and the social costs of providing for a rapidly growing proportion of the elderly in the population. There must also be doubt whether the traditional group cohesion, reinforced by the lifetime employment system in the large firms, will survive the effects of the technological revolution and the new culture of individualistic consumerism.

Economic changes and their social impact raise questions whether Japan will continue to be a wealthy, basically satisfied society, which runs reasonably smoothly and enjoys its economic primacy without a high diplomatic and military profile or becoming involved in messy international problems. On the other hand, there is little to suggest that the public is ready to abandon its opposition to the creation of a strong military machine and to any involvement in foreign adventures. That opposition no longer has the ideological content of the 1940s, 1950s and early 1960s, but is informed by the success of the 'Yoshida Doctrine'. Such attitudes represent a deeply conservative mood, symbolized by the favourable image of Switzerland in the minds of many Japanese. This may be due partly to its beautiful mountain scenery – similar to that of Japan – but chiefly because of its peacefulness and low military profile. They do not know how 'militarized' that country really is.

A Japanese defence lobby exists, but it is not a powerful grouping of the military, civilian bureaucrats, business interests and politicians. Although most defence production is concentrated in the hands of a few large firms, it forms a small percentage of their total output. The ambiguity of dual purpose technology also weakens any incentive to press for increased weapons production or the lifting of the ban on the export of arms. Furthermore, while the military may grumble, as they do, and some politicians urge a much more assertive foreign policy backed by military strength, the former remain under tight civilian control and the latter are a minority within parties that are too conscious of the public mood to risk going very far in promoting a more vigorous defence policy.

There is as yet little evidence that Japanese perceptions with regard to security policy and particularly its military dimension are about to change, but there is no doubt that nationalism is on the rise. It may be largely passive, but there are hints of it in a sense of superiority and a certain degree of arrogance towards the less developed countries as well as an impatience at being lectured from abroad over Japan's failure to act more positively in international affairs. At home there is some hostility to immigrants who perform the menial tasks Japanese are no longer willing to do. The nationalist sentiment remains unfocused, but could acquire a sharper edge under the impact of events in the region, especially those which might have a shock effect on Japan. A serious deterioration of domestic conditions in the context of a deepening world recession might have a similar effect. The constant stream of statements by government, politicians, the press and other opinion formers, that Japan has reached a stage where it must assume greater responsibility for world affairs is preparing the ground for a rapid acceptance of an assertive nationalism, always disguised as a contribution to international peace and stability, just as the drip-drip of the post-war argument that the constitution did not preclude the right to self-defence led to the almost universal acceptance of the legality of the SDF.

Clues to possible shifts in national policy and their acceptance by the public lie in the changing political scene. Observers are agreed that a redistribution of power and influence among the groups which constitute the policy-making élite – the bureaucracy, conservative politicians and the business community – is in progress. As noted in the introduction (see p. 11), it is misleading to think of each of these three categories as monolithic in outlook. Instead, policy formulation depends on *ad hoc* coalitions which cut across the boundaries and pit groups within one category against each other.[21]

For some time before the upset which brought a coalition government to power in the summer of 1993, ending thirty-eight years of unbroken rule by the Liberal-Democratic Party, it was no longer accurate to describe the LDP as a coalition of factions in which a powerful boss commands the unswerving loyalty of his followers or as being primarily rural based. The traditional distinction between urban and rural has been eroded, with the great majority of farming households earning their main income from sources other than agriculture.[22] Within the faction personal loyalty had become weaker and for younger members issues of policy were becoming more important and there was a greater interest in shaping its direction – a task traditionally in the hands of bureaucrats. Hence the rise of the so-called policy 'tribes' (zoku) in the LDP.[23] The bureaucracy, though still powerful and élitist, is on the defensive in some areas as a consequence of the opening of the economy, its increasing deregulation and its gradual internationalization, which have given the large multinational companies certain advantages. For example, information and its analysis in a firm like

Nomura Securities is sometimes superior to that available in government departments. Finally, there was a noticeable convergence of the LDP and some of the opposition parties in various fields, especially over national security. The only serious ideological confrontation in this respect is between the declining communist party and its fellow doctrinaires in the socialist party, on the one hand, and the rest of the political spectrum, on the other. The continuing and seemingly irreversible decline of the Marxist element in politics has shifted the focus of debate to specific issues such as parliamentary reform or the involvement of the SDF in UN peacekeeping operations. The line-up over these controversies often cuts across party boundaries.

The result of the general election to the Lower House in July 1993 produced the most dramatic shift on the political scene since the formation of the Liberal-Democratic Party in 1955. While it is expected that the upheaval will lead to a period of political instability with short-lived coalitions holding office, the loss of the LDP's undisputed dominance has to be assessed at several levels.

In terms of political arithmetic, the LDP's demise was more apparent than real. It remained by far the largest party in the House of Representatives with 227 seats, 29 short of an overall majority, while the SDPJ, the next largest party, won 70 seats. Though scandal-ridden, discredited and unpopular, the LDP did remarkably well. The unreformed electoral system and the continued importance of 'money power' undoubtedly helped to account for this paradox. Political reform may, therefore, weaken the party further.

It is more significant that the three new reformist parties which contested the election – Shinseitō (Japan Renewal Party), Nihon Shintō (Japan New Party) and Sakigake (Harbinger Party) – were all led by former politicians of the LDP. This is particularly true of Shinseitō and Sakigake, which broke away just before the election. Nihon Shintō made its appearance a year earlier, but its leader, Morihiro Hosokawa, had also been a prominent member of the LDP. In one sense, therefore, the split can be seen as a conflict between factions of the ruling party, especially as the power broker of Shinseitō, Ichirō Ozawa, was a rival of the Secretary-General of the LDP, Seiroku Kajiyama, for control over the largest faction in the party.[24] The sequence of events can be interpreted as an outcome of internecine conflict in the ruling party, which may turn out to be a passing phenomenon and lead to the eventual reintegration of the dissidents. Such an outcome would follow the pattern of the 1970s, when a much smaller group of LDP rebels left the party over a similar issue of bribery and corruption and formed the Shin Jiyū (New Liberal) Club. They were gradually reintegrated into the LDP, and one of their leaders, Yōhei Kōno, was Chief Cabinet Secretary in Mr Miyazawa's government before the July election. Subsequently he became President of the LDP in opposition.

The phenomenon of groups breaking away from a ruling coalition to form parties, ostensibly on points of principle, but really on personal and factional grounds, has been a feature of the Japanese political system ever since the Restoration of 1868. The primacy of personal loyalties and the leader–follower relationship over broad philosophical principles and policy objectives in party politics has distinguished the democratic system in Japan from that of other Western countries,[25] which brings us to another level of assessment.

The circumstances that brought about the political upset in 1993 arose from a growing malaise about the extent of corruption in the LDP, which was closely linked to the structure of an electoral system that encouraged the blatant use of money power. The central issue became one of political reform with strong ethical overtones. But, as noted, the issue was also a cover or mask for a power struggle within the LDP arising from the disintegration of its largest faction. Since the leaders of the reformist parties had been leading members of the LDP, many people thought that the effect of the political change was superficial. However, such cynicism overlooks an important dimension of the events, namely that they are a symbol of generational change. Nearly all the present leaders of the LDP and other parties are from the post-war generation and are thus psychologically and personally less burdened by the legacy of the militarist period in Japan's modern history. Miyazawa was probably the last leader whose outlook was influenced by the experience of the 1930s and 1940s.

The new generation of politicians has grown up with Japan's economic success and expansion. They are more familiar with the world outside than the previous generation. Many have travelled widely and some have lived abroad for lengthy periods of time. They are less inclined to look elsewhere for a model to emulate. They are less patient with lectures from foreigners on how Japan should behave. They have been nurtured on the hard-headed *Realpolitik* and strategic thinking that dominated American policy in the later phases of the Cold War. They are going to be more self-confident and assertive in dealing with foreign policy. This is not to say that the appearance of Japanese policy will be less hesitant and cautious than it has been in the past. The manner and pace of the decision-making process may still seem convoluted and painfully slow to outsiders, especially in a period of political uncertainty, but the underlying drive and purpose are likely to be more vigorous and determined.

There is a third level of assessment: the impact of the political changes on the external relations of Japan. Here, again, there may be no striking developments to begin with. For one thing, energies will be absorbed by the issues and consequences of electoral and political reform whose impact is unpredictable, given the entrenched power of the LDP and the fact that the political kaleidoscope continues to turn around its factions and ex-factions. None the less, the emergence of the new political generation is bound to lead to a less pliant attitude in international affairs.

So far, however, the rising nationalist mood has been a contented one. There is no evidence that the electorate is panting for revolutionary changes. In a survey conducted in November 1991, more than 70 per cent of the respondents indicated that they preferred a government of the LDP. Of that number 24.5 per cent favoured a stable regime with a substantial overall majority over the combined opposition parties. Although the LDP lost its majority in 1993, if one adds the votes cast for it to those for the other three parties led by former members of the party and for the independents who joined the LDP in the Diet after the election, then the proportion of the voters who supported these conservative candidates was almost 60 per cent. This suggests that Mr Ozawa's idea that Japan will eventually have two main conservative parties alternating in power may not be too far-fetched.

Since the election of 1993 there have been further indications that the dichotomy in post-war Japanese politics between left and right is disappearing. The conservative-dominated coalition which replaced the LDP was replaced by a new administration in April 1994 under the ostensible leadership of Mr Tsutomu Hata of Shinseitō, who had been Minister of Finance in the last LDP government, and the real leadership behind the scenes of Mr Ozawa. That government was much more 'conservative' than its predecessor as it did not include the socialists. Within two months Mr Hata's cabinet was out of office and replaced by a new coalition headed by Mr Tomiichi Murayama, chairman of the SDPJ, but dominated by the LDP which held 13 of the 21 ministerial portfolios. It can be confidently predicted that this coalition will not last long. Although it seems to mark a return of the LDP, it is not likely to be a return to the *status quo ante* in view of the accelerating fragmentation of that party and the prospect of schisms among the socialists.

In the continuing realignment of the political forces, a political reform (Kaishin) movement is emerging which is almost the opposite to what was labelled 'progressive' in the post-war era. Instead of upholding a strict interpretation of Article 9 of the Constitution, opposing any military build-up and advocating a neutralist/non-aligned foreign policy, today's political reformers think the time may be approaching when the Constitution should be revised to make it a more genuine Japanese product and when Japan should play a more prominent and assertive role on the international stage. The new reformers are not nostalgic for past imperial glory, but they are concerned to modernize the political structures of the country and to give Japan a place in world affairs commensurate with its economic importance.

The quiescent public mood could always change and become more strident and aggressive, especially if some major issue disturbed and galvanized the large percentage of people (33 per cent in the July 1993 election) who do not bother to vote and show little interest in politics. It could provoke a more forceful Japanese policy than the world has been accustomed to.

JAPAN'S OPTIONS

While the many variables in Japan's domestic and international environment make it difficult to predict with any confidence the future direction of Japan's external policy, it is possible to consider the kind of options open to Japan with the aim of establishing the parameters within which it is likely to operate at a time of flux and uncertainty. The options cluster around two distinct but closely related themes: the problems of national security and the relationship between the Asian and global dimensions of Japanese policy.

To take security first. It is a concept which has three components: the possession of values that one wants to protect; the perception of threats to those values; and the choice of means and the cost of defending those values. Leaving on one side the determination to keep itself in power, the supreme value for the Japanese government, as indeed for most governments, is the well-being of the national polity. There are at least three elements in the Japanese definition of that value. The first is the preservation of national homogeneity, which means excluding large-scale immigration and limiting the impact of foreign cultures. The second is the defence of national sovereignty and territorial integrity, and the third is freedom of access to the world's resources and markets upon which so much of Japan's post-war prosperity has been based.

Each of these elements requires different means to ensure its protection. The first is mainly, though not wholly, a matter of domestic policies and it raises the huge question whether in the end Japan will be able to withstand the tide of global cultural integration, which is outside the purview of this book. The second falls largely into the realms of diplomacy and military strategy and the third falls principally into the realms of diplomacy and economic policy. The following discussion concentrates on how the second and third elements are likely to influence Japanese security policy and relations with Asia.

Since the end of the Cold War it is no longer possible for the defence establishment to point to a specific threat to national security and, as a consequence, discussion in the 1990s has turned around potential threats. The most immediate of such threats is the volatile and possibly dangerous situation on the Korean peninsula, as discussed in chapter 4, which includes the nightmare scenario of huge numbers of Koreans trying to seek refuge in Japan in the event of an outbreak of hostilities in their own country. Among the less immediate threats are the prospect that a more belligerent and nationalist Russia will try to restore the military strength of the former Soviet Union in the Far East and use it as an instrument of pressure or that there might be a serious crisis between China and Taiwan which would involve the United States. Another potential threat, perhaps at the turn of the century and beyond, could come from an economically strong and militarily powerful China with unsatisfied territorial ambitions in the East and South China Seas. This list does not, of course, preclude as yet totally unforeseen 'threats' which might emerge suddenly, just as the collapse of the Soviet bloc within the space of three years had been totally unforeseen.

For reasons of professional gloom and also out of self-interest, the defence lobby will insist that all potential threats should be taken seriously. The government on the whole and especially the ministries dealing with finance, economic affairs, social welfare, and education may take a more detached view and demand that defence expenditure should be reduced in line with similar reductions in the budgets of the other industrial powers. From their point of view, threats in the future are more likely to be economic and social, for which military counter-measures will be largely irrelevant.

The alliance with the United States

In an atmosphere of uncertainty in which all threats may be regarded as hypothetical, the most persuasive argument is to continue to rely on the security alliance with the United States. Not only has that association seen Japan through the long post-war era with great success, it has also been the most sensible course to follow once the international order envisaged in the Charter of the United Nations had failed to materialize. Given the essentially American occupation from 1945 to 1952 and Japan's location in the direct firing line between the superpowers, a policy of non-alignment was not considered to be a viable option. Furthermore, the protective mantle of the United States provided the cover for economic and social recovery at the price of a modest rearmament programme, which was designed to keep the Americans reasonably satisfied while avoiding domestic upheaval because of the people's attachment to the 'Peace Constitution'.

In the early 1990s, the argument for a continuation of the special relationship with the United States was put forward as strongly as at the height of the Cold War. The context and nature of the relationship had changed and it is precisely because of these changes that the proponents of the Japanese-American alliance are calling for it to be maintained and deepened. They insist that collaboration between the two most dynamic societies in the world would best ensure global stability and peace. Together they account for some 40 per cent of the global GNP, with Japan's share standing at 15–16 per cent. The volume of their bilateral trade is larger than the trade of each with any other part of the world. Although Japan's trade with Asia has grown more rapidly than its trans-Pacific trade since 1986, the true gauge of the Japanese-American symbiosis is investment in the United States, whose share of Japan's total FDI rose to 45.9 per cent in the same period and was nearly triple the amount of Japanese investment in Asia. It is estimated that by the end of the century as many as one million Americans or more may be employed by Japanese enterprises.

In spite of economic friction caused by huge and apparently chronic balance of trade differences and mounting popular perceptions that competition and rivalry rather than cooperation and partnership will become the norm of the bilateral relationship, their basic interests and global outlook, which distinguish them from the other major industrialized states, point to a continuation of the alliance as the core of each nation's approach to the other.[26] Behind this reasoning there are less acknowledged motives on each side. A close alliance with Japan would be the surest guarantee from the American point of view that Japan would not become a dangerous maverick in the Asia–Pacific region. Ironically, the more nationalist-minded Japanese regard the association as a necessary stepping stone towards becoming a pre-eminent and genuinely independent Asian/Pacific power.

From a more immediate perspective, there are three distinct advantages in continuing with the American alliance as the cornerstone of Japan's foreign and security policy. The first is that it avoids the danger of isolation in the region and in the world at large. The fear of isolation has been an important motive in guiding Japan's post-war relations. The experience of the inter-war years, when Japan became effectively isolated in the negotiations over the Treaty of Versailles and over the insertion of a clause on racial equality in the draft text of the Covenant of the League of Nations, when the United States undermined the Anglo-Japanese Alliance, when the attack on China in the 1930s made Japan a pariah in the League of Nations, and when Japan challenged the most powerful nation in the world, was indelibly printed on the minds of the post-war leadership.

The second advantage is the deflation if not removal of suspicions among Japan's neighbours in East Asia. The United States is regarded as a restraining influence on any Japanese propensity to become an expansionist power. The alliance enables Japan to pursue its interests by removing the obstacles created by revived fears of Japanese militarism.

Finally, many Japanese see the close association with the United States as a bridge leading to an active role in the management of global affairs alongside the other leading industrial powers of the world. It marks a stage towards global integration. In the words of a commentator writing in 1991:

> The Japan–U.S. alliance is no longer needed to counter the Soviet threat, but it can still play a useful role in strengthening the integrationist camp. We should turn this bilateral partnership into a global alliance for dealing with environmental destruction, the North–South gap, the drug trade, and assorted other problems with global dimensions. With the arrival of the fortieth anniversary of the formation of this alliance, the time has come

> to reconsider it, and our choice should be to make it even broader and stronger.[27]

But there are at least as many disadvantages to balance this optimistic assessment. The first is the unspoken but widely held doubt about the strength of the American commitment to the alliance and to Japan; in particular, the fear of a return to a pro-China policy which would neglect Japanese interests and might even be directed against them. The intense American hostility towards China in the early post-war years, from which Japan had benefited, contained an element of the emotions aroused by a sense of love betrayed. In 1972 Nixon and Kissinger set off on the long road towards restoring the traditional friendly relationship and Japanese anxieties were heightened by the secretive manner in which the *volte face* was executed. A more recent example of the American tendency to change sides was the eagerness with which the United States embraced the reformed Soviet Union of Gorbachev and the strong support given to his successor and the new Russia. There had been a corresponding impatience with Japanese reservations over economic aid to Russia and an implied loss of interest in supporting Japan's territorial claims, in spite of formal statements to the contrary.

These doubts are linked to the second disadvantage. How can a relationship so full of contradictions be expected to continue, let alone be deepened and extended, when the main reason for its existence in the first place has fallen away? Can it withstand the clash of interests in the region? With regard to China, paradoxically in the light of what has been said above, the clash in the early 1990s was between American moralism over the issue of human rights and Japanese amoral realism, which they have turned into an 'Asian' versus 'Western' approach. Behind this clash there lies a long-term American unease over the creation of a Sino-Japanese bloc designed to exclude the United States from the region, an anxiety which could lead to the kind of reversal of American post-war policy described above. The conflict arising out of different objectives in the East Asian region would be sharpened once the communist/non-communist dichotomy, which has vanished in Europe, disappears in East Asia under the impact of market-orientated reforms in the remaining three communist countries. This would not necessarily remove the question of human rights from the agenda. On the contrary, the issue, which plays an important part in shaping American and West European attitudes and policies, may accentuate the differences between them and the 'Asian-centred' approach of the Japanese to such problems.

A third disadvantage in the eyes of a growing number of Japanese rests with the assumption that continued reliance on the bilateral alliance implies subordination in the political and military aspects of foreign policy, even though there might be equality or Japanese superiority in the economic sphere. Such a state of affairs would become increasingly unacceptable to the new mood of national assertiveness and run counter to all the rhetoric about the need for Japan to play a political role in world affairs. And yet, any attempt by Japan to reject American leadership would immediately arouse suspicions and fears in other countries and have the effect of creating that very isolation which Japan should avoid in order not to repeat the mistakes and disasters of the past.

The contradiction between a restiveness over Japan's subordinate role and the demand for a greater freedom in its foreign policy, on the one hand, and the wish to be embedded in an international security system, on the other, was addressed by a special study group on 'Japan's Role in the International Community', which was set up by the LDP and became known as the Ozawa Committee after its chairman, Ichirō Ozawa, at that time Secretary-General of the party.

The committee submitted a draft report in February 1992,[28] which is noteworthy not so much for its specific proposals as for the order of priorities which it sought to establish. Many of the recommendations in the draft had been around for some time. They included: the call for a reinterpretation of the constitution, particularly Article 9, which would permit Japan's participation in 'overseas peace-keeping and peacemaking operations'; more involvement in the United Nations, with the demand that Articles 53 and 107, with their references to 'enemy states', should be deleted from the Charter and that Japan should be given a permanent seat on the Security Council; insistence on restraint in arms production as a 'precondition' for Japanese economic assistance to a developing country; renewed efforts to overcome the fears of other countries based on the past behaviour of Japan; continued existence of the Mutual Security Treaty with the United States; and concentration on economic aid, cultural relations, the provision of education and training, and cooperation in humanitarian affairs in relations with Asian countries.

The order of the four principles which were proposed as the bases on which Japan should develop its new role in the changed international environment is interesting. The maintenance of close ties with the United States heads the list. 'These should be used to orient any roles Japan seeks to assume.' The second principle was to 'cooperate in and seek to strengthen the G-7 leadership set-up'. Third came the need to play an active part in the United Nations. The last principle stated that, '. . . as an Asian country, Japan must strive to preserve peace and maintain stability in the Asian region'.

At a more specific level, the report listed ways in which Japan could participate in ensuring international security. Most attention was devoted to the problem of involving the SDF in United Nations peacekeeping operations, albeit with many caveats and restrictions. The greatest restraint was urged on policy in Asia and the report concluded: 'It thus should go without saying that we must consult and cooperate closely with the United States.' However, it also stressed that 'From the standpoint of Japan's safety, conditions in Asia are more critical than those anywhere else.'

The tenor of the report underlines the predicament of Japan. Asia is clearly the main focus of security policy, but the legacy of the past, domestic inhibitions, and the expansion of its economic interests to include the whole world, compel Japan to keep a certain distance. This is the contemporary context of the Asia versus the West debate. The Ozawa Committee came down firmly on the side of those who argue that there is no alternative to the Japanese-American alliance as the main pillar of national security policy, with its promise of gradual integration into a Western-dominated global security system. It noted that 'discussions on regional security have now begun' and made passing reference to developments in ASEAN and in the Asia–Pacific Economic Cooperation Forum, but pointed out that little progress had been made towards integration when compared with the European Community or the Organization of American States.

A multilateral security organization

Some form of multilateral, regional security arrangement, which included the United States, is the only realistic alternative to the existing bilateral alliance, on the assumption that in the foreseeable future it will continue to be neither practicable nor desirable for Japan to stand alone and be self-sufficient in the pursuit of national security. One advantage of multilateralism is the greater flexibility it offers to the individual member in such a system than is possible in a bilateral relationship with a much stronger power. The North

Atlantic Alliance gave such flexibility to the more important European partners, enabling them to pursue policies at variance with those of the alliance hegemon, but without seriously threatening the basic unity of the alliance. When France withdrew from the integrated command system of NATO and expelled the foreign military presence from its soil in the mid-sixties, De Gaulle's policy caused much consternation, although it did not imperil the Alliance, of which France remained a member. If Japan had expelled the Americans during the Cold War, the mutual security system would have been destroyed with incalculable consequences. A multilateral alliance during the Cold War provided greater freedom in the conduct of foreign policy while still ensuring basic international stability in the context of the restrained confrontation between the superpowers.

Multilateral security structures in the post-Cold War era could not be expected to operate in such a stable environment and would therefore require a common purpose that was strong enough to withstand any deviation of its members. For example, the momentum of European integration provided such a common purpose, so that the existence of the European Community/Union was not imperilled by conflicting policies of the member states over the breakup of Yugoslavia. That kind of momentum does not yet exist in East Asia and a multilateral security system would have to be modest in the beginning, starting with a process of consultation and coordination and the setting up of very limited objectives.

The approach that seems most likely at the time of writing is the introduction of security issues as part of the agenda of the organized multinational consultations of ASEAN-PMC and APEC. The process is indeed already underway through the ASEAN Regional Forum. APEC also has become institutionalized with a permanent secretariat based in Singapore, but its focus remains essentially economic. ARF, on the other hand, was created specifically for the purpose of discussing a framework of common security and to study confidence-building measures (CBMs) such as the exchange of unclassified information, maritime cooperation, issues of nuclear non-proliferation, and the control of the transfer of conventional weapons, starting perhaps with participation in the UN Register of Conventional Arms that came into existence in January 1992 and in the promotion of which Japan had played a leading role. There is a very large overlap in the membership of ARF and APEC, although it would seem that ARF offers a better prospect of becoming the springboard for the development of a multilateral security system.

One benefit of multilateralism would be the participation of the major powers in the region. The way towards the establishment of such an all-embracing body is now open. It would have the added advantage of institutionalizing the role of the United States in East Asian security at a time when its obligations under existing bilateral agreements are becoming unpopular and burdensome for the Americans. However, there is no parallel to CSCE in East Asia which could serve as a model for an embryonic security system. Nor has the region the experience of Europe where a complex and elaborate architecture of mutual security was created during the decades of the Cold War. An Australian proposal for the establishment of a Conference on Security and Cooperation in Asia (CSCA) met with a cool reception. Most of the Asian states, including Japan, prefer a specific and sub-regional approach to the more general and amorphous structures of a CSCA. Moreover, the four major powers in the East Asian region have pursued policies in the past which conflicted and converged in kaleidoscopic fashion. This has been particularly true over the situation in the Korean peninsula, which remains a potential source of danger. The various territorial disputes in its neighbourhood present an additional problem for Japan. They raise an obstacle in the way of Japanese participation in any comprehensive security system, especially if such an arrangement were to follow the pattern of the Helsinki process and have the effect of freezing the existing borders and thus make the prospect of a settlement of the claim to the Northern Territories even more remote.

Another problem would be the role Japan could be expected to play in the system. The continued inhibitions towards its participation in international operations as a result of constitutional constraints, the legal prohibition under the Self-Defence Forces Law of 1954 on sending the SDF overseas, and the climate of public opinion all point to the role of paymaster as its contribution to a multilateral organization. It is one of the complaints of the Japanese that it was precisely such a role which they were expected to play, alongside Germany and the oil-rich Arab states, in the Gulf War of 1991, with little opportunity to influence the course of events. To add insult to injury, Japan earned much criticism for dithering and not assuming its share of responsibility, in spite of contributing some US$13 billion to the coalition. It would be unwilling to act as treasurer of an East Asian security organization without a corresponding say in its management. Finally, a deep involvement in sub-regional security structures without the United States would also conflict with the Japanese objective of closer identification with the Western powers.

The attractions and the difficulties of participation in a regional security system, in whatever form, throw further light on the tensions created by the Asian and global dimensions of Japan's policy options.

The global dimension

Throughout the book it has been suggested that economic, political, and security interests are drawing Japan closer to Asia in the post-Cold War era, but it has also been argued that this may involve a contradiction with its global interests and aspirations. To be more precise, we can describe the choice facing Japan as one between regional bloc-building and identification with a predominantly Euro-American grouping of the most advanced industrialized societies. The debate over the two tendencies echoes the debate which began in the mid-nineteenth century in very different historical circumstances. It would therefore be misleading to push the parallel too far. None the less, there is a real continuity in the Japanese predicament, which stems from the fact that, as a result of a far-sighted and determined policy, Japan became the first modern state in Asia and the only one which could claim to be one of the world's major powers.

The price of the transformation has been a permanent tension within Japanese society between ideas and methods introduced from the West and the search for a national identity based upon an indigenous heritage within the orbit of an East Asian culture. Externally it meant that Japan has not been fully accepted or trusted either in Asia or by the Western powers.

The circumstances at the end of the twentieth century raise the question whether this dichotomy has not become a false one. That there remains a tension in the direction of Japanese foreign policy cannot be denied, unless one takes the view that there is in fact no such thing as a Japanese foreign policy. That view could have been held legitimately during the early post-war period when the consequences of defeat, surrender and American occupation led to a Japan which was essentially inward turned and relied upon the United States to set the direction of its external relations. When economic expansion brought Japanese interests into conflict with those of the United States, the government, while turning a blind eye to unofficial initiatives which contradicted American policy or even quietly encouraging them, sought at all times to limit any damage to the foundations of Japanese-American relations and publicly continued to support the American line.

From the 1970s onwards, internal pressures from the rising post-war generation and expectations from the world outside have forced a foreign and security policy debate on the country's leadership. That debate has several strands. The most prominent concerns the economic issues in Japan's external relations. They have been the main focus of attention both inside and outside Japan and have become the subject of a truly enormous literature. Another strand is that of national security, whose main feature has been the Mutual Security Treaty with the United States. The third strand consists of more general political objectives, which include raising the status and influence of Japan in Asia and in the world as a whole. Finally, a fourth strand has to do with the impact of a universal, Americanized culture, spread by the means of modern communications. It has raised a debate about the essence of Japanese culture and how it might be preserved, adjusted to the conditions of the 'global village', and disseminated.

The discussion of economic issues has centred on the question of whether Japan is being drawn to form and lead an East Asian regional bloc or whether it is being driven to work for global integration. Leading commentators, captains of industry and spokesmen of large multinational enterprises generally oppose the construction of a protectionist yen-bloc. Their position has been expressed by Professor Seiichirō Saitō:

> The world in the 1990s will be moving in two directions. On the one hand, the logic of culture will be erecting borders. Aspiring for self-determination, ethnic groups will be espousing separatism and demanding autonomy. On the other, the logic of business will be dismantling borders. At present only a few countries, notably the United States, Japan and unified Germany, have big enough markets within their existing borders to make full use of economies of scale. To survive competition in the world's markets, companies will be pressing for the lowering of barriers to create a borderless economy.

He concludes:

> A global power like Japan should not make regionalism the cornerstone of its foreign policy. It should be an advocate of

> globalism and a protector of free trade everywhere. It should be working to undercut the foundations of regionalism by calling for cooperation from the leaders of the Western blocs and pulling them in a global direction.[29]

The reasons for opposition to the creation of exclusive economic areas are based on theoretical arguments, but also reflect the particular interests of large financial, commercial, and industrial enterprises. Data for trade and FDI in the decade of the 1980s tended to disprove the thesis of an emerging economic bloc in Asia. For example, Japan's FDI in East Asia, though rising, was still less than the cumulative totals in the United States and Europe. Although there was evidence of increasing Japanese influence in the financial markets of the East Asia/Pacific region, this reflected the growing impact of the yen on exchange rate policies and on interest rates. These developments were due less to a deliberate Japanese policy than to American policies which encouraged Japan to promote the yen globally as a unit of currency and pressed the East Asian NICs to open their financial markets.[30] All this points in the direction of a wider global economic integration rather than to a deliberate policy of promoting a new version of the Greater East Asia Co-prosperity sphere. Moreover, the increasing complexity of economic interaction within the region itself, where there has been a growth of trade intensity between the NICs (South Korea, Taiwan, Hong Kong and Singapore) and the other five members of ASEAN (Indonesia, Malaysia, Thailand, the Philippines and Brunei), on the one hand, and, on the other, a similar increase of trade intensity between the NICs and Japan, does not necessarily mean that Japan would be dominant merely because of the strength of the yen and the size of its investment.

The economic arguments for a more open global system are countered by political factors which could have the opposite effect. At the beginning of the 1990s the world economy was in a recession which might have far-reaching consequences. For the recession, taken together with the collapse of the Soviet bloc, has had the effect of strengthening protectionism in the form of regional exclusiveness as well as reviving more traditional forms of nationalism which have arisen from the ruins of Cold War ideological confrontation.

In Europe it is an open question whether the historic nationalism of its major states or a new form of regional identity will prevail. One could also point to the rise of a North American regionalism whose characteristic is an inward turning to the pressing domestic problems of the three countries involved. The complex pattern in

East Asia, which marks the economic relations between Japan and the NICs, between the NICs and the other countries of South-East Asia, and between all and China, adds to the uncertainty over Japan's role. Will it become an undisputed and accepted leader or a facilitator of a slow and complicated process of integration? Will it become a contestant with China for a dominant position in the region or a partner with China in managing it?

The Japanese face a variety of permutations and combinations when contemplating the future direction of their policy. Japan could become the leader or the most influential member of a regional economic bloc which would be one of three economic blocs in the northern hemisphere. The relationship between them could be mainly antagonistic, mainly cooperative or a mixture of competition and cooperation. On present evidence, the third course is the most likely one, which would suggest a gradual economic integration of the whole of the northern hemisphere, with APEC serving as a link between East Asia and the other economically advanced societies – a development assisted by the activities and evolution of giant multinational corporations.[31] The establishment of three major economic blocs and their eventual convergence would create a simple divide in the global economy with the prospect of sharpened and possibly violent conflict between a prosperous north and a deprived south. There are some who see this as the ultimate scenario of the next century, They point to the GATT agreement at the end of 1993 as confirmation of this trend, in that it favoured the interests of the advanced economies over the needs of the poorer countries.

MAKING THE CHOICE

Japan's part in the future direction of the global economy and politics will depend to some extent on the resolution of the current tension between its Asian inclinations and the pull of the West. The outcome may not be a clear-cut decision in favour of one or the other direction in its policy. Instead, it is likely to reflect the interplay and influence upon each other of four distinct courses that Japan could follow in theory. Each has its origin in past experience and the political culture of Japan.

Isolation

The first course is that of isolation. A return to Tokugawa seclusion is obviously ruled out, but the geographical position of the country, a popular desire for domestic order and tranquillity, a strong sense of national identity and exclusiveness, and an unwillingness to bc drawn into international conflicts would encourage a policy that sought to minimize the impact of the external world. Since total isolation would be impossible, a policy similar to that pursued by Switzerland might be attractive. However, given the giantism of the national economy, British policy in the nineteenth century – a mixture of detachment and of limited intervention at relatively low cost when the national interest seemed to be threatened – might be a more appropriate model. Japanese participation to preserve or make peace would parallel British gunboat diplomacy and imperial policing. There would be no acquisition of colonies as in the past, but Japanese financial power would make the local representative of a major bank or trading house the equivalent of the British 'resident' in a semi-independent state.

Neo-isolation would be a policy whose key features are detachment, neutrality, and a low-key posture in international affairs with limited interventions to safeguard Japanese interests and influence. It is a policy which has no open advocates today and is indeed rejected as a practicable course for Japan. Yet there exists a mood which is not unfavourable to such a stance. The reluctance of a large section of the population and of some political parties to accept any involvement of the SDF in international peacekeeping operations is expressive of this attitude.

A major international role

The second course is the exact opposite of the first and would imply a major international role for Japan and an ever increasing involvement in the affairs of the world. This is the publicly expressed view of many politicians, diplomats, commentators and academics. It tends to stress one or the other of two policy options: either building on the current relationship with the United States to construct a new world order or concentrating on Japan's involvement in the United Nations. The first approach is to be found in an article by Takakazu Kuriyama, a Vice-Minister of Foreign Affairs.[32] The Soviet Union was still in existence at the time and there was some doubt as to whether Gorbachev's *perestroika* was the beginning of a revolution which could lead to the end of the Cold War or whether it and the accompanying 'new thinking' in Soviet foreign policy merely marked another interlude of détente before a renewal of international tensions. None the less, the paper contained an outline of much that has become declaratory policy since. Although its sub-title was 'Making active Contributions to the Creation of a New International Order', there was no mention of the United Nations. Instead, the basic thrust of the argument was that the economic decline of the United States required Japan to play a major role in helping it to establish a new world order.

Mr Kuriyama pointed out that the United States and the European Community each accounted for a quarter of the world's GNP, while Japan accounted for approximately one seventh to one sixth, and that the share of the three economic giants together amounted to almost two thirds of the global figure. He converted these proportions into a 5–5–3 structure and likened it to the formula for capital ships worked out in the Washington Naval Treaty of 1922, which he described as symbolizing 'the responsibilities for the maintenance of the international order in the pre-war era'.[33] Recalling that Japan had tried to reverse this order with tragic consequences, he asked whether Japan could turn the new 5–5–3 ratio into a basis for genuine cooperation with its American and European partners. He went on to stress that Japan had become an 'important' member of the club of industrialized democracies and must actively participate in the construction of a new international order.

Several principles emerge from his discussion of the requirements of Japan's new role. It must work through the tripartite system; its role will be confined to non-military contributions; and within the tripartite structure the special relationship with the United States will be more important than Japan's relationship with Europe. Moreover, he emphasized that the Asia/Pacific region is the main theatre of Japan's foreign policy; '. . . their national interests dictate both Japan and the United States to share special interests and responsibilities for peace, stability, growth and prosperity' of that region.[34]

The article is noteworthy because it traced the path of Japan's contribution to the new world order along the route of traditional world politics. The circumstances at the end of the twentieth century required that the projection of Japanese power should be economic and financial rather than military, but that Japan should seek the fulfilment of its role through a close alliance with the world's greatest military power and in belonging to the club of the most advanced industrialized democracies.

The other line of approach is to focus on Japan's role in the United Nations. The fact that it has become the second largest financial contributor is seen as proof that Japan has become a major power. The amount of its financial support and its active participation in the work of the world body, especially in various initiatives over arms control such as the formulation of standards and guidelines to govern the trade in conventional arms,[35] and in the field of development assistance, are cited as evidence in support of the claim to a permanent seat on the Security Council.

Japan's first major involvement in United Nations peacekeeping operations came with its participation in the work of UNTAC. This was made possible by the passage of the International Peace Cooperation Law in June 1992 after protracted debates in the Diet and much political manoeuvring. The law and the operations in Cambodia highlight some of the issues which would arise from a decision to make the United Nations the central plank in its foreign policy.

The main features of the International Peace Cooperation Law are the strict limitations on the functions of the SDF. There are complicated procedures to go through before the dispatch of units can be authorized. They must not exceed two thousand personnel at any one time. Their specific tasks are confined to transportation, communications, construction (e.g. repairs to roads and bridges in Cambodia), and humanitarian relief. A separate bill governs the use of the SDF in disaster relief missions. The forces may also help in the supervision of elections and in an advisory capacity to the local administration and police. Side-arms can only be used for self-protection when unavoidable. Special authorization by the Diet is necessary each time the units are asked to perform additional tasks such as monitoring compliance with cease-fire arrangements, assisting in the demarcation of cease-fire lines or patrolling buffer zones. Japanese forces are only to be deployed after the establishment of a cease-fire. Should it break down or its imposition require the use of force, they would be withdrawn.[36]

The debate over the law is an illustration of the continuing importance of the underlying principles of the 'Peace Constitution' and, at the same time, of the extent to which the SDF have become an accepted though very limited instrument of national policy. In order to secure its passage, the Prime Minister had to gain the support of two of the smaller opposition parties, whose price was the inclusion of restraints that would set Japanese units apart from other national contingents. Even so, the bill was bitterly contested by the SDPJ and communists on the grounds that it violated the constitution. An obvious and possibly more palatable alternative, the establishment of an independent, civilian unit to participate in non-military peacekeeping operations, might have been preferred by Prime Minister Kaifu himself and would have been supported by the leaders of the socialists. However, it was opposed by their hardline, doctrinaire left-wingers as well as by the defence lobby.[37] The hierarchy of the SDF favoured deployment within a UN force – it would give them something to do other than the endless training for the remote contingency of an attack on the national territory. It would also provide valuable overseas experience. The enlisted men were less enthusiastic about giving up the comforts of life on the home bases for the discomfort and boredom of life in provincial Cambodia.

The rather modest Japanese effort immediately triggered expressions of concern and misgivings among Japan's neighbours. There was apprehension in Korea and China that participation in UN operations would provide the cover for a Japanese policy of trying to expand its political and military influence in the region. Similar anxieties had been voiced when Japan sent a minesweeping flotilla to the Gulf between June and September 1991, after the end of the war against Iraq.[38] In enabling the SDF to take part in UN peacekeeping, the government may well have seen an opportunity to circumvent legal restrictions on their dispatch abroad. However, as in all decisions affecting security policy, it was caught between opposition at home and in Asia and pressures from the United States and its allies.

The Cambodian experience had an interesting side-effect, for it also revealed a strain of internationalism among the public. There was a striking illustration of this in the reaction to the murder of Atsuhito Nakata on 8 April 1993. Nakata was a young civilian who worked with the UN Volunteers as an election monitor. He and his Cambodian interpreter had been ambushed and he was dead by the time help arrived. The casket containing his ashes was flown to Osaka, draped in the UN flag. His father decided to devote himself to the cause of the United Nations and international solidarity as a memorial to his son's idealism and selflessness.

> I want people throughout the world to know that there are so many people in Japan who were motivated in their efforts in Cambodia not by national interest, but by global citizenship, by the ideal of sharing global solidarity with the people of other countries.[39]

His stand met with an astonishing response. Apart from a flood of letters from young people expressing a desire to follow in Atsuhito's footsteps, Japan Overseas Cooperation Volunteers (JOCV) received nearly five thousand applications – the highest ever – in the two months following the father's appeal.

One could, of course, dismiss the episode as an isolated, emotional and sentimental response to a shocking incident, especially when it is set against the reaction to a similar event a month later, following the ambush and death of a Japanese police officer. On that occasion there was a demand for the withdrawal of the police contingent from their zone of operation. The request was rejected by Yasushi Akashi, the Japanese Head of UNTAC. He told the Minister of Home Affairs, who had flown to Phnom Penh to see him, that the Japanese police serving with UNTAC could not be given preferential treatment in this respect.[40]

The response to Nakata's death may nevertheless point to an element of idealism among the Japanese, especially younger people, which coexists with a largely dormant nationalism. The impression that internationalism is gaining ground was reinforced by the results of an opinion survey conducted by the Prime Minister's Office in October 1992. The questions were put in a multiple choice format. In response to one about Japan's role in the international community, 49.7 per cent said it should help to resolve global issues and 31.4 per cent opted for contributing to the maintenance of peace. On the question of how Japan might cooperate with the UN, 68.7 per cent referred to preserving international peace and security, while 61.9 per cent chose tackling environmental issues. On the other hand, considerably less than half the sample mentioned assistance to developing countries or aid to refugees.[41]

The emphasis on Japan's place in international organizations does not necessarily contradict the emphasis on its place in the American-led Western alliance. Indeed, they can be regarded as complementary because the UN, especially when it is concerned with peace and security, is largely led by the United States and other Western countries. The two approaches are usually linked in official statements on foreign policy, but whereas the emphasis on the alliance is a continuation of the pattern established after the war, the stress on working within and through the UN prepares the ground for the time when Japan may seek to play a more independent role in world affairs and when the alliance may be under strain or has outlived its usefulness. However, the focus on the United Nations should not be taken to mean that Japan has a clear vision of the new order. On the contrary, it should be seen as an attempt to adjust to the direction in which events seem to be moving at the moment.

An Asia policy

The third distinctive course would be a single-minded concentration on developing an Asia policy. Japan has already replaced the United States as Asia's principal market, source of investment and provider of development assistance. It has begun tentatively to stake out its political leadership with a claim to protect regional interests, especially as spokesman for ASEAN in the Group of Seven and through various attempts to mediate in regional conflicts, and it has played a leading role in launching a multilateral approach to regional security through the ARF. However, policies in North-East and South-East Asia are bound to differ.

Concern over national security is more directly involved in the formulation of policy towards North-East Asia. Pursuit of a settlement in Korea will be undertaken in concert with its other neighbours and might lead to the construction of a 'sub-regional mechanism for regional stability'.[42] China remains the crucial factor. It straddles both sub-regions and it is the only power which could challenge Japan for the leadership of East Asia. Policy towards China will continue to be cautious, with the objective of tying it closely to Japan through economic engagement. This has a twofold objective: to enable Japan to exercise a subtle influence over Chinese policy; and to avoid an alliance between China and third parties, such as Russia or the United States, which might be directed against Japan. Finally, any substantial movement in relations with Russia will depend on a resolution of the dispute over the Northern Territories, which still seems to be elusive.

Japan can afford to take a more detached view in South-East Asia. The integration of Vietnam into an ASEAN-based sub-regional grouping was an important objective to balance the political and economic weight of China in that part of the world. In addition to continued reliance on the mutual security arrangements with the United States, Japan will work through its association with the overlapping multilateral organizations of ASEAN and APEC. At a time of rapid change and great uncertainty, it has neither the confidence nor the desire to stand out as an independent and forceful actor. Nevertheless, such diffidence could evaporate quite quickly.

A balanced policy

The fourth course of action would really be a combination of the other three sketched above: a mixture of a semi-isolationist policy on the model of nineteenth-century Britain, but using different tools; an active policy of globalism within the framework of the Western alliance and/or the United Nations; and the development of Japanese influence and leadership in the East Asian region. Such a combination would be an 'omnidirectional' policy in the literal sense.

The term 'omnidirectional diplomacy' first made its appearance under Prime Minister Fukuda (1976–8) and was intended to replace the concept of 'equidistant diplomacy' of his predecessor, Takeo Miki (1974–6). Equidistance had been invented to describe Japan's relations with each of the communist titans on the Asian mainland at the height of their mutual hostility.[43] Fukuda used the expression 'omnidirectional' to counter internal political opposition to his handling of negotiations for the Peace and Friendship Treaty with China and to cover himself if they came to grief. It simply meant maintaining relations of mutual trust with countries in all directions, regardless of their political systems, size and geographical distance from Japan, something the Chinese would hardly approve of since they were trying to persuade Japan to accept a treaty that included an 'anti-hegemony' clause which was directed against the Soviet Union. 'Omnidirectional diplomacy' ceased to feature in the *Diplomatic Bluebook* of 1980. Under the influence of renewed Cold War tensions it was replaced by an emphasis on Japan's membership of the 'Free World', which laid stress on the relationship with the United States as the 'axis' of its foreign policy and on the need to improve the nation's self-defence capabilities.[44]

An omnidirectional approach at the end of the century would require the pursuit of all options on the basis of a fundamentally independent stance in world politics, so that Japan remains in the best position to adjust to a rapidly changing environment. Consolidation of its position as a leading power in East Asia, cooperation with the United States in the shaping of APEC and the creation of a global economic order, an active role in the development of the United Nations and its international agencies might all bc pursued simultaneously, with a shift of emphasis from one to another as circumstances dictate.

The concept of the direction of foreign policy should not be taken to mean tactical manoeuvres in pursuit of some carefully defined and overriding objective, such as leadership of an East Asian bloc, domination of the global economy, the creation of a particular world order or some other grand design. Instead, the idea of steering the ship of state through the uncharted seas of international relations is a more accurate reflection of Japanese thinking about the conduct of foreign policy. Another metaphor would be the progress of a portable shrine (mikoshi) during a festival. Policy, like the carriers of the mikoshi, moves forward and backward. It lurches from side to side and occasionally lands in a ditch, but its general direction is not in doubt.[45] From this one may infer that while Japan is aware of its potential as a major actor in world affairs, its policies remain uninformed by a very clear concept of the kind of regional or world order which it wants to shape.

The Japanese intellectual tradition has not equipped the country's politicians and bureaucrats to take a leading role in international politics. They failed to do so in the first half of the twentieth century with their attempt to imitate the imperial powers of the West under the guise of a pseudo-*mission civilisatrice*. For, alongside the emphasis on national self-interest and the never-ending competition among sovereign states, Western political thought includes a tradition of grappling with the need to create some kind of international order out of anarchy. The rule of international law or of a universal empire, the establishment of an international organization to keep the peace or the pursuit of comprehensive disarmament also have their roots in Western philosophy. Such architectonic visions have been absent from the Japanese approach to the world outside. The absence of a universalism, which is often accompanied by an aggressive missionary zeal, can be attributed to Japan's geographical isolation, its historical development, its religious and philosophical traditions, and its social structures with their 'we inside' and 'they outside' perceptions.[46] On the other hand, Japan's post-war tradition of flexibility and pragmatic adjustment, coupled with a measure of international idealism, might be just the right kind of mixture which would enable it to make a constructive contribution to world affairs at the end of the twentieth century.

7 Conclusion

No single factor has been more important in shaping the course of Japan's post-war external relations than its political dependence on the United States. The impact of this relationship, though declining, will continue to influence the course of Japanese policy to the end of the century and possibly beyond. Japan's own 'special relationship' with the United States enabled it to concentrate on economic and social reconstruction after the war and then to expand economically within a world system regulated by the United States.

Once recovery had been achieved, there were intimations that Japan would not continue in a subordinate role for ever. At the diplomatic/strategic level there was no serious divergence from the American position until 1973, when Japan took a more independent line over the Palestinian question. An earlier and more subtle indication that Japan would not follow the American lead blindly, was the continuation and growth of trade with the Chinese mainland throughout the two decades between 1952 and 1972, in spite of an overall Sino-Japanese relationship which swung between the deep freeze of hostility and a slight thaw. Economic ties were fostered and developed by independent and unofficial associations of Japanese enterprises without the public support of a government which was tied to the American policy of recognizing the Kuomintang regime in Taipei as the legitimate government of China. Nevertheless, the pro-mainland commercial and industrial lobby did receive some indirect encouragement from sympathetic politicians in the LDP and elements in the bureaucracy, especially in MITI.

One could cite other cases where non-governmental initiatives pushed official policy in a particular direction, which modify the conventional perception of Japanese policy-making. Instead of consensus as a precondition of decision, they point to *post facto* agreement over policy and raise the possibility that in the future the activities of large Japanese corporations with worldwide interests may push government into decisions which bring it into line with the actions taken by bodies beyond its direct control; a situation analogous to the pre-war influence of the military over policy through their initiatives in Manchuria and China. It is also important to bear in mind the intricate and often close personal ties between members of the government, whether politicians or bureaucrats, and so-called non-governmental actors such as financiers, merchants, industrialists, journalists and even members of opposition parties. Ties which blur the distinction between what is official and what is unofficial.

In spite of probings for autonomy in foreign policy, Japan remained a political outsider in Asia throughout the four decades of the Cold War. It was generally accepted as such by its neighbours and regarded as little more than an appendage of the United States in matters of regional security.

As long as the international system, which had emerged in the 1940s, continued to exist, Japan could steer its policy in a reasonably certain and predictable environment. Nor were the basic structures seriously undermined by the development of Kissinger's triangular diplomacy in the 1970s, involving the United States, the Soviet Union and China. The rough nuclear strategic parity between the United States and the Soviet Union in the 1970s and their mutual global reach, following the development of the Soviet navy, had made the superpowers 'limited adversaries' with a shared interest in avoiding direct confrontation. They had every incentive to avoid a repetition of the hair-raising experience of the Cuban missile crisis in 1962. Their open competition for power and influence was accompanied by quiet cooperation designed to ensure that they retained their primacy in world politics – a discreet collusion which General de Gaulle had been one of the first to spot and to exploit in the 1960s. The relationship between the superpowers was governed by an intricate and complex set of rules, some explicit such as those governing the arms race, others implicit such as the recognition of each other's spheres of influence, which ensured a remarkably stable political and strategic environment in both Europe and North-East Asia.

In this context it did not matter much whether Japan had a specific foreign policy or not. Once it had begun to make inroads in the world's markets and to accumulate mounting trade surpluses, there were grumbles and suspicions, coupled with calls, led by the

United States, that it should do more to support the West in the struggle against the communist powers. The Japanese government was able to buy off such criticism with token measures to curb the commercial imbalances and by a policy of rearmament which, after 1960, skilfully blended appeasement of American opinion with reassurances to the Japanese public that there was no basic shift from adherence to the 'Peace Constitution'. From the American point of view, Japan was too important an ally to alienate and, after all, it was preferable to have an inoffensive Japan than one whose rearmament would frighten the neighbours in Asia. Moreover, Japan was making a growing contribution to the cost of Western security through its payments for American military facilities on its soil, through an increasing share in financing the American national debt, and through ODA targeted at countries considered to be of strategic importance for Western security.

With the first signs of change in the post-war economic and political order in the 1970s and 1980s, the Japanese began to question the objectives and direction of their foreign policy. The debate was rather leisurely and academic at first, but gained momentum and relevance in the late 1980s when it became clear that the Cold War might be coming to an end and that American policy could no longer serve as the sole point of reference for the conduct of Japan's external relations. The dramatic events since 1989 lent urgency to this questioning and have brought it into the realm of practical politics.

The size and spread of the Japanese economy will continue to tie it into an increasingly interdependent world. The general drift towards global integration in one form or another is not likely to be a straightforward, linear process. It will be accompanied by upheavals and setbacks. Whether Japan will find itself at the hub of an Asia–Pacific economic zone, as the leader of an East Asian regional bloc, with or without China, or integrated into the network of the world's industrialized powers (including the dynamic economies of East Asia), it cannot return to the isolation of the past, to which it might be inclined by its historical and cultural tradition. And yet, despite global interests, domestic politics continue to impede Japanese governments from exercising a decisive leadership in world affairs.

Competitive urges and a desire for status and power will strengthen the demand that Japan should not only be recognized as one of the most important states in the world, but also seen as decisively engaged in shaping the international system. These expectations are bound to grow as a new generation of leaders takes over the business of government, unfettered by the psychological burdens of the past, although it does not follow that they will repeat the mistakes of the past. The pattern and conduct of international relations at the end of the century are fundamentally different from those at the beginning. The Japanese are also good learners from their own experience and that of others.

However, without a precise programme and the missionary zeal to establish a new world order, Japan will proceed along the lines of flexible adjustment to the external environment, an approach in tune with its political culture. The realignment of domestic politics in 1993 was more dramatic in appearance than in reality. Nevertheless, the changes were in line with fundamental shifts in world politics: old orders and certainties are being replaced by new issues and patterns of interaction.

All this does not signify and probably never meant inaction or merely *ad hoc* reaction to what is happening elsewhere. The ship of state is not drifting through a foggy international environment. Broad objectives exist. They may be summed up as the prosperity and stability of the national polity, an open international economic system in which Japan has free access to resources and markets, and the enhancement and extension of Japanese influence in the world. The prevailing uncertainty of the post-Cold War years requires adaptation as well as planning for a variety of contingencies. The foundations are being laid for the 'soft' leadership of an East Asian economic bloc, for close cooperation with China or for competition and rivalry with it, for joint leadership with the United States of the Asia–Pacific region or for acting without the US, for the exercise of independent national power or for a major part in helping to create a more cohesive world order. None of these is certain to happen and new, unexpected developments may blow Japan off course, but it has the resources to pursue each of these objectives.

So, where does this leave the debate over Asia and the West? It continues, but on different terms from those which governed it a century or half a century ago. In geography, history and culture there can be no doubt where Japan belongs. In terms of its perceived national interest, the economy, and social development, there is more doubt. The context of the dialogue between Orient and Occident has changed. Traditional patterns of social, political and international behaviour are breaking down throughout the world and old cultural distinctions are dissolving under the impact of a technological revolution. However, when people are losing their bearings as the familiar landmarks crumble around them and threaten to disappear, they will often cling more tenaciously and fervently than ever before to what they believe to be their historic identity and traditions. Hence the return to intolerant fundamentalism in some of the major world religions and the rise of a neo-conservatism which looks back on a golden age of harmony. More ominous still is the revival of a primitive tribalism of the blood and soil variety with its call for ethnic exclusivity.

The impact of these forces will have its effect on Japanese attitudes and policies. They would find fertile ground among people who see themselves as racially and culturally unique. If the reactionary tendencies prevail, then Japan will seek refuge in a neo-isolationism or in creating some kind of Asian bloc as a protection against a hostile and threatening environment. If the changes making for global integration turn out to be more powerful, then the dichotomy between Asia and the West will gradually lose its meaning and Japan is likely to adapt to loosely structured regional associations, wider economic groupings and global organizations. The policies of Japan will reflect changes in the international environment, but the Japanese response to those changes will have an important influence in shaping it.

Appendix I

Treaty of Mutual Cooperation and Security Between the United States of America and Japan, Washington DC, 19 January 1960

The United States of America and Japan,

Desiring to strengthen the bonds of peace and friendship traditionally existing between them, and to uphold the principles of democracy, individual liberty, and the rule of law,

Desiring further to encourage closer economic cooperation between them and to promote conditions of economic stability and well-being in their countries,

Reaffirming their faith in the purposes and principles of the Charter of the United Nations, and their desire to live in peace with all peoples and all governments,

Recognizing that they have the inherent right of individual or collective self-defense as affirmed in the Charter of the United Nations,

Considering that they have a common concern in the maintenance of international peace and security in the Far East,

Having resolved to conclude a treaty of mutual cooperation and security,

Therefore agree as follows:

Article I

The Parties undertake, as set forth in the Charter of the United Nations, to settle any international disputes in which they may be involved by peaceful means in such a manner that international peace and security and justice are not endangered and to refrain in their international relations from the threat or use of force against the territorial integrity or political independence of any state, or in any other manner inconsistent with the purposes of the United Nations.

The Parties will endeavor in concert with other peace-loving countries to strengthen the United Nations so that its mission of maintaining international peace and security may be discharged more effectively.

Article II

The Parties will contribute toward the further development of peaceful and friendly international relations by strengthening their free institutions, by bringing about a better understanding of the principles upon which these institutions are founded, and by promoting conditions of stability and well being. They will seek to eliminate conflict in their international economic policies and will encourage economic collaboration between them.

Article III

The Parties, individually and in cooperation with each other, by means of continuous and effective self-help and mutual aid will maintain and develop, subject to their constitutional provisions, their capacities to resist armed attack.

Article IV

The Parties will consult together from time to time regarding the implementation of this Treaty, and, at the request of either Party, whenever the security of Japan or international peace and security in the Far East is threatened.

Article V

Each Party recognizes that an armed attack against either Party in the territories under the administration of Japan would be dangerous to its own peace and safety and declares that it would act to meet the common danger in accordance with its constitutional provisions and processes.

Any such armed attack and all measures taken as a result thereof shall be immediately reported to the Security Council of the United Nations in accordance with the provisions of Article 51 of the Charter. Such measures shall be terminated when the Security Council has taken the measures necessary to restore and maintain international peace and security.

Article VI

For the purpose of contributing to the security of Japan and the maintenance of international peace and security in the Far East, the United States of America is granted the use by its land, air and naval forces of facilities and areas in Japan.

The use of these facilities and areas as well as the status of United States armed forces in Japan shall be governed by a separate agreement, replacing the Administrative Agreement under Article III of the Security Treaty between the United States of America and Japan, signed at Tokyo on February 28, 1952, as amended, and by such other arrangements as may be agreed upon.

Article VII

This Treaty does not affect and shall not be interpreted as affecting in any way the rights and obligations of the Parties under the Charter of the United Nations or the responsibility of the United Nations for the maintenance of international peace and security.

Article VIII

This Treaty shall be ratified by the United States of America and Japan in accordance with their respective constitutional processes and will enter into force on the date on which the instruments of ratification thereof have been exchanged by them in Tokyo.

Article IX

The Security Treaty between the United States of America and Japan signed at the city of San Francisco on September 8, 1951, shall expire upon the entering into force of this Treaty.

Article X

This Treaty shall remain in force until in the opinion of the Governments of the United States of America and Japan there shall have come into force such United Nations arrangements as will satisfactorily provide for the maintenance of international peace and security in the Japan area.

However, after the Treaty has been in force for ten years, either Party may give notice to the other Party of its intention to terminate the Treaty, in which case the Treaty shall terminate one year after such notice has been given.

Source: *U.S. Department of State Bulletin*, vol. XLII, no. 1076, 8 February 1960, pp. 184–5.

Appendix II

Treaty of Peace with Japan, 8 September 1951

Whereas the Allied Powers and Japan are resolved that henceforth their relations shall be those of nations which, as sovereign equals, coöperate in friendly association to promote their common welfare and to maintain international peace and security, and are therefore desirous of concluding a Treaty of Peace which will settle questions still outstanding as a result of the existence of a state of war between them;

Whereas Japan for its part declares its intention to apply for membership in the United Nations and in all circumstances to conform to the principles of the Charter of the United Nations; to strive to realize the objectives of the Universal Declaration of Human Rights; to seek to create within Japan conditions of stability and well-being as defined in Articles 55 and 56 of the Charter of the United Nations and already initiated by post-surrender Japanese legislation; and in public and private trade and commerce to conform to internationally accepted fair practices;

Whereas the Allied Powers welcome the intentions of Japan set out in the foregoing paragraph;

The Allied Powers and Japan have therefore determined to conclude the present Treaty of Peace, and have accordingly appointed the undersigned Plenipotentiaries, who, after presentation of their full powers, found in good and due form, have agreed on the following provisions:

CHAPTER I

PEACE

Article 1

(a) The state of war between Japan and each of the Allied Powers is terminated as from the date on which the present Treaty comes into force between Japan and the Allied Power concerned as provided for in Article 23.

(b) The Allied Powers recognize the full sovereignty of the Japanese people over Japan and its territorial waters.

CHAPTER II

TERRITORY

Article 2

(a) Japan, recognizing the independence of Korea, renounces all right, title and claim to Korea, including the islands of Quelpart, Port Hamilton and Dagelet.

(b) Japan renounces all right, title and claim to Formosa and the Pescadores.

(c) Japan renounces all right, title and claim to the Kurile Islands, and to that portion of Sakhalin and the islands adjacent to it over which Japan acquired sovereignty as a consequence of the Treaty of Portsmouth of September 5, 1905.

(d) Japan renounces all right, title and claim in connection with the League of Nations Mandate System, and accepts the action of the United Nations Security Council of April 2, 1947, extending the trusteeship system to the Pacific Islands formerly under mandate to Japan.

(e) Japan renounces all claim to any right or title to or interest in connection with any part of the Antarctic area, whether deriving from the activities of Japanese nationals or otherwise.

(f) Japan renounces all right, title and claim to the Spratly Islands and to the Paracel Islands.

Article 3

Japan will concur in any proposal of the United States to the United Nations to place under its trusteeship system, with the United States as the sole administering authority, Nansei Shoto south of 29° north latitude (including the Ryukyu Islands and the Daito Islands), Nanpo Shoto south of Sofu Gan (including the Bonin Islands, Rosario Island and the Volcano Islands) and Parece Vela and Marcus Island. Pending the making of such a proposal and affirmative action thereon, the United States will have the right to exercise all and any powers of administration, legislation and jurisdiction over the territory and inhabitants of these islands, including their territorial waters.

Article 4

(a) Subject to the provisions of paragraph (b) of this Article, the disposition of property of Japan and of its nationals in the areas referred to in Article 2, and their claims, including debts, against the authorities presently administering such areas and the residents (including juridical persons) thereof, and the disposition in Japan of property of such authorities and residents, and of claims, including debts, of such authorities and residents against Japan and its nationals, shall be the subject of special arrangements between Japan and such authorities. The property of any of the Allied Powers or its nationals in the areas referred to in Article 2 shall, insofar as this has not already been done, be returned by the administering authority in the condition in which it now exists. (The term nationals whenever used in the present Treaty includes juridical persons.)

(b) Japan recognizes the validity of dispositions of property of Japan and Japanese nationals made by or pursuant to directives of the United States Military Government in any of the areas referred to in Articles 2 and 3.

(c) Japanese owned submarine cables connecting Japan with territory removed from Japanese control pursuant to the present Treaty shall be equally divided, Japan retaining the Japanese terminal and adjoining half of the cable, and the detached territory the remainder of the cable and connecting terminal facilities.

CHAPTER III

SECURITY

Article 5

(a) Japan accepts the obligations set forth in Article 2 of the Charter of the United Nations, and in particular the obligations

(i) to settle its international disputes by peaceful means in such a manner that international peace and security, and justice, are not endangered;

(ii) to refrain in its international relations from the threat or use of force against the territorial integrity or political independence of any State or in any other manner inconsistent with the Purposes of the United Nations;

(iii) to give the United Nations every assistance in any action it takes in accordance with the Charter and to refrain from giving assistance to any State against which the United Nations may take preventive or enforcement action.

(b) The Allied Powers confirm that they will be guided by the principles of Article 2 of the Charter of the United Nations in their relations with Japan.

(c) The Allied Powers for their part recognize that Japan as a sovereign nation possesses the inherent right of individual or collective self-defense referred to in Article 51 of the Charter of the United Nations and that Japan may voluntarily enter into collective security arrangements.

Article 6

(a) All occupation forces of the Allied Powers shall be withdrawn from Japan as soon as possible after the coming into force of the present Treaty, and in any case not later than 90 days thereafter. Nothing in this provision shall, however, prevent the stationing or retention of foreign armed forces in Japanese territory under or in consequence of any bilateral or multilateral agreements which have been or may be made between one or more of the Allied Powers, on the one hand, and Japan on the other.

(b) The provisions of Article 9 of the Potsdam Proclamation of July 26, 1945, dealing with the return of Japanese military forces to their homes, to the extent not already completed, will be carried out.

(c) All Japanese property for which compensation has not already been paid, which was supplied for the use of the occupation forces and which remains in the possession of those forces at the time of the coming into force of the present Treaty, shall be returned to the Japanese Government within the same 90 days unless other arrangements are made by mutual agreement.

CHAPTER IV

POLITICAL AND ECONOMIC CLAUSES

Article 7

(a) Each of the Allied Powers, within one year after the present Treaty has come into force between it and Japan, will notify Japan which of its prewar bilateral treaties or conventions with Japan it wishes to continue in force or revive, and any treaties or conventions so notified shall continue in force or be revived subject to such amendments as may be necessary to ensure conformity with the present Treaty. The treaties and conventions so notified shall be considered as having been continued in force or revived three months after the date of notification and shall be registered with the Secretariat of the United Nations. All such treaties and conventions as to which Japan is not so notified shall be regarded as abrogated.

(b) Any notification made under paragraph (a) of this Article may except from the operation or revival of a treaty or convention any territory for the international relations of which the notifying Power is responsible, until three months after the date on which notice is given to Japan that such exception shall cease to apply.

Article 8

(a) Japan will recognize the full force of all treaties now or hereafter concluded by the Allied Powers for terminating the state of war initiated on September 1, 1939, as well as any other arrangements by the Allied Powers for or in connection with the restoration of peace. Japan also accepts the arrangements made for terminating the former League of Nations and Permanent Court of International Justice.

(b) Japan renounces all such rights and interests as it may derive from being a signatory power of the Conventions of St. Germain-en-Laye of September 10, 1919, and the Straits Agreement of Montreux of July 20, 1936, and from Article 16 of the Treaty of Peace with Turkey signed at Lausanne on July 24, 1923.

(c) Japan renounces all rights, title and interests acquired under, and is discharged from all obligations resulting from, the Agreement between Germany and the Creditor Powers of January 20, 1930, and its Annexes, including the Trust Agreement, dated May 17, 1930; the Convention of January 20, 1930, respecting the Bank for International Settlements; and the Statutes of the Bank for International Settlements. Japan will notify to the Ministry of Foreign Affairs in Paris within six months of the first coming into force of the present Treaty its renunciation of the rights, title and interests referred to in this paragraph.

Article 9

Japan will enter promptly into negotiations with the Allied Powers so desiring for the conclusion of bilateral and multilateral agreements providing for the regulation or limitation of fishing and the conservation and development of fisheries on the high seas.

Article 10

Japan renounces all special rights and interests in China, including all benefits and privileges resulting from the provisions of the final Protocol signed at Peking on September 7, 1901, and all annexes, notes and documents supplementary thereto, and agrees to the abrogation in respect to Japan of the said protocol, annexes, notes and documents.

Article 11

Japan accepts the judgments of the International Military Tribunal for the Far East and of other Allied War Crimes Courts both within and outside Japan, and will carry out the sentences imposed thereby upon Japanese nationals imprisoned in Japan. The power to grant clemency, to reduce sentences and to parole with respect to such prisoners may not be exercised except on the decision of the Government or Governments which imposed the sentence in each instance, and on the recommendation of Japan. In the case of persons sentenced by the International Military Tribunal for the Far East, such power may not be exercised except on the decision of a majority of the Governments represented on the Tribunal, and on the recommendation of Japan.

Article 12

(a) Japan declares its readiness promptly to enter into negotiations for the conclusion with each of the Allied Powers of treaties or agreements to place their trading, maritime and other commercial relations on a stable and friendly basis.

(b) Pending the conclusion of the relevant treaty or agreement, Japan will, during a period of four years from the first coming into force of the present Treaty

(1) accord to each of the Allied Powers, its nationals, products and vessels

(i) most-favored-nation treatment with respect to customs duties, charges, restrictions and other regulations on or in connection with the importation and exportation of goods;

(ii) national treatment with respect to shipping, navigation and imported goods, and with respect to natural and juridical persons and their interests – such treatment to include all matters pertaining to the levying and collection of taxes, access to the courts, the making and performance of contracts, rights to property (tangible and intangible), participation in juridical entities constituted under Japanese law, and generally the conduct of all kinds of business and professional activities;

(2) ensure that external purchases and sales of Japanese state trading enterprises shall be based solely on commercial considerations.

(c) In respect to any matter, however, Japan shall be obliged to accord to an Allied Power national treatment, or most-favored-nation treatment, only to the extent that the Allied Power concerned accords Japan national treatment or most-favored-nation treatment, as the case may be, in respect of the same matter. The reciprocity envisaged in the foregoing sentence shall be determined, in the case of products, vessels and juridical entities of, and persons domiciled in, any non-metropolitan territory of an Allied Power, and in the case of juridical entities of, and persons domiciled in, any state or province of an Allied Power having a federal government, by reference to the treatment accorded to Japan in such territory, state or province.

(d) In the application of this Article, a discriminatory measure shall not be considered to derogate from the grant of national or most-favored-nation treatment, as the case may be, if such measure is based on an exception customarily provided for in the commercial treaties of the party applying it, or on the need to safeguard that party's external financial position or balance of payments (except in respect to shipping and navigation), or on the need to maintain its essential security interests, and provided such measure is proportionate to the circumstances and not applied in an arbitrary or unreasonable manner.

(e) Japan's obligations under this Article shall not be affected by the exercise of any Allied rights under Article 14 of the present Treaty; nor shall the provisions of this Article be understood as limiting the undertakings assumed by Japan by virtue of Article 15 of the Treaty.

Article 13

(a) Japan will enter into negotiations with any of the Allied Powers, promptly upon the request of such Power or Powers, for the conclusion of bilateral or multilateral agreements relating to international civil air transport.

(b) Pending the conclusion of such agreement or agreements, Japan will, during a period of four years from the first coming into force of the present Treaty, extend to such Power treatment not less favorable with respect to air-traffic rights and privileges than those exercised by any such Powers at the date of such coming into force, and will accord complete equality of opportunity in respect to the operation and development of air services.

(c) Pending its becoming a party to the Convention on International Civil Aviation in accordance with Article 93 thereof, Japan will give effect to the provisions of that Convention applicable to the international navigation of aircraft, and will give effect to the standards, practices and procedures adopted as annexes to the Convention in accordance with the terms of the Convention.

CHAPTER V

CLAIMS AND PROPERTY

Article 14

(a) It is recognized that Japan should pay reparations to the Allied Powers for the damage and suffering caused by it during the war. Nevertheless it is also recognized that the resources of Japan are not presently sufficient, if it is to maintain a viable economy, to make complete reparation for all such damage and suffering and at the same time meet its other obligations.

Therefore,

1. Japan will promptly enter into negotiations with Allied Powers so desiring, whose present territories were occupied by Japanese forces and damaged by Japan, with a view to assisting to compensate those countries for the cost of repairing the damage done, by making available the services of the Japanese people in production, salvaging and other work for the Allied Powers in question. Such arrangements shall avoid the imposition of additional liabilities on other Allied Powers, and, where the manufacturing of raw materials is called for, they shall be supplied by the Allied Powers in question, so as not to throw any foreign exchange burden upon Japan.
2. (I) Subject to the provisions of sub-paragraph (II) below, each of the Allied Powers shall have the right to seize, retain, liquidate or otherwise dispose of all property, rights and interests of

(a) Japan and Japanese nationals,

(b) persons acting for or on behalf of Japan or Japanese nationals, and

(c) entities owned or controlled by Japan or Japanese nationals, which on the first coming into force of the present Treaty were subject to its jurisdiction. The property, rights and interests specified in this sub-paragraph shall include those now blocked, vested or in the possession or under the control of enemy property authorities of Allied Powers, which belonged to, or were held or managed on behalf of, any of the persons or entities mentioned in (a), (b) or (c) above at the time such assets came under the controls of such authorities.

(II) The following shall be excepted from the right specified in sub-paragraph (I) above:

(i) property of Japanese natural persons who during the war resided with the permission of the Government concerned in the territory of one of the Allied Powers, other than territory occupied by Japan, except property subjected to restrictions during the war and not released from such restrictions as of the date of the first coming into force of the present Treaty;

(ii) all real property, furniture and fixtures owned by the Government of Japan and used for diplomatic or consular purposes, and all personal furniture and furnishings and other private property not of an investment nature which was normally necessary for the carrying out of diplomatic and consular functions, owned by Japanese diplomatic and consular personnel;

(iii) property belonging to religious bodies or private charitable institutions and used exclusively for religious or charitable purposes;

(iv) property, rights and interests which have come within its jurisdiction in consequence of the resumption of trade and financial relations subsequent to September 2, 1945, between the country concerned and Japan, except such as have resulted from transactions contrary to the laws of the Allied Power concerned;

(v) obligations of Japan or Japanese nationals, any right, title or interest in tangible property located in Japan, interests in enterprises organized under the laws of Japan, or any paper evidence thereof; provided that this exception shall only apply to obligations of

Japan and its nationals expressed in Japanese currency.

(III) Property referred to in exceptions (i) through (v) above shall be returned subject to reasonable expenses for its preservation and administration. If any such property has been liquidated the proceeds shall be returned instead.

(IV) The right to seize, retain, liquidate or otherwise dispose of property as provided in sub-paragraph (I) above shall be exercised in accordance with the laws of the Allied Power concerned, and the owner shall have only such rights as may be given him by those laws.

(V) The Allied Powers agree to deal with Japanese trademarks and literary and artistic property rights on a basis as favorable to Japan as circumstances ruling in each country will permit.

(b) Except as otherwise provided in the present Treaty, the Allied Powers waive all reparations claims of the Allied Powers, other claims of the Allied Powers and their nationals arising out of any actions taken by Japan and its nationals in the course of the prosecution of the war, and claims of the Allied Powers for direct military costs of occupation.

Article 15

(a) Upon application made within nine months of the coming into force of the present Treaty between Japan and the Allied Power concerned, Japan will, within six months of the date of such application, return the property, tangible and intangible, and all rights or interests of any kind in Japan of each Allied Power and its nationals which was within Japan at any time between December 7, 1941, and September 2, 1945, unless the owner has freely disposed thereof without duress or fraud. Such property shall be returned free of all encumbrances and charges to which it may have become subject because of the war, and without any charges for its return. Property whose return is not applied for by or on behalf of the owner or by his Government within the prescribed period may be disposed of by the Japanese Government as it may determine. In cases where such property was within Japan on December 7, 1941, and cannot be returned or has suffered injury or damage as a result of the war, compensation will be made on terms not less favorable than the terms provided in the draft Allied Powers Property Compensation Law approved by the Japanese Cabinet on July 13, 1951.

(b) With respect to industrial property rights impaired during the war, Japan will continue to accord to the Allied Powers and their nationals benefits no less than those heretofore accorded by Cabinet Orders No. 309 effective September 1, 1949, No. 12 effective January 28, 1950, and No. 9 effective February 1, 1950, all as now amended, provided such nationals have applied for such benefits within the time limits prescribed therein.

(c) (i) Japan acknowledges that the literary and artistic property rights which existed in Japan on December 6, 1941, in respect to the published and unpublished works of the Allied Powers and their nationals have continued in force since that date, and recognizes those rights which have arisen, or but for the war would have arisen, in Japan since that date, by the operation of any conventions and agreements to which Japan was a party on that date, irrespective of whether or not such conventions or agreements were abrogated or suspended upon or since the outbreak of war by the domestic law of Japan or of the Allied Power concerned.

(ii) Without the need for application by the proprietor of the right and without the payment of any fee or compliance with any other formality, the period from December 7, 1941, until the coming into force of the present Treaty between Japan and the Allied Power concerned shall be excluded from the running of the normal term of such rights; and such period, with an additional period of six months, shall be excluded from the time within which a literary work must be translated into Japanese in order to obtain translating rights in Japan.

Article 16

As an expression of its desire to indemnify those members of the armed forces of the Allied Powers who suffered undue hardships while prisoners of war of Japan, Japan will transfer its assets and those of its nationals in countries which were neutral during the war, or which were at war with any of the Allied Powers, or, at its option, the equivalent of such assets to the International Committee of the Red Cross which shall liquidate such assets and distribute the resultant fund to appropriate national agencies, for the benefit of former prisoners of war and their families on such basis as it may determine to be equitable. The categories of assets described in Article 14 (a) 2(II) (ii) through (v) of the present Treaty shall be excepted from transfer, as well as assets of Japanese natural persons not residents of Japan on the first coming into force of the Treaty. It is equally understood that the transfer provision of this Article has no application to the 19,770 shares in the Bank for International Settlements presently owned by Japanese financial institutions.

Article 17

(a) Upon the request of any of the Allied Powers, the Japanese Government shall review and revise in conformity with international law any decision or order of the Japanese Prize Courts in cases involving ownership rights of nationals of that Allied Power and shall supply copies of all documents comprising the records of these cases, including the decisions taken and orders issued. In any case in which such review or revision shows that restoration is due, the provisions of Article 15 shall apply to the property concerned.

(b) The Japanese Government shall take the necessary measures to enable nationals of any of the Allied Powers at any time within one year from the coming into force of the present Treaty between Japan and the Allied Power concerned to submit to the appropriate Japanese authorities for review any judgement given by a Japanese court between December 7, 1941, and such coming into force, in any proceedings in which any such national was unable to make adequate presentation of his case either as plaintiff or defendant. The Japanese Government shall provide that, where the national has suffered injury by reason of any such judgment, he shall be restored in the position in which he was before the judgment was given or shall be afforded such relief as may be just and equitable in the circumstances.

Article 18

(a) It is recognized that the intervention of the state of war has not affected the obligation to pay pecuniary debts arising out of obligations and contracts (including those in respect of bonds) which existed and rights which were acquired before the existence of a state of war, and which arc due by the Government or nationals of Japan to the Government or nationals of one of the Allied Powers, or are due by the Government or nationals of one of the Allied Powers to the Government or nationals of Japan. The intervention of a state of war shall equally not be regarded as affecting the obligation to consider on their merits claims for loss or damage to property or for personal injury or death which arose before the existence of a state of war, and which may be presented or re-presented by the Government of one of the Allied Powers to the Government of Japan, or by the Government of Japan to any of the Governments of the Allied Powers. The provisions of this paragraph are without prejudice to the rights conferred by Article 14.

(b) Japan affirms its liability for the prewar external debt of the Japanese State and for debts of corporate bodies subsequently declared to be liabilities of the Japanese State, and expresses its intention to enter into negotiations at an early date with its creditors with respect to the resumption of payments on those debts; to encourage negotiations in respect to other prewar claims and obligations; and to facilitate the transfer of sums accordingly.

Article 19

(a) Japan waives all claims of Japan and its nationals against the Allied Powers and their nationals arising out of the war or out of actions taken because of the existence of a state of war, and waives all claims arising from the presence, operations or actions of forces or authorities of any of the Allied Powers in Japanese territory prior to the coming into force of the present Treaty.

(b) The foregoing waiver includes any claims arising out of actions taken by any of the Allied Powers with respect to Japanese ships between September 1, 1939, and the coming into force of the present Treaty, as well as any claims and debts arising in respect to Japanese prisoners of war and civilian internees in the hands of the Allied Powers, but does not include Japanese claims specifically recognized in the laws of any Allied Power enacted since September 2, 1945.

(c) Subject to reciprocal renunciation, the Japanese Government also renounces all claims (including debts) against Germany and German nationals on behalf of the Japanese Government and Japanese nationals, including inter-governmental claims and claims for loss or damage sustained during the war, but excepting (a) claims in respect of contracts entered into and rights acquired before September 1, 1939, and (b) claims arising out of trade and financial relations between Japan and Germany after September 2, 1945. Such renunciation shall not prejudice actions taken in accordance with Articles 16 and 20 of the present Treaty.

(d) Japan recognizes the validity of all acts and omissions done during the period of occupation under or in consequence of directives of the occupation authorities or authorized by Japanese law at that time, and will take no action subjecting Allied nationals to civil or criminal liability arising out of such acts or omissions.

Article 20

Japan will take all necessary measures to ensure such disposition of German assets in Japan as has been or may be determined by those powers entitled under the Protocol of the proceedings of the Berlin Conference of 1945 to dispose of those assets, and pending the final disposition of such assets will be responsible for the conservation and administration thereof.

Article 21

Notwithstanding the provisions of Article 25 of the present Treaty, China shall be entitled to the benefits of Articles 10 and 14(a)2; and Korea to the benefits of Articles 2, 4, 9 and 12 of the present Treaty.

CHAPTER VI

SETTLEMENT OF DISPUTES

Article 22

If in the opinion of any Party to the present Treaty there has arisen a dispute concerning the interpretation or execution of the

Treaty, which is not settled by reference to a special claims tribunal or by other agreed means, the dispute shall, at the requcst of any party thereto, be referred for decision to the International Court of Justice. Japan and those Allied Powers which are not already parties to the Statute of the International Court of Justice will deposit with the Registrar of the Court, at the time of their respective ratifications of the present Treaty, and in conformity with the resolution of the United Nations Security Council, dated October 15, 1946, a general declaration accepting the jurisdiction, without special agreement, of the Court generally in respect to all disputes of the character referred to in this Article.

CHAPTER VII

FINAL CLAUSES

Article 23

(a) The present Treaty shall be ratified by the States which sign it, including Japan, and will come into force for all the States which have then ratified it, when instruments of ratification have been deposited by Japan and by a majority, including the United States of America as the principal occupying Power, of the following States, namely Australia, Canada, Ceylon, France, Indonesia, the Kingdom of the Netherlands, New Zealand, Pakistan, the Republic of the Philippines, the United Kingdom of Great Britain and Northern Ireland, and the United States of America. The present Treaty shall come into force for each State which subsequently ratifies it, on the date of the deposit of its instrument of ratification.

(b) If the Treaty has not come into force within nine months after the date of the deposit of Japan's ratification, any State which has ratified it may bring the Treaty into force between itself and Japan by a notification to that effect given to the Governments of Japan and the United States of America not later than three years after the date of deposit of Japan's ratification.

Article 24

All instruments of ratification shall be deposited with the Government of the United States of America which will notify all the signatory States of each such deposit, of the date of the coming into force of the Treaty under paragraph (a) of Article 23, and of any notifications made under paragraph (b) of Article 23.

Article 25

For the purposes of the present Treaty the Allied Powers shall be the States at war with Japan, or any State which previously formed a part of the territory of a State named in Article 23, provided that in each case the State concerned has signed and ratified the Treaty. Subject to the provisions of Article 21, the present Treaty shall not confer any rights, titles or benefits on any State which is not an Allied Power as herein defined; nor shall any right, title or interest of Japan be deemed to be diminished or prejudiced by any provision of the Treaty in favor of a State which is not an Allied Power as so defined.

Article 26

Japan will be prepared to conclude with any State which signed or adhered to the United Nations Declaration of January 1, 1942, and which is at war with Japan, or with any State which previously formed a part of the territory of a State named in Article 23, which is not a signatory of the present Treaty, a bilateral Treaty of Peace on the same or substantially the same terms as are provided for in the present Treaty, but this obligation on the part of Japan will expire three years after the first coming into force of the present Treaty. Should Japan make a peace settlement or war claims settlement with any State granting that State greater advantages than those provided by the present Treaty, those same advantages shall be extended to the parties to the present Treaty.

Article 27

The present Treaty shall be deposited in the archives of the Government of the United States of America which shall furnish each signatory State with a certified copy thereof.

Source: Treaty of Peace with Japan, Signed at San Francisco on 8 September 1951 (*United Nations Treaty Series,* vol. 136, no. 1832, 1952, pp. 46–77).

Appendix III

Japan–Korea Treaty on Basic Relations,* Tokyo, 22 June 1965

TREATY ON BASIC RELATIONS BETWEEN JAPAN AND THE REPUBLIC OF KOREA

Japan and the Republic of Korea,

Considering the historical background of relationship between their peoples and their mutual desire for good neighborliness and for the normalization of their relations on the basis of the principle of mutual respect for sovereignty;

Recognizing the importance of their close cooperation in conformity with the principles of the Charter of the United Nations to the promotion of their mutual welfare and common interests and to the maintenance of international peace and security; and

Recalling the relevant provisions of the Treaty of Peace with Japan signed at the city of San Francisco on September 8, 1951 and the Resolution 195(III) adopted by the United Nations General Assembly on December 12, 1948;

Have resolved to conclude the present Treaty on Basic Relations and have accordingly appointed as their Plenipotentiaries,

Japan:
Etsusaburo Shiina, Minister for Foreign Affairs of Japan
Shinichi Takasugi

The Republic of Korea:
Tong Won Lee, Minister of Foreign Affairs of the Republic of Korea

* Reproduced from the official English text, provided by the Embassy of Japan in Washington, DC. On 22 June 1965, agreements were also concluded between Japan and Korea on fisheries, property and claims, Korean residents in Japan, cultural assets, and settlement of disputes. These agreements were concluded in Japanese and Korean only.

Dong Jo Kim, Ambassador Extraordinary and Plenipotentiary of the Republic of Korea

Who, having communicated to each other their full powers found to be in good and due form, have agreed upon the following articles:

Article I

Diplomatic and consular relations shall be established between the High Contracting Parties. The High Contracting Parties shall exchange diplomatic envoys with the Ambassadorial rank without delay. The High Contracting Parties will also establish consulates at locations to be agreed upon by the two Governments.

Article II

It is confirmed that all treaties or agreements concluded between the Empire of Japan and the Empire of Korea on or before August 22, 1910 are already null and void.

Article III

It is confirmed that the Government of the Republic of Korea is the only lawful Government in Korea as specified in the Resolution 195(III) of the United Nations General Assembly.

Article IV

(a) The High Contracting Parties will be guided by the principles of the Charter of the United Nations in their mutual relations.

(b) The High Contracting Parties will cooperate in conformity with the principles of the Charter of the United Nations in promoting their mutual welfare and common interests.

Article V

The High Contracting Parties will enter into negotiations at the earliest practicable date for the conclusion of treaties or agreements to place their trading, maritime and other commercial relations on a stable and friendly basis.

Article VI

The High Contracting Parties will enter into negotiations at the earliest practicable date for the conclusion of an agreement relating to civil air transport.

Article VII

The present Treaty shall be ratified. The instruments of ratification shall be exchanged at Seoul as soon as possible. The present Treaty shall enter into force as from the date on which the instruments of ratification are exchanged.

IN WITNESS WHEREOF, the respective Plenipotentiaries have signed the present Treaty and have affixed thereto their seals.

DONE in duplicate at Tokyo, this twenty-second day of June of the year one thousand nine hundred and sixty-five in the Japanese, Korean, and English languages, each text being equally authentic. In case of any divergence of interpretation, the English text shall prevail.

FOR JAPAN:
Etsusaburo Shiina
Shinichi Takasugi

FOR THE REPUBLIC OF KOREA:
Tong Won Lee
Dong Jo Kim

AGREEMENT BETWEEN JAPAN AND THE REPUBLIC OF KOREA CONCERNING FISHERIES,* Tokyo, 22 June 1965

Japan and the Republic of Korea

Desiring that the maximum sustained productivity of the fishery resources in waters of mutual interest be maintained;

Firmly believing that the conservation of such resources and their rational exploitation and development will serve the interests of both countries;

* Translated for *International Legal Materials* by Dr. Sung Yoon Cho, Legal Specialist, Far Eastern Law Division, Library of Congress.

Confirming that the principle of freedom of the high seas shall be respected unless otherwise prescribed by special provisions in the present Agreement;

Recognizing the desirability of eliminating the causes of disputes which may arise from their geographical proximity and the intermingling of their respective fisheries; and

Desiring mutual cooperation for the development of their fisheries,

Have agreed as follows:

Article I

1. The High Contracting Parties mutually recognize that each High Contracting Party has the right to establish a sea zone (hereinafter 'fishery zone'), extending not more than 12 nautical miles from its respective coastal base line, over which it will have exclusive jurisdiction with respect to fisheries. However, in case either High Contracting Party uses the straight base line for the establishment of its fishery zone, the straight base line shall be determined through consultation with the other High Contracting Party.
2. The High Contracting Parties shall not present objections when one Party excludes the fishing vessels of the other Party from engaging in fishing operations in its fishery zone.
3. Areas where the fishery zones of the High Contracting Parties overlap shall be divided in two by straight lines joining the ends of the overlapping areas with the mid-points of straight lines drawn across the areas at their widest points.

Article II

1. The High Contracting Parties shall establish a joint control zone encircled by the lines described below (excluding territorial waters and the Republic of Korea's fishery zone).

   (a) A line north on the 124th E meridian north of 37°30' N.

   (b) Thence, a line joining the following coordinates in order:

(I)	37° 30' N,	124° E
(II)	36° 45' N,	124° 30' E
(III)	33° 30' N,	124° 30' E
(IV)	32° 30' N,	126° E
(V)	32° 30' N,	127° E
(VI)	34° 34' 30" N,	129° 2' 50" E
(VII)	34° 44' 10" N,	129° 8' E
(VIII)	34° 50' N,	129° 14' E
(IX)	35° 30' N,	130° E
(X)	37° 30' N,	131° 10' E
(XI)	High peak of Uamnyong	

Article III

Until conservation measures necessary for maintaining the maximum sustained productivity of fishery resources are implemented on the basis of exhaustive scientific research, the provisional fishery control measures listed in the Annex, which forms an integral part of this Agreement, shall be enforced in the joint control zones with respect to dragnet fishing and surrounding net fishing, and mackerel fishing by fishing vessels of not less than 60 tons. (Ton represents gross ton. The tonnage shall be indicated by deducting the tonnage permitted for improving living quarters on the vessels.)

Article IV

1. The right of control (including the right to halt and inspect vessels) and jurisdiction in waters outside the exclusive fishery zone shall be exercised only by the High Contracting Party to which the ship belongs.
2. The High Contracting Parties shall exercise appropriate guidance and supervision in order to guarantee the faithful observance of the provisional fishery control measures by their own nationals and fishing vessels, and shall carry out domestic measures, including appropriate penalties against violations thereof.

Article V

Joint resources survey zones shall be established outside of the joint control zones. The scope of the said zones and the surveys to be conducted within these zones shall be determined through consultation between the two High Contracting Parties, on the basis of recommendations made by the Joint Fisheries Commission provided for in Article VI.

Article VI

1. The High Contracting Parties shall establish and maintain the Japan–Republic of Korea Joint Fisheries Commission (hereinafter referred to as the 'Commission') in order to realize the purposes of this Agreement.
2. The Commission shall be composed of two national sections, each consisting of three members appointed by the Governments of the respective High Contracting Parties.
3. All resolutions, recommendations, and other decisions of the Commission shall be made only with the concurrence of the national sections.
4. The Commission may decide upon and revise, as occasion may require, rules for the conduct of its meetings.
5. The Commission shall meet at least once each year and, in addition, it may meet as requested by one of the national sections. The date and place of the first meeting shall be determined by agreement between the High Contracting Parties.
6. At its first meeting, the Commission shall select a Chairman and Vice-Chairman, one from each national section. The Chairman and Vice-Chairman shall hold office for a period of one year. During the succeeding years selection of a Chairman and a Vice-Chairman from the national sections shall be made in such a manner as will provide each High Contracting Party in turn with representation in those offices.
7. A standing secretariat shall be established under the Commission to carry out the business of the Commission.
8. The official languages of the Commission shall be Japanese and Korean. Proposals and data may be presented in either official language, or, if necessary, they may be presented in English.
9. In the event that the Commission concludes that joint expenses are necessary, such expenses shall be paid by the Commission through contributions made by the High Contracting

Parties in the form and proportion recommended by the Commission and approved by the High Contracting Parties.

10. The Commission may delegate the disbursement of funds for the joint expenses of the Commission.

Article VII

1. The Commission shall perform the following functions:

(a) The Commission shall make recommendations to the High Contracting Parties concerning scientific research for the purpose of studying the fishery resources in the sea areas of mutual interest and concerning control measures within the joint control zones to be carried out on the basis of the results of such research and study;

(b) The Commission shall make recommendations to the High Contracting Parties on the scope of the joint resources survey zones;

(c) When it is deemed necessary, the Commission shall review matters concerning provisional fishery control measures and make recommendations to the High Contracting Parties concerning measures to be taken as a result of such review (including the revision of the provisional control measures);

(d) The Commission shall review necessary matters concerning safe operations and order among the fishing vessels of the High Contracting Parties and general policies for settling accidents occurring at sea between the fishing vessels of the High Contracting Parties, and shall make recommendations to the High Contracting Parties concerning measures to be taken as a result of such review;

(e) The Commission shall compile and study data, statistics, and records which the High Contracting Parties submit at the request of the Commission;

(f) The Commission shall consider and make recommendations to the High Contracting Parties concerning the enactment of schedules of equivalent penalties for violations of this Agreement;

(g) The Commission shall submit annually its business report to the High Contracting Parties; and

(h) The Commission shall study the various technical questions arising in connection with the implementation of this Agreement, and shall, when it is deemed necessary, make recommendations to the High Contracting Parties on the steps to be taken.

2. The Commission may establish such subsidiary organs as it deems necessary for the performance of its functions.
3. The Governments of the High Contracting Parties shall respect to the extent possible the recommendations made by the Commission in accordance with the provisions of paragraph 1.

Article VIII

1. The High Contracting Parties shall take measures as may be appropriate to guarantee the observance of international practices concerning navigation by their nationals and fishing vessels, to promote safe operations between the fishing vessels of the High Contracting Parties, to maintain proper order among them, and to achieve smooth and speedy settlements of accidents arising at sea between the fishing vessels of the High Contracting Parties.
2. In order to achieve the objective of paragraph 1, the authorities concerned of the two High Contracting Parties shall maintain as closely as possible mutual contact and cooperation.

Article IX

1. Any dispute between the High Contracting Parties concerning the interpretation or implementation of this Agreement shall be settled primarily through diplomatic channels.
2. Any dispute which cannot be settled under the provision of paragraph 1 shall be submitted for decision to an arbitration commission of three arbitrators; one to be appointed by the Government of each High Contracting Party within a period of thirty days from the date of receipt by the Government of either High Contracting Party from that of the other High Contracting Party of a note requesting arbitration of the dispute; and the third to be agreed upon by the two arbitrators so chosen or to be nominated by the Government of a

third power as agreed upon by the two arbitrators within a further period of thirty days. However, the third arbitrator must not be a national of either High Contracting Party.

3. If, within the periods respectively referred to, the Government of either High Contracting Party fails to appoint an arbitrator, or the third arbitrator of the third nation is not agreed upon, the arbitration commission shall be composed of one arbitrator to be nominated by the Government of each of two nations respectively chosen by the Government of each High Contracting Party within a period of thirty days, and the third arbitrator to be nominated by the Government of a third power decided upon by agreement between the Governments so chosen.
4. The Governments of the High Contracting Parties shall accept decisions rendered by the arbitration commission established in accordance with the provisions of this Article.

Article X

1. The present Agreement shall be ratified. The instruments of ratification shall be exchanged at Seoul as soon as possible. This Agreement shall enter into force as from the date on which the instruments of ratification are exchanged.
2. The present Agreement shall continue in force for a period of five years and thereafter until one year from the day on which a High Contracting Party shall give notice to the other High Contracting Party of an intention to terminate the Agreement.

In witness whereof, the undersigned, duly authorized by the respective Governments, have signed the present Agreement.

Done in duplicate at Tokyo, this twenty-second day of June of the year one thousand nine hundred and sixty-five in the Japanese and Korean languages, each text being equally authentic.

For Japan

Etsusaburo Shiina
Shinichi Takasugi

For the Republic of Korea

Tong Won Lee
Dong Jo Kim

AGREEMENT BETWEEN JAPAN AND THE REPUBLIC OF KOREA CONCERNING THE SETTLEMENT OF PROBLEMS IN REGARD TO PROPERTY AND CLAIMS AND ECONOMIC CO-OPERATION,* Tokyo, 22 June 1965

Japan and the Republic of Korea

Desiring to settle problems regarding the property of both countries and their peoples and the claims between both countries and between their peoples; and

Desiring to promote economic co-operation between the two countries,

Have agreed as follows:

Article I

1. Japan shall supply the Republic of Korea with:

   (a) Products of Japan and the services of Japanese people, free of charge, the total value of which will be so much in yen as shall be equivalent to three hundred million United States dollars ($300,000,000), at present computed at one hundred and eight billion yen (¥108,000,000,000), within a period of ten years of the date on which the present Agreement enters into force. The supply of products and services each year shall be limited to so much in yen as shall be equivalent to thirty million United States dollars ($30,000,000), at present computed at ten billion eight hundred million yen (¥10,800,000,000); when the supply of any one year falls short of this amount, the remainder shall be added to the amount for the next and subsequent years. However, the maximum amount supplied for any one year may be increased by agreement between the Governments of the High Contracting Parties.

   (b) Long-term and low-interest loans up to so much in yen as shall be equivalent to two hundred million United States dollars ($200,000,000), at present computed at seventy-two billion yen (¥72,000,000,000), which are requested by the Government of the Republic of Korea and which will be

* Translated for *International Legal Materials* by Dr. Sung Yoon Cho, Legal Specialist, Far Eastern Law Division, Library of Congress.

covered by procuring the products of Japan and the services of Japanese people necessary for implementing the enterprises to be decided upon in accordance with arrangements to be concluded under paragraph 3 within a period of ten years of the date on which the present Agreement enters into force. These loans shall be extended by the Overseas Economic Co-operation Fund of Japan, and the Government of Japan shall take the necessary measures to enable the Fund to secure the funds for equal annual loans. The aforesaid supply and loans must serve the economic development of the Republic of Korea.

2. There shall be established a Joint Committee composed of representatives of the two Governments as an organ for consultation between them, with the power to make recommendations on matters concerning the implementation of the present Agreement.

3. The two Governments of the High Contracting Parties shall take measures necessary for the implementation of this Article.

Article II

1. The High Contracting Parties confirm that the problems concerning property, rights, and interests of the two High Contracting Parties and their peoples (including juridical persons) and the claims between the High Contracting Parties and between their peoples, including those stipulated in Article IV(a) of the Peace Treaty with Japan signed at the city of San Francisco on September 8, 1951, have been settled completely and finally.

2. The provisions of this Article shall not affect the following (excluding those which become the objects of special measures taken by either of the High Contracting Parties prior to the date of the signing of the present Agreement):

   (a) The property, rights, and interests of the people of either High Contracting Party who have ever resided in the territory of the other High Contracting Party in the period between August 15, 1947, and the date of the signing of the present Agreement; and

   (b) The property, rights, and interests of either High Contracting Party and its people which were acquired or brought under the control of the other High Contracting Party in the course of ordinary contacts after August 15, 1945.

3. As a condition to comply with the provisions of paragraph 2 above, no claims shall be made with respect to the measures relating to the property, rights, and interests of either High Contracting Party and its people which were brought under the control of the other High Contracting Party on the date of the signing of the present Agreement, or to all the claims of either High Contracting Party and its people arising from the causes which occurred prior to that date.

Article III

1. Any dispute between the High Contracting Parties concerning the interpretation or the implementation of this Agreement shall be settled primarily through diplomatic channels.
2. Any dispute which cannot be settled under the provision of paragraph 1 above shall be submitted for decision to an arbitral commission of three arbitrators; one to be appointed by the Government of each High Contracting Party within a period of thirty days from the date of receipt by the Government of either High Contracting Party from that of the other High Contracting Party of a note requesting arbitration of the dispute; and the third to be agreed upon by the two arbitrators so chosen or to be nominated by the Government of a third power as agreed upon by the two arbitrators within a further period of thirty days. However, the third arbitrator must not be a national of either High Contracting Party.
3. If, within the periods respectively referred to, the Government of either High Contracting Party fails to appoint an arbitrator, or the third arbitrator or the third nation is not agreed upon, the arbitral commission shall be composed of one arbitrator to be nominated by the Government of each of two nations respectively chosen by the Government of each High Contracting Party within a period of thirty days, and the third arbitrator to be nominated by the Government of a third power decided upon by agreement between the Governments so chosen.

4. The Governments of the High Contracting Parties shall accept decisions rendered by the arbitral commission established in accordance with the provisions of this Article.

Article IV

1. The present Agreement shall be ratified. The instruments of ratification shall be exchanged at Seoul as soon as possible. The present Agreement shall enter into force as from the date on which the instruments of ratification are exchanged.

In witness whereof, the undersigned, duly authorized thereto by their respective Governments, have signed the present Agreement.

Done in duplicate at Tokyo, this twenty-second day of June of the year one thousand nine hundred and sixty-five in the Japanese and Korean languages, each text being equally authentic.

For Japan	For the Republic of Korea
Etsusaburo Shiina	Tong Won Lee
Shinichi Takasugi	Dong Jo Kim

AGREEMENT BETWEEN JAPAN AND THE REPUBLIC OF KOREA CONCERNING THE LEGAL STATUS AND TREATMENT OF THE PEOPLE OF THE REPUBLIC OF KOREA RESIDING IN JAPAN,* Tokyo, 22 June 1965

Japan and the Republic of Korea

Considering the fact that the nationals of the Republic of Korea residing in Japan for many years have come to possess a special relationship with Japanese society; and

Recognizing that enabling the nationals of the Republic of Korea to lead a stabilized life under the Japanese social order will contribute to the promotion of friendly relations between the two countries and their peoples,

Have agreed as follows:

* Translated for *International Legal Materials* by Dr. Sung Yoon Cho, Legal Specialist, Far Eastern Law Division, Library of Congress.

Article I

1. The Government of Japan will permit a national of the Republic of Korea falling under any one of the following categories to reside permanently in Japan if within five years of the date on which the present Agreement enters into force he applies, in accordance with the procedures determined by the Government of Japan for the implementation of the present Agreement, for permission for permanent residence:

   (a) A person who resided in Japan prior to August 15, 1945, and who has continuously resided there until the application has been filed; and

   (b) A person who is born on or after August 16, 1945, and within five years of the date on which the present Agreement enters into force, who is a lineal descendant of a person mentioned in (a) above, and who has continuously resided in Japan therefrom until the application has been filed.

2. The Government of Japan will permit a national of the Republic of Korea, born after the lapse of five years from the date on which the present Agreement enters into force, and who is the child of a person permitted to reside permanently in Japan in accordance with the provisions of paragraph 1 above, to reside permanently in Japan when permission for permanent residence is applied for within sixty days of the date of his birth in accordance with the procedures determined by the Government of Japan for the implementation of the present Agreement.
3. The term within which application for permission for permanent residence is to be filed for a person falling under paragraph 1(b) above and who is born after the lapse of 4 years and 10 months from the date on which the present Agreement enters into force shall be 60 days beginning from the date of his birth notwithstanding the provisions of paragraph 1 above.
4. No fee shall be levied on the aforesaid application and permission.

Article II

1. The Government of Japan agrees to enter into consultations, if requested by the Government of the Republic of Korea,

within 25 years of the date on which the present Agreement enters into force, with a view to the residence in Japan of a national of the Republic of Korea born in Japan as a lineal descendant of a person who has been permitted to reside permanently in Japan in accordance with the provisions of Article I.

2. In the consultations under paragraph 1 above, the spirit and purposes which form the basis of the present Agreement shall be respected.

Article III

A national of the Republic of Korea who has been permitted to reside permanently in Japan in accordance with the provisions of Article I shall not be forcibly deported from Japan unless after the date on which the present Agreement enters into force he commits an act whereby he falls under any one of the following categories:

(a) A person who has been punished with a penalty heavier than imprisonment in Japan for crimes concerning insurrection or crimes concerning foreign aggression (excluding a person whose sentence has been suspended or one who has been punished on charges of joining in an insurrection);

(b) A person who has been punished with a penalty heavier than imprisonment in Japan for crimes relating to diplomatic relations, and a person who has been punished with a penalty heavier than imprisonment for criminal acts against the chief of State, a diplomatic envoy, or a diplomatic mission of a foreign country and thereby causing an injury to the important diplomatic interests of Japan;

(c) A person who has been punished with penal servitude or imprisonment for life or for not less than three years (excluding a person whose sentence has been suspended) on charges of violation of Japanese laws and ordinances concerning control of narcotics for the purpose of gain, and a person who has been punished three or more times (twice or more for one who has been punished three or more times for acts committed prior to the date on which the present Agreement enters into force) on charges of violation of Japanese laws and ordinances; and

(d) A person who has been punished with penal servitude or imprisonment for life or for seven or more years on charges of violation of Japanese laws and ordinances.

Article IV

The Government of Japan will give due consideration to the following matters:

(a) Matters concerning the education, livelihood protection, and national health insurance in Japan for a national of the Republic of Korea who has been permitted to reside permanently in Japan in accordance with the provisions of Article I; and

(b) Matters concerning the carrying of property and the remitting of funds to the Republic of Korea in the case of a national of the Republic of Korea who has been permitted to reside permanently in Japan in accordance with the provisions of Article I (including one who is qualified to apply for permission for permanent residence in accordance with the provisions of the same Article), who has abandoned the intention to reside permanently in Japan, and who returns to the Republic of Korea.

Article V

It is confirmed that a national of the Republic of Korea who has been permitted to reside permanently in Japan in accordance with the provisions of Article I shall be subject to the application of Japanese laws and ordinances applicable equally to all aliens, concerning all matters including emigration, immigration, and residence, except for the cases specifically prescribed in the present Agreement.

Article VI

The present Agreement shall be ratified. The instruments of ratification shall be exchanged at Seoul as soon as possible. The present Agreement shall enter into force thirty days after the date on which the instruments of ratification are exchanged.

In witness whereof, the undersigned, being duly authorized thereto by their respective Governments, have signed the present Agreement.

Done in duplicate at Tokyo, this twenty-second day of June of the year one thousand nine hundred and sixty-five in the Japanese and Korean languages, each text being equally authentic.

For Japan
Etsusaburo Shiina
Shinichi Takasugi

For the Republic of Korea
Tong Won Lee
Dong Jo Kim

(Agreed minutes interpreting the Agreement have been omitted)

Appendix IV

Treaty of Peace and Friendship between Japan and the People's Republic of China, 12 August 1978

Japan and the People's Republic of China, recalling with satisfaction that, since the Government of Japan and the Government of the People's Republic of China issued a joint communiqué in Peking on 29th September 1972, the friendly relations between the two Governments and the peoples of the two countries have developed greatly on a new basis, confirming that the abovementioned joint communiqué constitutes the basis of the relations of peace and friendship between the two countries and that the principles enunciated in the joint communiqué should be strictly observed, confirming that the principles of the Charter of the United Nations should be fully respected, hoping to contribute to peace and stability in Asia and in the world, for the purpose of solidifying and developing the relations of peace and friendship between the two countries, have resolved to conclude a Treaty of Peace and Friendship and for that purpose have appointed as their plenipotentiaries:

Japan	Minister for Foreign Affairs Sunao Sonoda
People's Republic of China	Minister for Foreign Affairs Huang Hua

who, having communicated to each other their full powers, found to be in good and due form, have agreed as follows:

Article 1

1. The contracting parties shall develop relations of perpetual peace and friendship between the two countries on the basis of the principles of mutual respect for sovereignty and territorial integrity,

mutual non-aggression, non-interference in each other's internal affairs, equality and mutual benefit and peaceful coexistence.

2. The contracting parties confirm that, in conformity with the foregoing principles and the principles of the Charter of the United Nations, they shall in their mutual relations settle all disputes by peaceful means and shall refrain from the use or threat of force.

Article 2

The contracting parties declare that neither of them should seek hegemony in the Asia-Pacific region or in any other region and that each is opposed to efforts by any other country or group of countries to establish such hegemony.

Article 3

The contracting parties shall, in good-neighbourly and friendly spirit and in conformity with the principles of equality and mutual benefit and non-interference in each other's internal affairs, endeavour to further develop economic and cultural relations between the two countries and to promote exchanges between the peoples of the two countries.

Article 4

The present Treaty shall not affect the position of either contracting party regarding its relations with third countries.

Article 5

1. The present Treaty shall be ratified and shall enter into force on the date of the exchange of instruments of ratification which shall take place at Tokyo. The present Treaty shall remain in force for ten years and thereafter shall continue to be in force until terminated in accordance with the provisions of paragraph 2.

2. Either contracting party may, by giving one year's written notice to the other contracting party, terminate the present Treaty at the end of the initial ten year period or at any time thereafter.

In witness whereof the respective plenipotentiaries have signed the present Treaty and have affixed thereto their seals.

Source: *Japan* (London, Embassy of Japan), no. 21, 16 August 1978

NOTES

1 INTRODUCTION

1 For a discussion of the origins and development of the line of policy associated with Yoshida, see Michio Muramatsu and Ellis S. Krauss, 'The Conservative Party Line and the Development of Patterned Pluralism', in Kōzō Yamamura and Yasukichi Yasuba, eds, *The Political Economy of Japan*: vol. I *The Domestic Transformation* (Stanford, California, Stanford University Press, 1987), pp. 517–36. Also Kenneth B. Pyle, *The Japanese Question: Power and Purpose in a New Era* (Washington, DC, The AEI Press, 1992), pp. 25–8, 32–6. Muramatsu and Krauss use the term 'Hoshu – Honryū' – literally, 'Mainstream Conservatism', to refer to 'a policy line that may . . . be traced back to Yoshida' (p. 518).

2 Yoshida had always been opposed to labelling the distinctive Japanese policy line of the post-war era as the 'Yoshida Doctrine' (Pyle, pp. 25–6, footnote).

3 A recent exposition of the neo-mercantilist thesis is to be found in William R. Nester, *Japan's Growing Power over East Asia and the World Economy* (Basingstoke, The Macmillan Press, 1990).

4 For a succinct argument that Japan '. . . will not, . . ., take a strong leadership role for one simple reason: it does not have to do so', see Bill Emmott, 'The Economic Source of Japan's Foreign Policy' (*Survival*, vol. 34 no. 2, Summer 1992, pp. 50–70), p. 69.

5 See, for example, Masahide Shibusawa, *Japan and the Asian Pacific Region: Profile of Change* (London, Croom Helm for the Royal Institute of International Affairs (RIIA), 1984); Shirō Saitō, *Japan at the Summit: Its Role in the Western Alliance and in Asian Pacific Co-operation* (London, Routledge for RIIA, 1990).

6 Adam Smith, *The Wealth of Nations* (1776); Herbert Spencer, *The Principles of Sociology*, vol. II/2 (New York, Appleton, 1925–1929), pp. 568–602; E. F. Hecksher, *Mercantilism* (London, Allen & Unwin; New York, Macmillan, 2 vols, rev. edn, 1955); Harold Lasswell, 'The Garrison State and Specialists in Violence', (*American Journal of Sociology*, vol. XLVI no. 4, Jan. 1941, pp. 455–68); Paul Kennedy, *The Rise and Fall of the Great Powers: Economic change and Military Conflict from 1500 to 2000* (New York, Random House, 1987).

7 Akira Iriye, *Power and Culture: The Japanese American War, 1941–1945* (Cambridge, Mass., Harvard University Press, 1981), p. vii.
8 George Sansom, *Japan in World History* (London, George Allen & Unwin Ltd, 1952), pp. 33–4, 36; Junichi Kyōgoku, *The Political Dynamics of Japan* (translated by Nobutaka Ike, Tokyo, University of Tokyo Press, 1987), pp. 80–1, 130–2, 145, 153–74.
9 Gerald L. Curtis, *The Japanese Way of Politics* (New York, Columbia University Press, 1988), pp. 236, 248.

2 THE HISTORICAL DIMENSION OF JAPAN'S ASIA POLICY

1 See J. K. Fairbank, ed., *The Chinese World Order: Traditional China's Foreign Relations* (Cambridge, Mass., Harvard University Press, 1968); M. Frederick Nelson, *Korea and the Old Orders in Eastern Asia* (Baton Rouge, Louisiana State University Press, 1946).
2 Ryūsaku Tsunoda, Wm. Theodore de Bary and Donald Keene, eds, *Sources of Japanese Tradition:* vol. I (New York, Columbia University Press, 1964), p. 10.
3 Ibid, p. 9.
4 George Sansom, *Japan: a Short Cultural History* (London, The Cresset Press, 2nd edn revised, October, 1952), pp. 36, 54–5, 62 note 2, 64–9, 83–109.
5 Heita Kawakatsu, 'The National Seclusion Policy Reappraised' (*Japan Echo*, vol. XIX no. 2, Summer 1992), pp. 68–9.
6 George Sansom, *A History of Japan to 1334* (London, The Cresset Press, 1958), pp. 136–7, 422–3; *A History of Japan 1334–1615* (London, The Cresset Press, 1961), pp. 9, 166–77, 266–70.
7 *Sources of Japanese Tradition:* vol. I, pp. 316–19; Delmer M. Brown, *Nationalism in Japan: an Introductory Historical Analysis* (New York, Russell & Russell, 1971), p. 47.
8 Miao-Ling M. Tjoa, 'Korean Embassies in the Tokugawa Period' (*Japan Foundation Newsletter*, vol. XXI no. 1, 1993), pp. 17–18, 23 note 4. See also p. 23 note 2 for a discussion of the origin and use of the term 'sakoku'.
9 Brown, p. 61.
10 *Sources of Japanese Tradition:* vol. II, pp. 9–22, 70–3; Martin Collcutt, 'The Legacy of Confucianism in Japan', in Gilbert Rozman ed., *The East Asian Region: Confucian Heritage and its Modern Adaptation* (Princeton, N.J., Princeton University Press, 1991), pp.111–54.
11 *Sources of Japanese Tradition:* vol. II, pp. 41–2.
12 Ibid, p. 50, also pp. 51–6.
13 George A. Lensen, *The Russian Push toward Japan: Russo-Japanese Relations, 1697–1875* (Princeton, N.J., Princeton University Press, 1959), pp. 316–18.
14 Joseph R. Levenson, *Confucian China and its Modern Fate: The Problem of Intellectual Continuity* (London, Routledge and Kegan Paul, 1965), pp. 53–69.

15 *Sources of Japanese Tradition:* vol. II, pp. 122–3. See also Terumasa Nakanishi, 'Japan's Place in the World' (*Japan Echo*, vol. XIX, Special Issue, 1992), p. 5; Hiroshi Momose, 'Perceptions of the Small States in the Post War Japan, 1945–1987' (Tsudajuku Daigaku, *Kokusaikankeigaku Kenkyū*, no. 17, March 1991), p. 4.
16 *Sources of Japanese Tradition:* vol. II, pp. 148–55.
17 Ibid, pp. 294–8.
18 Ibid, pp. 250–1; Iriye, op. cit., p. 2.
19 *Sources of Japanese Tradition:* vol. II, pp. 206–9.
20 Iriye, pp. 169–70, 222–3; Ian Nish, *The Anglo-Japanese Alliance: The Diplomacy of Two Island Empires: 1894–1907* (London, The Athlone Press, 1968), pp. 19, 69–71, 78, 167–8; George A. Lensen, *The Strange Neutrality: Soviet-Japanese Relations during the Second World War 1941–1945* (Tallahassee, Florida, The Diplomatic Press, 1972), pp. 14, 105–21, 133.
21 For the text of the 1946 Constitution, compared with the text of the Meiji Constitution of 1889, see Hugh Borton, *Japan's Modern Century* (New York, The Ronald Press Company, 1955), pp. 490–507.
22 Edwin O. Reischauer, *The United States and Japan* (New York, The Viking Press, 3rd edn, 1972), pp. 286–7.
23 *Lensen, The Russian Push Toward Japan*, pp. 316–18; *The Strange Neutrality*, pp. 214–16; Savitri Vishwanathan, *Normalization of Japanese-Soviet Relations 1945–1970* (Tallahassee, Florida, The Diplomatic Press, 1973), pp. 49–50; *Foreign Relations of the United States (FRUS) 1950:* vol. VI: *East Asia and the Pacific* (Washington, D.C., United States Government Printing Office, 1976), p. 1196.
24 See Ian Nish, *Alliance in Decline: A Study of Anglo-Japanese Relations, 1908–1923* (London, The Athlone Press, 1972).
25 *Defense of Japan* (Tokyo, Defense Agency, 1976), p. 129.
26 See Saitō, op. cit., passim.
27 Hanna Newcombe, Michael Ross and Alan G. Newcombe, 'United Nations Voting Patterns' (*International Organization*, vol. XXIV no. 1, Winter 1970, pp. 100–21), pp. 106–9.
28 See Wolf Mendl, *Issues in Japan's China Policy* (London and Basingstoke, The Macmillan Press for RIIA, 1978); pp. 101–2.
29 Wolf Mendl, *Western Europe and Japan between the Superpowers* (London and Sydney, Croom Helm, 1984), pp. 134–5.
30 Gilbert Rozman, 'Comparisons of Modern Confucian Values in China and Japan', in Rozman, op. cit., p. 182.
31 *Sources of Japanese Tradition:* vol. II, p. 394.

3 THE BREAKDOWN OF THE POST-WAR INTERNATIONAL SYSTEM AND ITS IMPACT ON JAPAN'S ASIA POLICY

1 Edward J. Lincoln, *Japan Facing Economic Maturity* (Washington, DC, The Brookings Institution, 1988), pp. 74–5.
2 Wolf Mendl, *Western Europe and Japan between the Superpowers*, op. cit., pp. 61–2.

3 For this historical phenomenon, see O. Edmund Clubb, *China and Russia: The 'Great Game'* (New York, Columbia University Press, 1971).
4 Stuart Schram, *Mao Tse-tung* (Harmondsworth, Middlesex, Penguin Books, 1970), pp. 220–1.
5 Levenson, op. cit., pp. 129, 134, 141, 144–5, 162–3.
6 Benjamin Schwartz, 'The Chinese Perception of World Order, Past and Present', in Fairbank, op. cit., pp. 284–8.
7 *International Herald Tribune (IHT)*, 16 February 1990.
8 Leszek Buszynski, *Gorbachev and Southeast Asia* (London and New York, Routledge, 1992), especially chs 3 and 4.

4 REGIONAL INTERESTS AND POLICY IN NORTH-EAST ASIA

1 For the background of Japan's relations with Russia and the Soviet Union, see Lensen, *The Russian Push toward Japan*, op. cit.; *The Strange Neutrality*, op. cit.; *Japanese Recognition of the U.S.S.R.: Soviet-Japanese Relations 1921–1930* (Tokyo, Sophia University; Tallahassee, Florida, The Diplomatic Press, 1970); John J. Stephan, *The Kuril Islands: Russo-Japanese Frontier in the Pacific* (Oxford, The Clarendon Press, 1974); *Sakhalin: A History* (Oxford, The Clarendon Press, 1971); Wolf Mendl, 'Stuck in a Mould: The Relationship between Japan and the Soviet Union', in Kathleen Newland, ed., *The International Relations of Japan* (Basingstoke and London, Macmillan, 1990, pp. 174–205); 'Japan and the Soviet Union: towards a deal?' (*The World Today*, vol. XLVII no. 11, November 1991, pp. 196–200); Gilbert Rozman, *Japan's Response to the Gorbachev Era, 1985–1991: A Rising Superpower Views a Declining One* (Princeton, N.J., Princeton University Press, 1992); Joachim Glaubitz, *Fremde Nachbarn: Tokyo und Moskau: Ihre Beziehungen vom Beginn der 70er Jahre bis zum Ende der Sowjetunion* (Baden-Baden, Nomos Verlagsgesellschaft, 1992); Hiroshi Kimura, ed., *Hoppō Ryōdo o Kangaeru* (Sapporo, Hokkaidō Shimbun, 1982); Haruki Wada, *Hoppō Ryōdo Mondai o Kangaeru* (Tokyo, Iwanami Shoten, 1990).
2 For the text of the Cairo Declaration, see Stephan, *The Kuril Islands . . .*, p. 240; for the text of the Potsdam Proclamation, see *International Declarations* (London, National Peace Council, September 1945), pp. 27–8. See also Mendl, 'Stuck in a Mould,' pp. 182–3, 185.
3 Article 2(c) of the Treaty of Peace with Japan. For the full text of the Treaty, see Appendix II.
4 See Articles 25 and 26 of the Treaty, ibid.
5 Kenichi Itō, 'Hoppōryōdo Henkan eno Senryaku' (*Voice*, March 1986, pp. 134–47); Fuji Kamiya, 'The Northern Territories: 130 Years of Japanese Talks with Czarist Russia and the Soviet Union', in Donald S. Zagoria, ed., *Soviet Policy in East Asia* (New Haven and London, Yale University Press, 1982), p. 128.
6 Stephan, *The Kuril Islands . . .*, p. 247.

7 Glaubitz, pp. 224–35; see also Myles L.C. Robertson, *Soviet Policy towards Japan: An Analysis of Trends in the 1970s and 1980s* (Cambridge, Cambridge University Press, 1988), ch. 2.
8 Lensen, *The Russian Push toward Japan*, pp. 444–5, 448–52.
9 Lensen, *Japanese Recognition of the U.S.S.R. . . .*, pp. 137–9, 145–6, 318, 353–8, 361.
10 Glaubitz, pp. 237–42; Kenichi Nakamura, 'Soren Kyōiron Karano Dakkyaku' (*Sekai*, April 1985, pp. 56–73).
11 Lensen, *Japanese Recognition of the U.S.S.R. . . .*, pp. 363–73; V.I. Lenin, *On the Foreign Policy of the Soviet State* (Moscow, Progress Publishers, n.d.), pp. 190, 301–8.
12 *The Japan Times Weekly* (*JTW*) 23–29 April, 30 April–6 May, 7–13 May 1990; *The Japan Times (JT)*, 25 April, 1 May 1990.
13 Hiroshi Takeuchi, 'East Asia's Uncertain Future' (*Japan Echo*, vol. XIX, Special Issue, 1992), p. 25. For a more positive assessment of the prospects, see Twu Jaw-Yann, 'The Coming Era of the Sea of Japan' (ibid), pp. 6–13.
14 Glaubitz, pp. 195–7.
15 Sansom, *A History of Japan 1334–1615*, op. cit., pp. 352–62.
16 Sansom, *A History of Japan to 1334*, op. cit., pp. 59, 438–50.
17 See Chapter 2, note 8; Chong-Sik Lee, *Japan and Korea: The Political Dimension* (Stanford, California, Hoover Institution Press, Stanford University, 1985), p. 154.
18 Lee, p. 155.
19 Ibid, pp. 153–7.
20 Ibid, pp. 157–61.
21 Ibid, pp. 141–51, 161–3.
22 Ibid, pp. 5–22.
23 Ibid, p. 181; *JTW*, 17 February, 14 July 1979, 20 March 1982, 16–22 April 1990; *JT*, 12 December 1979.
24 Richard B. Finn, *Winners in Peace: MacArthur, Yoshida and Postwar Japan* (Berkeley, University of California Press, 1992), p. 310; Lazar Focsaneanu, 'Les Relations Nippo-Coréennes et les Traités de Tokio du 22 Juin 1965' (*Politique Etrangère*, nos. 4–5, 1965, pp. 369–409), pp. 384–7.
25 Kim Sam-Kyu, 'A Korean View of Ratification' (*Japan Quarterly*, vol. XII no. 4, October–December 1965, pp. 445–53); Fumio Ikematsu, 'The ROK–Japan Treaty and Political Parties' (*Contemporary Japan*, vol. XXVIII no. 3, May 1966, pp. 494–519).
26 Lee, pp. 69–72, 75–6, 94–6.
27 Brian Bridges, *Japan and Korea in the 1990s: From Antagonism to Adjustment* (Aldershot, Hants, Edward Elgar, 1993), pp. 10–11; Focsaneanu, pp. 381–2, 398.
28 Lee, pp. 76–80; Bridges, p. 59.
29 Bridges, pp. 45–6, 87–8.
30 Ibid, pp. 93–4.
31 Ibid, p. 71.
32 Ibid, p. 88.
33 *JT*, 21 February 1992, 17 and 18 September 1992.

34 Zengo Ōhira, 'The Territorial Problems of the Peace Treaty with Japan' (*The Annals of the Hitotsubashi Academy*, vol. VII no. 2, April 1957), pp. 120–1.
35 Focsaneanu, pp. 384–91, 401–5.
36 Lee, p. 120; *JTW*, 12 February 1977, 20 May and 17 June 1978, 2–8 April 1990; *The Guardian*, 12 February 1977.
37 Bridges, pp. 40, 118–27.
38 Ibid, p. 17; Focsaneanu, pp. 407–9; Soon Sung Cho, 'Japan's Two Korea Policy and the Problems of Korean Unification' (*Asian Survey*, vol. VII no. 10, October 1967, pp. 703–25), pp. 708–10; *Japan Echo*, vol. XXI no. 2, Summer 1994, pp. 47–8.
39 *JT*, 3 February, 2,4,7 and 19 May 1993; *The Guardian*, 24 February, 13 and 17 March, 28 May, 12 June, 4 August, 26 October 1993; *Frankfurter Allgemeine Zeitung*, 19 March 1993; Katsumi Satō, 'The Danger of appeasing Pyongyang' (*Japan Echo*, vol. XXI no. 2, Summer 1994, pp. 49–56).
40 Jin Park, 'Japan-North Korean *Rapprochement*: Issues and Prospects' (*Japan Forum*, vol. 4 no. 2, October 1992, pp. 329–44); James Cotton, 'The Two Koreas and *Rapprochement*: Foundations for Progress?' (*The Pacific Review*, vol. 5 no. 2, 1992, pp. 162–6).
41 Marius B. Jansen, *The Japanese and Sun Yat-Sen* (Stanford, California, Stanford University Press, 1970), pp. 202–4, 213.
42 John Hunter Boyle, *China and Japan at War, 1937–1945: The Politics of Collaboration* (Stanford, California, Stanford University Press, 1972), especially pp. 140–1, 167–74, 177–8, 181–2, 187–92.
43 Mendl, *Issues in Japan's China Policy*, op. cit., pp. 2–5.
44 Quoted in Boyle, pp. 34, 368 note 33; see also Sun Yat-Sen, *The Vital Problem of China* (Taipei, China Cultural Service, 1953), pp. 123–4.
45 Shigeru Yoshida, 'Japan and the Crisis in Asia' (*Foreign Affairs*, January 1951), p. 179.
46 *Nixon–Chou Communiqué* (London, United States Information Service, American Embassy, 28 February 1972); 'Joint Communiqué on the Establishment of Diplomatic Relations between the People's Republic of China and the United States of America, 1 January 1979' (*Xinhua News Agency*, 16 December 1978); Henry Kissinger, *The White House Years* (London, Weidenfeld & Nicolson and Michael Joseph, 1979), p. 783; Fumio Matsuo, 'The U.S. and China – their Shrewd Relationship' (*Bungei Shunjū*, August 1978 – Tokyo, U.S. Embassy Office of Translation Services, October 1978); *Yomiuri*, 10 October 1971; *Joint Statement of the Government of the People's Republic of China and the Government of Japan*, Peking, September 29, 1972, Articles (2), (3) and (7), Mendl, p. 143.
47 For the background of the dispute over the Senkaku Islands and details of the incidents, see Mendl, pp. 88–91; *JTW*, 15 April, 6 May, 23 September, 4 November 1978; *The Times*, 13, 15, 17 and 22 April 1978; *JT*, 18 March, 2 and 8 April 1992; *Liberal Star* (Tokyo, The Liberal Democratic Party, vol. 21 no. 241, 15 April 1992), p. 4.
48 *International Herald Tribune* (*IHT*), 9 and 11 July 1990; see also *Asahi Evening News*, 23 and 27 August 1988; *JTW*, 13 January 1990; *The Guardian*, 12 July 1990.

49 *Political Declaration*, The Economic Summit of Industrialized Nations, Houston, Texas, 10 July 1990 (US Press Release, Washington, D.C., 734 Jackson Place).
50 Mendl, *Western Europe and Japan between the Superpowers*, op. cit., p. 28.
51 Wolf Mendl, 'Japans Aussen- und Sicherheitspolitik in Ostasien', in Hanns W. Maull, ed., *Japan und Europa: Getrennte Welten?* (Frankfurt/New York, Campus Verlag, 1993), pp. 201–3.
52 Ying-Jeou Ma, *The Republic of China's Policy towards the Mainland* (Taipei, National Day Press Conference, 9 October 1991); *JT*, 28 April 1993; George T. Crane, 'China and Taiwan: not yet "Greater China"' (*International Affairs*, vol. 69 no. 4, October 1993, pp. 705–23).
53 *Far Eastern Economic Review*, 4 March 1993, pp. 17–18.
54 Mendl, *Issues in Japan's China policy*, p. 124.
55 *JT*, 24 and 26 October 1992; *IHT*, 26 October 1992.

5 REGIONAL INTERESTS AND POLICY IN SOUTH-EAST ASIA

1 Sansom, *A History of Japan 1334–1615*, op. cit., pp. 377–8.
2 Ibid, p. 180.
3 Ibid, pp. 267–70.
4 Jansen, op. cit., pp. 14–16, 68.
5 G.C. Allen, *A Short Economic History of Modern Japan* (London, George Allen & Unwin Ltd, 2nd rev. edn, 1962), pp. 177–9, 217.
6 Chitoshi Yanaga, *Big Business in Japanese Politics* (New Haven and London, Yale University Press, 1968), pp. 202–28.
7 Lawrence Olson, *Japan in Postwar Asia* (New York, Praeger Publishers for the Council on Foreign Relations, 1970), p. 194. See also pp. 198–200, 203–4, 209, 211, for a discussion of relations with other South-East Asian states.
8 Ibid, p. 185.
9 *Le Monde*, 14 November 1972; *JTW*, 16 September 1978.
10 Masahide Shibusawa, Zakaria Haj Ahmad, Brian Bridges, *Pacific Asia in the 1990s* (London and New York, Routledge for RIIA, 1992), p. 19 table 7. For patterns of trade see pp. 13–18.
11 *Diplomatic Bluebook 1991* (Tokyo, Ministry of Foreign Affairs, 1991), p. 225.
12 Ibid, p. 230.
13 *Defense of Japan 1983* (Tokyo, Japan Defense Agency), pp. 73–7; *JTW*, 18 July 1981, 3 April 1982.
14 *Diplomatic Bluebook 1991*, p. 230.
15 For references to Burma's relations with Japan and ASEAN, see Robert M. Orr, *The Emergence of Japan's Foreign Aid Power* (New York, Columbia University Press, 1990), pp. 84–6; Saitō, *Japan at the Summit: . . .*, op. cit., pp. 23–4, 28, 33–4, 53; Michael Leifer, *ASEAN and the Security of South-East Asia* (London and New York, Routledge, 1989), pp. 63, 140.

16 Orr, pp. 85–6.
17 Michio Takeyama, *Harp of Burma* (Translated by Howard Hibbett, Rutland, Vt. and Tokyo, Charles E. Tuttle Company, 1972).
18 Leifer, p. 81. For the text of the Zone of Peace, Freedom and Neutrality Declaration, see ibid, pp. 163–4.
19 Olson, pp. 156–7; Saitō, p. 33.
20 Saitō, p. 23.
21 For the text of the Bangkok Declaration, see Leifer, pp. 160–2.
22 For the text of Fukuda's speech in Manila on August 18, 1977, see *JTW*, 27 August 1977.
23 For a list of the projects and details of other economic assistance, see the *Bulletin of the Anglo-Japanese Economic Institute*, no. 190, September 1977, p. 6.
24 Saitō, pp. 71, 142.
25 For a full text of the Declaration issued by the 4th ASEAN Summit in Singapore, 27–28 January 1992, see *JT*, 29 January 1992, p. 5.
26 For the text of the Treaty of Amity and Co-operation in Southeast Asia, see Leifer, pp. 170–4.
27 See note 18.
28 Policy Speech by Prime Minister Miyazawa, *The New Era of the Asia–Pacific and Japan-ASEAN Co-operation* (Bangkok, 16 January 1993, p. 14, provisional translation).
29 Ibid, p. 3.
30 Ibid, p. 4. See also Eiichi Furukawa, 'Changes in Southeast Asian Views of Japan' (*Japan Echo*, vol. XX no. 3, Autumn 1993, pp. 45–52), pp. 50–2; *JT*, 26 July 1992.
31 Ibid, p. 7.
32 Ibid, p. 5.
33 Ibid, p. 7.
34 Ibid, p. 10.
35 Ibid, p. 12.
36 Ibid, p. 14.
37 Donald Lancaster, *The Emancipation of French Indochina* (London, Oxford University Press for RIIA, 1961) pp. 91–121. See also George McTurnan Kahin and John W. Lewis, *The United States in Vietnam* (Delta, 1967), pp. 14–19, for an overview of Japanese policy in Indochina during the Pacific War.
38 Lancaster, p. 73. For a contemporary French reaction to the Russo-Japanese War and especially for an analysis of a potential Japanese threat to Indochina, see Roger Dorient, *Le Japon et la Politique Française* (Paris, Librairie Plon, 1906), pp. 257–65, 268–9, 274–311.
39 Bernard B. Fall, *The Two Vietnams: A Political and Military Analysis* (London and Dunmow, Pall Mall Press, 1963), p. 194.
40 *JTW*, 3 and 17 February, 31 March, 29 September 1973; *Le Monde*, 26 January, 21 February 1973; *The Guardian*, 31 March 1973.
41 Kaoru Murakami, 'The Postwar Defense Debate in Review' (*Japan Echo*, vol. V no. 4, Winter 1978, pp. 18–31), p. 23.
42 *The Guardian*, 31 March 1973.
43 Shibusawa, *Japan and the Asian Pacific Region*, op. cit., pp. 31–3, 102–3. For the wartime experience in China, see Dick Wilson, *When*

Tigers Fight: The Story of the Sino-Japanese War, 1937–1945 (London, Hutchinson, 1982).

44 *JTW*, 27 January 1979; *Japan* (London, Embassy of Japan), no. 42, 24 January 1979.

45 Buszynski, *Gorbachev and Southeast Asia*, op. cit., pp. 121–46.

46 *The Guardian*, 19 July 1990.

47 *JTW*, 4 July 1987.

48 *Japan* (London, Embassy of Japan), no. 148, 24 June 1981.

49 Ibid, no. 531, 31 March 1992; *JT*, 23 June 1992.

50 *Mainichi*, 24 February 1973.

51 *JTW*, 12 December 1987.

52 Ibid, 23 February 1985.

53 *The Times*, 12 June 1991; *The Guardian*, 13 June 1991; *JT*, 19 November 1991.

54 *JT*, 29 September 1992; *The Guardian*, 7 November 1992.

55 *JT*, 14 April 1993.

56 Ibid, 17 February 1993.

57 *Diplomatic Bluebook 1991*, pp. 233–4.

58 Isami Takeda, 'A New Dialogue for Japan, ASEAN, and Oceania' (*Japan Echo*, vol. XX Special Issue, 1993, pp. 72–6), p. 75.

59 See for example, Hisahiko Okazaki, 'Southeast Asia in Japan's National Strategy' (Ibid, pp. 52–63), p. 62.

6 REGIONAL POLICY IN THE GLOBAL CONTEXT

1 Emmott, 'The Economic Source of Japan's Foreign Policy', op. cit., p. 50.

2 Ibid, p. 66.

3 Ibid, p. 67.

4 Hugh Lofting, *The Story of Doctor Dolittle* (Harmondsworth, Middx, Penguin Books, 1968), pp. 76, 79.

5 For a discussion of what I mean by 'strategic thinking', see Wolf Mendl, 'Strategic Thinking in Diplomacy: a Legacy of the Cold War', in Michael Clarke, ed., *New Perspectives on Security* (London, Brassey's (UK) for The Centre for Defence Studies, 1993), pp. 1–16.

6 Orr, *The Emergence of Japan's Foreign Aid Power*, op. cit., p. 1.

7 *JT*, 3 September 1990; *IHT*, 19 September 1990; *The Financial Times*, 19 September 1990 Until 1989, the expression 'potential threat' (senzaiteki kyōkan) had been used with reference to the Soviet Union. It disappeared from subsequent White Papers.

8 *Defense of Japan 1991* (Tokyo, Defense Agency of Japan), p. 30.

9 Ibid, pp. 26–8.

10 One of the earliest and most influential books to discuss this theme was by Ezra Vogel, *Japan as Number One, Lessons for America* (Cambridge, Mass., Harvard University Press, 1979). See also Ronald Dore, *Taking Japan Seriously: a Confucian Perspective on Leading Economic Issues* (Stanford, Stanford University Press, 1987).

11 See, for example, George Friedman and Meredith Legard, *The Coming War with Japan* (New York, St Martin's Press, 1991).

12 A good example of this kind of analysis is to be found in Pyle, *The Japanese Question: . . .*, op. cit.

13 The most celebrated of such writings is by Shintarō Ishihara and Akio Morita, *'No' to ieru Nihon* (Tokyo, Kobunsha, 1989), translated as *The Japan that can say No* (New York, Simon and Schuster, 1991).

14 Ronald Dore, *Flexible Rigidities: Industrial Policy and Structural Adjustment in Japan 1970–1980* (London, Athlone Press, 1986).

15 John E. Endicott, *Japan's Nuclear Option: Political, Technical, and Strategic Factors* (New York, Praeger Publishers, 1975), pp. 127–8, 140–1; *JTW*, 19 December 1987, 14 May 1988.

16 *JT*, 19 March 1986; *JTW*, 16 May 1987, 17 December 1988, 20 May 1989.

17 Katsuto Ushihashi, 'Truth on overheating of Japanese Defence Industry' (*Bungei Shunjū*, May 1982 – Full Translation, US Embassy, Tokyo, July 1982, pp. 7–8).

18 Hisashi Nakamura and Malcolm Dando, 'Japan's Military Research and Development: a High Technology Deterrent' (*The Pacific Review*, vol. 6 no. 2, 1993, pp. 177–90).

19 Ibid, pp. 187–8.

20 J.M. Chapman, R. Drifte and I.T.M. Gow, *Japan's Quest for Comprehensive Security: Defence – Diplomacy – Dependence* (London, Frances Pinter, 1983), pp. xiv–xviii, 71, 92–4.

21 A good corrective to generalizations about how decisions are reached is to be found in T.J. Pempel, ed., *Policymaking in Contemporary Japan* (Ithaca and London, Cornell University Press, 1977), especially chs 2, 3 and 9.

22 Curtis, *The Japanese Way of Politics*, op. cit., pp. 54–6.

23 Ibid, p. 248.

24 For a discussion of the pattern of intra-faction fighting following the loss of its leader, see Chie Nakane, *Japanese Society* (London, Weidenfeld & Nicolson, 1970), pp. 40–8.

25 E. Herbert Norman, *Japan's Emergence as a Modern State: Political and Economic Problems of the Meiji Period* (New York, Institute of Pacific Relations, 1940), pp. 85–8.

26 Kent E. Calder, 'The United States–Japan Relationship: A Post-Cold War Future' (*The Pacific Review*, vol. 5 no. 2, 1992, pp. 125–34); Shin'ichi Kitaoka, 'Opting for a Global Alliance' (*Japan Echo*, vol. XIX, Special Issue, 1992, pp. 26–36). The article by Kent Calder is a well-balanced and persuasive statement of a point of view which is largely that of the political leadership in both countries.

27 Kitaoka, p. 36.

28 Draft Report, Special Study Group of the LDP, 'Japan's Role in the International Community' (*Japan Echo*, vol. XIX no. 2, Summer 1992, pp. 49–58).

29 Seiichirō Saitō, 'The Pitfalls of the New Asianism' (*Japan Echo*, vol. XIX, Special Issue 1992, pp. 14–19), pp. 18–19.

30 Jeffrey Frankel, 'Is a Yen Bloc forming in Pacific Asia?' (*The AMEX Bank Review*, November 1991, pp. 2–3).

31 For a discussion of such a prospect, see Kenichi Ohmae, *Triad Power: The Coming Shape of Global Competition* (New York, The Free Press; London, Collier Macmillan Publishers, 1985).

32 Takakazu Kuriyama, 'New Directions for Japanese Foreign Policy in the Changing World of the 1990s: Making Active Contributions to the Creation of a New International Order' (Text of a paper distributed on the occasion of his visit to the Royal Institute of International Affairs, London, 5 December 1991, p. 30), being the translation of an article in *Gaiko Forum*, May 1990, pp. 12–21.
33 Ibid, p. 13.
34 Ibid, pp. 12 and 23.
35 For an overview of Japan's arms control and disarmament policies in the 1980s, see Reinhard Drifte, *Japan's Rise to International Responsibilities: The Case of Arms Control* (London and Atlantic Highlands, N.J., The Athlone Press, 1990).
36 *JT*, 16 June 1992.
37 *JT*, 12 June 1992.
38 *The Guardian*, 4 December 1991; *Süddeutsche Zeitung*, 4 Dezember 1991; *Xinhua*, 14 April 1991; Joachim Glaubitz, *Japan, China und der Golf-Konflikt* (Ebenhausen, Stiftung Wissenschaft und Politik, KA 2677, Januar 1991), p. 3.
39 Kunio Nishimura, 'Sweat and Blood' (*Look Japan*, August 1993, pp. 5–6). See also Takehiko Nakata, 'Coming to Terms with my Son's Death' (*Japan Echo*, vol. XX no. 3, Autumn 1993, pp. 19–22).
40 *JT*, 9 and 11 May 1993.
41 *Japan* (London, Embassy of Japan), no. 545, 9 February 1993.
42 Hisashi Owada, 'Prospects for Cooperation in the Asia–Pacific Region', *IHJ Bulletin* (Tokyo, International House of Japan), vol. XII no. 2, Spring 1992, p. 3.
43 *JTW*, 29 July 1978.
44 *JTW*, 30 August 1980.
45 London, Far Eastern Department of the Foreign Office, Report No. 2173, 23 April 1943. Quoted in Chihiro Hosoya, 'Characteristics of the Foreign Policy Decision-making System in Japan' (*World Politics*, vol. XXVI no. 3, April 1974), p. 357.
46 Wolf Mendl, 'Independence and Interdependence: Japan in a Changing International Environment', *Annals of the Institute of Social Science* (Tokyo, University of Tokyo), Special Issue, 1989, p. 28.

Select bibliography of books in English

G.C. Allen, *A Short Economic History of Modern Japan* (London, George Allen & Unwin Ltd, second revised edn., 1962).

Hugh Borton, *Japan's Modern Century* (New York, The Ronald Press Company, 1955).

John Hunter Boyle, *China and Japan at War, 1937–1945: The Politics of Collaboration* (Stanford, California, Stanford University Press, 1972).

Brian Bridges, *Japan and Korea in the 1990s: From Antagonism to Adjustment* (Aldershot, Hants, Edward Elgar, 1993).

Delmer M. Brown, *Nationalism in Japan: An Introductory Historical Analysis* (New York, Russell & Russell, 1971).

Leszek Buszynski, *Gorbachev and Southeast Asia* (London and New York, Routledge, 1992).

J.M. Chapman, R. Drifte and I.T.M. Gow, *Japan's Quest for Comprehensive Security: Defence – Diplomacy – Dependence* (London, Frances Pinter, 1983).

Gerald Curtis, *The Japanese Way of Politics* (New York, Columbia University Press, 1988).

Ronald Dore, *Flexible Rigidities: Industrial Policy and Structural Adjustment in Japan 1970–1980* (London, Athlone Press, 1986).

—— *Taking Japan Seriously: A Confucian Perspective on Leading Economic Issues* (Stanford, Stanford University Press, 1987).

Reinhard Drifte, *Japan's Rise to International Responsibilities: The Case of Arms Control* (London and Atlantic Highlands, N.J., The Athlone Press, 1990).

John E. Endicott, *Japan's Nuclear Option: Political, Technical, and Strategic Factors* (New York, Praeger Publishers, 1975).

J.K. Fairbank, ed., *The Chinese World Order: Traditional China's Foreign Relations* (Cambridge, Mass., Harvard University Press, 1968).

Richard B. Finn, *Winners in Peace: MacArthur, Yoshida, and Postwar Japan* (Berkeley, University of California Press, 1992).

Akira Iriye, *Power and Culture: The Japanese-American War, 1941–1945* (Cambridge, Mass., Harvard University Press, 1981).

Marius B. Jansen, *The Japanese and Sun Yat-sen* (Stanford, California, Stanford University Press, 1970).

Junichi Kyōgoku, *The Political Dynamics of Japan* (Tokyo, University of Tokyo Press, 1987).
Donald Lancaster, *The Emancipation of French Indochina* (London, Oxford University Press for the Royal Institute of International Affairs, 1961).
Chong-Sik Lee, *Japan and Korea: The Political Dimension* (Stanford, California, Hoover Institution Press, 1985).
Michael Leifer, *ASEAN and the Security of South-East Asia* (London and New York, Routledge, 1989).
George R. Lensen, *The Russian Push toward Japan: Russo-Japanese Relations, 1697–1875* (Princeton, N.J., Princeton University Press, 1959).
—— *The Strange Neutrality: Soviet-Japanese Relations during the Second World War 1941–1945* (Tallahassee, Florida, The Diplomatic Press, 1972).
Joseph R. Levenson, *Confucian China and its Modern Fate: vol. I: The Problem of Intellectual Continuity* (London, Routledge and Kegan Paul, 1965).
Edward J. Lincoln, *Japan Facing Economic Maturity* (Washington, D.C., The Brookings Institution, 1988).
Wolf Mendl, *Issues in Japan's China Policy* (London and Basingstoke, The Macmillan Press for The Royal Institute of International Affairs, 1978).
—— *Western Europe and Japan between the Superpowers* (London, Croom Helm; New York, St Martin's Press, 1984).
Chie Nakane, *Japanese Society* (London, Weidenfeld & Nicolson, 1970).
M. Frederick Nelson, *Korea and the Old Orders in Eastern Asia* (Baton Rouge, Louisiana State University Press, 1946).
William R. Nester, *Japan's Growing Power over East Asia and the World Economy* (Basingstoke, The Macmillan Press, 1990).
Kathleen Newland, ed., *The International Relations of Japan* (Basingstoke and London, Macmillan, 1990).
Ian Nish, *The Anglo-Japanese Alliance: The Diplomacy of Two Island Empires: 1894–1907* (London, The Athlone Press, 1968).
—— *Alliance in Decline: A Study of Anglo-Japanese Relations, 1908–1923* (London, The Athlone Press, 1972).
Kenichi Ohmae, *Triad Power: The Coming Shape of Global Competition* (New York, The Free Press, Macmillan Inc.; London, Collier Macmillan Publishers, 1985).
Lawrence Olson, *Japan in Postwar Asia* (New York, Praeger Publishers for the Council on Foreign Relations, 1970).
Robert Orr, *The Emergence of Japan's Foreign Aid Power* (New York, Columbia University Press, 1990).
T.J. Pempel, ed., *Policymaking in Contemporary Japan* (Ithaca and London, 1977).
Kenneth B. Pyle, *The Japanese Question: Power and Purpose in a New Era* (Washington, D.C., The AEI Press, 1992).
Edwin O. Reischauer, *The United States and Japan* (New York, The Viking Press, 3rd edn, 1972).
L.C. Robertson, *Soviet Policy towards Japan: An Analysis of Trends in the 1970s and 1980s* (Cambridge, Cambridge University Press, 1988).
Gilbert Rozman, ed., *The East Asian Region: Confucian Heritage and its Modern Adaptation* (Princeton, N.J., Princeton University Press, 1991).

—— *Japan's Response to the Gorbachev Era, 1985–1991: A Rising Superpower Views a Declining One* (Princeton, N.J., Princeton University Press, 1992).

Shiro Saitō, *Japan at the Summit: Its Role in the Western Alliance and in Asian Pacific Co-operation* (London, Routledge for the Royal Institute of International Affairs, 1990).

George Sansom, *Japan in World History* (London, George Allen & Unwin Ltd, 1952).

—— *Japan: A Short Cultural History* (London, The Cresset Press, Second Edition Revised, 1952).

—— *A History of Japan to 1334* (London, The Cresset Press, 1958).

—— *A History of Japan 1334–1615* (London, The Cresset Press, 1961).

Stuart Schram, *Mao Tse-Tung* (Harmondsworth, Middx, Penguin Books, 1970).

Masahide Shibusawa, *Japan and the Asian Pacific Region: Profile of Change* (London, Croom Helm for the Royal Institute of International Affairs, 1984).

Masahaide Shibusawa, Zakaria Haj Ahmad and Brian Bridges, *Pacific Asia in the 1990s* (London and New York, Routledge for the Royal Institute of International Affairs, 1992).

John J. Stephan, *The Kuril Islands: Russo-Japanese Frontier in the Pacific* (Oxford, The Clarendon Press, 1974).

—— *Sakhalin: A History* (Oxford, The Clarendon Press, 1971).

Ryūsaku Tsunoda, Wm. Theodore de Bary and Donald Keene, eds, *Sources of Japanese Tradition: vols. I and II* (New York, Columbia University Press, 1964).

Ezra F. Vogel, *Japan as Number One, Lessons for America* (Cambridge, Mass., Harvard University Press, 1979).

Kōzō Yamamura and Yasukichi Yasuba, eds, *The Political Economy of Japan: vol. I: The Domestic Transformation* (Stanford, California, Stanford University Press, 1987).

Chitoshi Yanaga, *Big Business in Japanese Politics* (New Haven and London, Yale University Press, 1968).

INDEX

Adenauer, Konrad 2
Akashi, Yasushi 157
Aleutian Islands 20
Arafat, Yasser, visit to Tokyo 32
Argentina 56
ASEAN Regional Forum (ARF) 111–12, 147–8; China and 122; given go ahead by Miyazawa 111; Japan and 158
Ashikaga, Yoshimitsu (1358–1408) 17
Ashikaga, Yoshimochi (1386–1428) 17
Asia-Pacific Economic Cooperation Forum (APEC) 147, 152; Japan and 158–9; Miyazawa speech and 112; Ozawa Committee report and 146
Association of South-East Asian Nations (ASEAN) 7, 67, 96, 97, 100, 115, 123, 146; Brunei member of 102; Cambodia and 47, 106–7, 116; dialogue partners 109; East Asian Economic Caucus (EAEC) 109; foreign ministers meeting in Manila (July 1992) 109; public attitudes toward Japan 120–1; relations with Japan 99, 103, 104–12, 116, 120; relations with Vietnam 8, 109; Singapore summit (January 1992) 108–9; stages in the development of 105–8; Zone of Peace, Freedom and Neutrality (ZOPFAN) 104, 110; *see also under* ASEAN Regional Forum
Atlantic Alliance 43–4, 146–7
Australia 7, 100, 109, 118; proposes Conference on Security and Cooperation in Asia (CSCA) 148

Baker, James 84
Bangkok 100, 103; Bangkok Declaration (August 1967) 106; speech by Miyazawa (January 1993) 111
Belgrade 44
Berlin Wall, breach of 41, 127–8
Bismarck, Otto von 10
Boxer Rebellion 78
Bretton Woods Conference (July 1944) 39–40
Britain 23, 52, 56, 100; Anglo-Japanese Alliance 25, 28, 38, 78, 143; British and Commonwealth Occupation Forces in Japan 28; model for Japan 153, 159; policy towards Europe 1, 10, 95, 124–5; 'special relationship' with US 1, 124
Brunei 96, 120; relations with Japan 102
Burma 7, 96, 100, 105; ASEAN and 103; relations with Japan 103–4, 120; reparation agreements 97

Bush, George 86, 90; sale of fighter planes to Taiwan 89

Cairo Declaration (November 1943) 54
Cambodia 47–8, 96, 128, 129; Japan and 98, 113, 155–7; Paris Peace Agreement (October 1991) 48, 116; Vietnamese occupation of 106–8, 116
Canada 52, 109, 118
Chekhov, Anton 58
Chiang Kai-shek 54, 78–9; *see also under* Kuomintang; Taiwan
Chien, Frederick, visit to Japan (February 1993) 90
China 7–8, 37, 42, 60, 64–5, 67, 76, 96, 103, 109, 126, 129, 134; ambitions in East and South China Seas 141; attitude to ARF 111–12, 122; Cambodia and 47–8, 106–7, 116; Ch'in dynasty 15; communism in 44–6, 94; economic relations with Japan 29, 82–3, 86–7, 90–1, 97; 'Greater China' (south China, Hong Kong, Taiwan) 8, 87; Korea and 17, 77; National People's Congress 82; Peace and Friendship Treaty with Japan (1978) 81, 83, 115, 159, 204–5; relations with: Japan 5, 8, 14–18, 31, 50–1, 61, 77–91, 93, 115–16, 156, 158, 161, 164, Russia 44, South Korea 47, 66, Soviet Union 43, 46–8, 94, US 12, 80–1, 85, 127, 144; Taiwan and 88–9, 141; Tiananmen Square massacre 85, 128; traditional conception of world order 14–16, 46; *see also under* Kuomintang
China Committee (CHINCOM) 92
Chongnyon 71
Chungking 113
Churchill, Winston 54
Clark airbase 101
Conference on Security and Cooperation in Europe (CSCE) 44, 148
Co-ordinating Committee (COCOM) 92
Cuban missile crisis 162
Cultural Revolution 45

Daewoo 67
Deng Xiaoping 82, 89
Deshima island 18
Dore, Ronald 130
Dostoyevsky, Fyodor 58

Edo 20, 62; *see also under* Tokyo
Etorofu 50, 52, 55, 58
European Community 44, 106, 146, 147, 154; ASEAN and 109; Britain and 1, 10; France and 1; Japan and 33, 41; *see also under* European Union
European Union 60, 147; *see also under* European Community

Falkland Islands (Malvinas), compared to the Northern Territories issue 56, 94
Food and Agricultural Organization (FAO) 30
France 1, 10, 25, 52, 100, 133; invests in Vietnam 118; Taiwan and 89; tripartite intervention and 52; withdrawal from NATO 147; *see also under* Gaulle, Charles de; Indochina
Fukuda, Takeo 159; 'Fukuda Doctrine' 106
Fukuzawa, Yukichi (1834–1901) 22

Gaimushō – *see under* Ministry of Foreign Affairs
Gaulle, Charles de 2, 10, 147, 162; *see also under* France
General Agreement on Trade and Tariffs (GATT) 40; favours interests of advanced economies 152; Japan joins 31, 38
Geneva 44
Germany 10, 53, 60, 133, 148; contrasted to Japan 1, 27; model for Korean unification 77; tripartite intervention and 52; West Germany 1, 41

Gorbachev, Mikhail 32, 41, 144, 153; attitude to Northern Territories issue 56; policy towards Cambodia 116; withdrawal from South-East Asia 48
Greater East Asia Co-prosperity Sphere 23, 104, 121, 151
Group of Seven (G-7) industrialized powers 31, 38, 86; Japan as spokesman for ASEAN 107, 112, 158; summits: Bonn (1978) 107, Houston (1990) 83–4, Ottawa (1981) 107
Gulf 101 – War, Japan and 86, 148, 156

Habomai group of islands 50, 53, 55–6
Haiphong 112–13
Hanoi 119
Hata, Tsutomu 75, 139
Hatoyama, Ichirō 92
Helsinki 44 – process 148
Herter, Christian 42
Hiroshima, atomic bombing of 25–6, 93
Ho Chi Minh City 118
Hokkaidō 20, 52; Shikotan and Habomai islands as part of 50, 55
Honda, investment in Vietnam 117–18
Hong Kong 7, 45, 67, 87, 96, 118; importance of in China's relations with Taiwan 88–9; links of merchants with Japanese businesses 107
Hosokawa, Morihiro 68, 137
Hu Yaobang 82
Hyundai 67

India 96, 109
Indian Ocean 51, 100
Indochina 7, 96, 105; Japanese occupation of 112–13; Japanese policy towards 106, 112, 122; under French rule 97, 100, 112–13, 120
Indonesia 7, 96, 101, 105–6; Dutch East Indies 113; Japanese reparations 97; public attitudes towards Japan 120; relations with Japan 40–1, 99–100, 102; *see also under* Association of South-East Asian Nations (ASEAN)
INF (Intermediate Nuclear Forces) negotiations 127
International Atomic Energy Agency (IAEA) 73–4; Japan joins 31
International Bank for Reconstruction and Development (IBRD) 39, 84, 88, 126; Japan becomes member of 30–1
International Court of Justice 55; proposal to submit dispute over Takeshima to 69–70
International Labour Office (ILO), Japan becomes member of 30
International Monetary Fund (IMF) 39; Japan becomes member of 30
Iraq 86, 156; *see also under* Gulf
Iriye, Akira 10–11
Ishikawajima Harima Industries 101
Israel 89
Italy 25
Itō, Masayoshi 85

Japan: American Occupation 1, 26–8, 30, 97, 142; Asia v. the West debate 5–7, 21–5, 33, 36–7, 38, 87, 111–12, 123, 127, 146, 149, 164–5; Association of South- East Asian Nations (ASEAN) and 99, 103, 104–12, 116, 119, 120, 122; Axis powers and 38, 53; 'catching up' syndrome 9, 37, 95; Chamber of Commerce and Industry 98; characteristics of foreign policy vii–ix, 8–13, 159–60; Chinese entrepreneurs and 102–3, 107–8; Chinese Nationalists and 78–80, 92, 161; communist party 137, 155; compared with: Britain 1, 95, 124–5, 159, France 1, Germany 1, 27; 'Comprehensive Security' policy 134; culture of 10–11, 36, 62–3; debate over security 33–5, 142, 163; dependence on US for security 3, 94, 134, 142, 146; Dutch traders and 18, 20; economic friction with US 30, 41, 43, 128–9, 142–3, 149–50, 162–3; economic relations with: China 11, 29, 61, 79, 82–3, 85–7, 90–1, 97, 161, Russia 57, 60–1, South-East Asia 99, 102–3, 106, 109–10, 121, South Korea 65–8; economy 39–41, 66–7, 134–5; educational and cultural diplomacy 133–4; emperor 11, 19–20, 26–7, 91, 93; 'equidistant diplomacy' 81, 159; ethnocentrism viii–ix, 5, 165; Foreign Direct Investment (FDI) 99, 102, 133, 142, 151; FS–X procurement 131–2; Group of Seven (G–7) and 31, 38, 146; human rights and 85–6, 103–4, 144–5; independence of US policy 32–3, 64–5, 79–80, 83–5, 87–8, 91–2, 115, 117–18, 121, 145, 161; influence of Confucian ideas 19, 22, 36, 62; influence of media on policy 11–12; international idealism and 156–7, 160; Iran-hostage and Afghan crises 33, 84–5; isolation of 18–20, 36, 143, 145, 152–3, 163; Korean minority in 70–1, 92; Korean War and 29, 32, 98; League of Nations and 24–5, 38; Meiji Restoration 9, 23, 62, 87, 95; member of international agencies 30–1, 38, 126, 157; Middle East and 12, 32, 51, 100, 161; Mongolia and 31; nationalism of 5, 10–11, 18–21, 37, 93, 135–6, 157; nuclear policy of 34, 130–1; Official Development Assistance (ODA) 102, 103, 107–8, 112, 133, 163; 'oil shocks' and 40–1, 102, 121, 130, 134; 'omnidirectional diplomacy' 159; Peace and Friendship Treaty with China 81, 83, 115, 159, 204–5; 'Peace Constitution' 26–7, 30, 132, 140, 142, 145, 155, 163; political reform (Kaishin) movement 140; post-war reforms 1–2, 26–8; post-war reparation agreements 97–9, 113, 121, 178–84, 196–9; process of decision-making 2, 11, 130, 136, 138–9, 161–2, 163; rearmament policy 30, 34–5, 128, 131–3, 135, 163; relations with: China 5, 15–17, 31, 77–91, 115–16, 121–3, 144–5, 158, 161, 164, Korea 16–18, 25, 38, 52, 61–3, 77, 156, 158, North Korea (DPRK) 31, 64–5, 72, 74–6, North Vietnam 31, 33, 114–15, 117, 121, Russia 20–1, 25, 38, 52, 56–61, 158, South Korea (ROK) 29–30, 63–71, 92, 187–203, South Vietnam 97–8, 113–14, Soviet Union 31, 33, 43, 52–6, 59, 92, 127–8, US 11, 20–1, 25, 94–5, 105, 117–18, 121, 124, 126–9, 142–6, 154, 159–63, 164, Vietnam 46, 110, 113–19, 120; security of South-East Asia and 103, 110, 111–12; Security Treaty with US 12, 33–5, 42–3, 48, 104, 111, 115, 134, 142, 145, 150, 158, 166–9; self-image of 10–11; Taiwan and 11, 33, 79–82, 89–90, 92; theses on post-war policy 4–5; triangular relationship with US and W. Europe 31, 33, 41, 126, 154; United Nations and 30–1, 80, 117, 118, 145–6, 153–7, 159; Vietnam War and 30, 113–15; Vietnamese occupation of Cambodia and 107, 115–18; view of the world 20–1, 157–8, 160, 164; 'Western alliance' and

31, 43, 48, 84–5, 88, 157, 159; *see also under* Britain; Liberal-Democratic Party; 'Northern Territories'; Treaty of San Francisco; Yoshida, Shigeru
Japan Defence Agency (JDA) 11, 128, 131
Japan English Teaching Programme (JET) 133
Japan Foreign Trade Association 98
Japan Foundation 133
Japan International Cooperation Agency (JICA) 133
Japan Overseas Cooperation Volunteers (JOVC) 157
Japan-Vietnam Economic and Technical Joint Committee 117
Japan-Vietnam Trade Association (JVTA) 117
Java 96
Jiang Zemin 82
Jingu, Empress 62
Jurang Shipyard 101

Kaifu, Toshiki 86, 128, 156
Kajiyama, Seiroku 137
Kamchatka 20, 52
Kamei, Katsuichirō (1907–1966) 36–7
Kanemaru, Shin 60, 75
Keidanren (Federation of Economic Organizations) 98
Keiretsu (enterprise groups) 2
Kim Il-sung 46; death of 76
Kim Jong-il 76
Kishi, Nobusuke, Asian tour (1957) 103, 105; exchange of letters with Christian Herter 42; forced out of office 12
Kissinger, Henry 144; *détente* and 12; triangular diplomacy of 162
Kojiki 19
Kōno, Yōhei 138
Konoe, Fumimaro 78
Korea 7, 37, 47–8, 50–3, 93, 96, 128, 129, 141, 148; 'comfort women' 68–9; Demilitarized Zone 47; factor in Sino-Japanese relations 14, 16, 17–18; Korean War 29, 32, 97; relations with Japan 16–18, 25, 38, 52, 61–3, 77, 156, 158; strategic importance of 18, 61–2; unification of 67–8, 75–7; *see also under* North Korea; Saigō, Takamori; South Korea
'Korea clause', *see under* Nixon-Satō joint communiqué
Korean Central Intelligence Agency (KCIA) 70
Korean Workers Party 71, 75
Kunashiri 50, 55, 58
Kuomintang 79, 81, 92, 161; *see also under* Chiang Kai-shek; Taiwan
Kurile Islands 8, 20, 50, 52–5; Japan renounces 55, 171; *see also under* 'Northern Territories'
Kuriyama, Takakazu 153–4
Kwantung Army 53
Kyūshū 17, 78, 96

Laos 96, 97, 112, 113
League of Nations 24–5, 143
Lee Kuan Yew 101
Lenin 59
Liaotung peninsula 52
Liberal-Democratic Party (LDP) 2, 11, 60, 70, 75, 114, 136–40, 145; and China policy 35, 79–82, 91, 161; *see also under* Ozawa, Ichirō
Luchu Islands, *see under* Ryūkyū Islands
Lucky Goldstar 67
Lytton Commission 25; *see also under* Manchuria

MacArthur, Douglas 26; 'MacArthur Line' 69
Mahathir, Mohamad 101
Malaysia 7, 96, 105, 106, 113; East Asian Economic Caucus and 109; public opinion and Japan 120; relations with Japan 98, 100–1
Manchuria 38, 63, 162; 'Manchurian Incident' 25, 52–3

Manila 109; Fukuda's speech in (1977) 106
Mao Zedong 45
Maritime Self-Defence Force (MSDF) 102
Marshall Plan 40
Marx, Karl 58
Marxism 44–5, 122, 137
Meiji Restoration 9, 23, 62, 87, 95, 138
mercantilism 9; neo-mercantilism 4
Middle East 8, 43, 51, 100; source of Japan's oil imports 32, 40–1
Miki, Takeo 159
Mimana, principality of 63
Mindan 71
Ming dynasty 17; and Japan 96–7
Ministerial Conference on the Economic Development of South-East Asia (MEDSEA) 104–5
Ministry of Education 133; authorization of textbooks 63
Ministry of Finance (Ōkurashō) 2, 11, 110, 131
Ministry of Foreign Affairs (Gaimushō) 2, 11, 91, 114, 120, 133; policy towards: ASEAN 104, FS-X procurement 131, Northern Territories 60, relations with China over Senkaku Islands 82, US 35, 88; trainees 29
Ministry of International Trade and Industry (MITI) 2, 104, 110; China policy 161; conflict of interests with Foreign Ministry 11, 35, 131
Mishima, Yukio (1925–1970) 37
Miyazawa, Kiichi 82, 138; North Korea's nuclear armament and 74; speech in Bangkok (1993) 111–12
Mongolia 31, 44, 72; *see also under* Nomonhan
Motoori, Norinaga (1730–1817) 20
Murayama, Tomiichi 68, 139
Myanmar, *see under* Burma

Nagasaki 18; atomic bombing of 25–6, 93
Naha 96
Nakasone, Yasuhiro 63, 93; prime minister 2–3; security policy and 12
Nakata, Atsuhito 156–7
Nakayama, Tarō 118
Nanking 78; massacre (1937) 82
NATO 31; Declaration of London summit (1990) 127
New Zealand 7, 109
Nihongi 19
Niigata 68
Nisshō Iwai 117
Nixon, Richard 144; *détente* and 12; visits China 32, 80
Nixon-Satō joint communiqué (1969) 64, 72
Nixon-Zhou communiqué (1972) 80–1
Nomonhan, battle of (1939) 53
Nomura Securities 136–7
North Korea (DPRK) 44, 46–7; communism in 94; Korean minority in Japan and 70–1; nuclear armament of 73–5; relations with: Japan 31, 64–5, 72, 74–6, US 72–4; Sino-Soviet rivalry for influence over 47
North Sumatra Oil Development Company (NOSODECO) 99
North Vietnam, relations with Japan 31, 33, 114–15, 117–18, 121
'Northern Territories' 50, 53–61, 92–3, 94, 148, 158; *see also under* Japan: relations with Russia; Soviet Union
Nuclear Non-Proliferation Treaty (NPT), and North Korea 73–4

Ōhira, Masayoshi 86
Okinawa 81
Ōkubo, Toshimichi (1830–1878) 23
Organization for Economic Cooperation and Development (OECD) 31, 38

Organization of American States 146
Osaragi, Jirō (1897–1973) 37
Overseas Economic Cooperation Fund (OECF) 133
Ozawa, Ichirō 137, 139; Ozawa Committee draft report 145–6

Pacific War 53, 59, 63, 100, 119, 125
Palestine Liberation Organization (PLO) 32
Papua New Guinea 112
Park Chung Hee 63
Penang 101
Perry, Commodore 21
Persia 96
Phibul Songkhram 100
Philippines 96; Japanese reparations 97; relations with Japan 101–2; US annexation of 6; *see also under* Manila; Subic Bay
Poland 62
Potsdam Proclamation to Japan 54
Prai 101
Pridit Phanomyong 100
Pushkin, Alexander 58
Pyongyang, *see under* North Korea

Rangoon 103–4
Red Army 53
Republic of China 92; *see also under* Chiang Kai-shek; Kuomintang; Taiwan
Rhee, Syngman 69; 'Rhee Line' 69–70
Roosevelt, Franklin 53
Russia 7–8, 44, 50, 141; ASEAN and 109, 112; attitude to Korea 77; relations with: China 61, Japan 20–1, 25, 38, 52, 56–61, 158, North Korea 72–3, South Korea 60–1, 66, US 59, 144; Russo-Japanese War 52, 58, 113; *see also under* 'Northern Territories'; Soviet Union
Ryūkyū Islands 50, 81, 96; relations with China and Japan 18, 96–7, 119

Saigō, Takamori (1827–1877) 23
Sakhalin 20, 52–3
Sakigake (Harbinger Party) 137
Samsung 67
Satō, Eisaku 103, 114; *see also under* Nixon-Satō joint communiqué
Satō, Nobuhiro (1769–1850) 20
Sea of Japan 50, 74; emerging economic zone 8, 60, 67–8, 95
Sea of Okhotsk 8
Self-Defence Forces (SDF) 33, 74, 123, 128; Law (1954) 34, 148; public opinion and 12, 136; UN peacekeeping operations and 137, 146, 153, 155–6
Senkaku (Diaoyu) Islands 50–1, 81–2, 97
Seventh Fleet 51
Shikotan 50, 53, 55–6
Shimazu clan 96
Shimizu, Ikutarō (1907–1988) 37
Shin Jiyū (New Liberal) Club 138
Shinseitō (Japan Renewal Party) 137, 139
Shintō (Japan New Party) 137
Shintō religion 19, 27, 62–3
Siberia 60; economic development of 57, 60; Japanese occupation of (1918–1922) 52, 59; prisoner-of-war camps in 53, 93
Singapore 7, 44, 67, 96, 102, 106, 113, 123; relations with Japan 98, 100, 103; summit (1992) 108–9
Social Democratic Party of Japan (SDPJ) 137, 139, 155; and North Korea 72, 75
Sonoda, Sunao 115, 117
South Korea (ROK) 31, 44–5, 101, 102, 109; American military presence in 47, 51; economic relations with US 65; economy 65–7, 134; Korean minority in Japan and 70–1; relations with: China 47, 66, Russia 60–1, 66, Soviet Union 47; Treaty and Agreements with Japan (1965) 29–30, 70–1, 187–203

South Vietnam, Japanese reparations 97–8, 113; relations with Japan 113–15
Soviet Union 44, 46, 51, 122; collapse of 5, 9, 13, 41, 43–4, 56, 58, 122, 128, 151; relations with: China 43, 48, 116, Japan 25, 29, 31, 33, 43, 52–6, 59, 92, 127–8, South Korea 47, US 41–2, 144, 162; South-East Asia and 48, 116; Soviet-Japanese Neutrality Pact (1941) 53; *see also under* 'Northern Territories'; Russia
Soviet-Japanese Joint Declaration (1956) 55–6
Soviet-Japanese Neutrality Pact (1941) 53
Soya/La Pérouse Strait 8
Spratly Islands 111, 123
Stalin, Josef 53–4
Stockholm 44
Straits of Formosa 51
Straits of Malacca and Singapore 7, 101
Subic Bay 101, 123
Sukarno 99
Sumatra 96
Sun Yat-sen 78, 79
Supreme Commander Allied Powers (SCAP) 3, 26; and ownership of Takeshima 69
Suzuki, Zenko 32
Switzerland 135, 153

Taiwan 7, 44, 50–1, 60, 67, 118, 129; economy 87–8, 90, 134; factor in Japan's relations with China 33, 79–81, 89–90; Japanese economic interest in 11, 35, 107; *see also under* Kuomintang; Republic of China
Taipei–*see under* Taiwan
Takeshima 50–1, 69–70, 92
Takeshita, Noboru 83
Takeyama, Michio 104
Tanaka, Kakuei, visit to China (1972) 81; visit to Moscow (1973) 33
Tanizaki, Junichirō (1886–1965) 37
Tehran 54
Thailand 96; popular attitudes towards Japan 120; relations with Japan 100, 102–3; Vietnam and 106, 123
Thatcher, Margaret 2
Tiananmen Square, massacre of 83; Japan's response to 85–8
Tokyo 20, 62, 86, 112, 118, 121; Arafat visit to 32; arrival of Perry's squadron in Tokyo Bay 21; MEDSEA conference 104–5; Olympics 126; Yeltsin visit to 56–7
Tokyo Declaration on Japan-Russia relations (1993) 57
Tolstoy, Leo 58
Tōshiba, export of machine tools to USSR (1987) 35
Toyotomi, Hideyoshi (1536–1598) 18, 62, 96
Treaty of St Petersburg (1875) 52, 58
Treaty of San Francisco (1951) 32, 69, 113, 170–86; Kurile Islands and 54–5, 171
Treaty of Shimoda (1855) 20, 52, 54–5, 57
Treaty of Versailles (1919) 25, 38, 143
Trilateral Commission 31
tripartite intervention (1895) 52, 58
Truman Doctrine (1947) 41
Tsugaru strait 8
Tsushima, Daimyō of 62; incident 70; straits of 8
Tumen river 67
Twenty One Demands (1916) 38

UNESCO 30
United Nations 43, 72, 86, 100, 142; Japan's admission to 31; Japan's voting record 31–2, 80, 118; Japanese policy towards 123, 145–6, 153–7, 159; Japanese public opinion and 157; Security Council 74, 155
United Nations High Commission for Refugees (UNHCR) 117

United Nations Transitional Authority in Cambodia (UNTAC) 117, 155; Japan's contribution to 117, 155–7
UN Register of Conventional Arms 147
United States 1, 8, 25, 48, 51, 52, 89, 100, 105, 148, 157; anti-Japanese feeling in California 24; dominates Japan's foreign policy 28–9, 64, 91–2, 149, 161; economic weakness of 40, 122, 126, 154; Kasten Resolution (Sept. 1987) 118; Korea and 77; Northern Territories issue and 54–5, 92, 144; occupation of Japan 1, 26–8, 30, 97, 142; policy over North Korean nuclear armament 73–5; policy towards China 12, 80–1, 127, 144; policy towards Japan 20–1, 28–9, 61; Russia and 144; Security Treaty with Japan 12, 33–5, 42–3, 48, 104, 111, 115, 134, 142, 145, 150, 158, 166–9; Seventh Fleet 51; South-East Asia and 100–3, 116; Soviet Union and 41–2, 144, 162; Taiwan and 80, 89–90, 141
Urup 52

Vienna 44
Vietnam 43, 44, 47, 96, 111, 112, 123; Cambodia and 47–8, 106, 116; China and 94; communism and nationalism of 94; integration with ASEAN 158; Japan and 46, 110, 113–19, 120; Viet Minh 113; *see also* North Vietnam; South Vietnam
Vo Van Kiet 118–19

Wang Ching-wei 78
Warsaw Pact 43, 127
Washington 74–5, 103, 105; naval treaties 24, 154
West Germany, *see under* Germany
Western European Union (WEU) 44
Wilson, Woodrow 24
World Bank, *see under* International Bank for Reconstruction and Development
World Health Organization (WHO) 30

Yalta agreement 53–4
Yamagata, Aritomo (1838–1922) 24–5
Yangtze 7
Yawata Steel 101
Yeltsin, Boris 56, 59; American support for 128; government of 59; visit to Japan 56–7, 59, 61
Yi dynasty 62
Yokohama 101
Yongbyon 73
Yon Hyong Muk 68
Yoshida, Shigeru 2–3, 79; 'Yoshida Doctrine' 3–5, 9, 29, 36, 80, 98, 135
Yugoslavia 44, 51, 147

Zaibatsu 2
Zaikai 98
Zhirinovsky, Vladimir 57
Zhong-nanhai 46
Zone of Peace, Freedom and Neutrality (ZOPFAN) 104, 110